# THE RIVER MEN

Robert Carse

# THE RIVER MEN

Charles Scribner's Sons · NEW YORK

THE IROQUOIS PEOPLE CAME BROKEN AND IN RE-
treat to the Mohawk River. They were driven by the Algonquins, their implacable enemies. Their original home was at the site of
Montreal on the St. Lawrence.

But they found this stream to the south beautiful, and the valley
fertile. They called the river Te-non-an-at-che. It meant "the river flowing through mountains." The French, Dutch and English changed the
name, shortened it to Mohawk.

The presence of the Iroquois along the Mohawk was to have an
almost incalculable effect upon the history of the continent. The river
carved through the vast rock barrier of the Appalachian plateau the single
entrance to the western territories between the St. Lawrence and the
Cumberland Gap in Virginia. It flowed across central New York State to
join the Hudson, and formed the most strategic valley anywhere near the
Atlantic seaboard.

Seneca doctor's mask

During the long conflict between the French and the English, it was the tribes of Iroquois stock, in particular the confederation of the Five Nations, the Senecas, Cayugas, Onondagas, Oneidas and Mohawks, which organized large mobile forces and helped secure the victory. They remained steadfast in their friendship with the English, and bitterly fought the French, who from the beginning had been allied with the Algonquins.

Hatred of the Algonquins increased after the Iroquois left the St. Lawrence. Raids were made repeatedly upon the Mohawk River settlements. Algonquin warriors came from the St. Lawrence to the north, the Hudson to the east, and from the Niagara on the western flank. The Iroquois were surrounded by their enemies. They were forced to fortify their towns.

They built stockades of heavy logs to protect the fifty or more longhouses that formed a community. Each longhouse held from eight to ten families. The longhouses were made of saplings covered with elm-bark slabs. They were often 100 feet in length, and resembled Quonset huts because of the curved shape of their roofs. Fireplaces shared by two families were along the center line of the earthen floor. Smoke slits were in the roof, but when the wind was wrong, they failed to work, and the occupants were miserable.

There were vestibules for storage, though, and the structures were much more substantial than the usual Indian *tipis* made of reed mats or animal skins set on poles. The sweat lodge was near the longhouses in an Iroquois town, and the stockade was high, the gate narrow. Three wooden figures, big, solemn and strange, surmounted the gate. These were carved to look like men, and as a breeze moved in the valley, scalps taken from Algonquin warriors fluttered above them at the tops of posts.

The Five Nations had tried to live in peace. Their holdings extended to the Genesee River and the Finger Lakes. They prospered, and in the confederation council the sachems talked of the Great Binding Law which would bring all Indian nations together. But the Algonquins and the Algonquins' new allies, the French, would not let them be. The Iroquois turned their full strength to the waging of war.

2

Samuel de Champlain and two French companions were with an Algonquin war party in 1609 when it met an Iroquois force. Champlain was a veteran soldier, canny and cool-headed. He was in charge of all northern French exploration, and unwilling to enter combat unless completely prepared for it.

But now he felt himself committed. He and a group of twenty Frenchmen had come up the Richelieu River from the St. Lawrence and the settlement at Quebec which Champlain had founded the year before. They were aboard a French-built shallop that carried trade goods, moved in company with sixty Algonquin warriors in twenty-four canoes.

Iroquois raids were increasing in the St. Lawrence region. The Hurons and the Montagnais and other tribes that lived along the river had asked the French for assistance. Champlain believed that he should give it. Without possession of the St. Lawrence, the entire French position in Canada was untenable. Still, he was doubtful about his decision.

Mohawk face mask

The Algonquin war with the Iroquois had deep and terrible roots, was certain to continue for a long time to come. There was a chance, too, that the Algonquins might lose despite their greatly superior numbers. Donnaconna, the sagamore of the Huron tribe that lived at Quebec, had complained bitterly to Jacques Cartier years before, in 1535, about the fierceness of the Iroquois.

Here, on the Richelieu, the falls of Chambly finished the upstream progress of the shallop. She could not navigate them. Champlain sent her back to Quebec with seventeen men. But he asked for volunteers and got a pair of tough Normans. They rode the canoes among the warriors with Champlain, their broad-muzzled arquebuses across their knees.

The party moved for several days up the river, and along the magnificent lake that was to bear Champlain's name. Then, during the starlit evening of July 29th, as the Algonquins softly paddled the big birchbark war canoes around a dark cape, there were loud shouts and cries. This was Ticonderoga, where so much American history was to

3

take place. Ahead in the spirals of mist over the water were Iroquois of the Mohawk nation. They were on their way north in their unwieldy elm-bark canoes to raid the Algonquins.

The Mohawk steersmen immediately swung their craft towards shore. They knew how much faster the enemy canoes were in action. The Mohawks cut down trees when they landed, built a barricade. The Algonquin flotilla lay off, beyond arrow range, the canoes held together by long poles. These were taken aboard and the warriors crouched with their weapons ready as two canoes came out from the beach.

The Mohawks shouted that they wanted to parley. They asked if the Algonquins really sought a fight. The answer to that was affirmative. But, the Algonquins added, it was too dark now for combat.

The Mohawks agreed. They said that at sunrise they would attack. The Algonquin chiefs told them it was a good time.

A large fire was started on the beach by the Mohawks. The warriors danced there all night long. They sang, and shouted insults at the Algonquins. The Algonquins kept the flotilla in formation offshore, but they sang their own chants, and answered the Mohawk insults. With dawn rising over the lake, they paddled to the beach, hauled up the canoes and advanced towards their enemy.

Champlain was a man of incomplete education. It was quite possible he was unaware that this combat resembled, with the formality of ritual, a confrontation between Athenians and Trojans, or Roman gladiators, medieval champions who engaged in chivalric feats of arms. But he and his two companions belonged to another age.

They wore steel corselets. Their sword scabbards glinted in the morning sun. The arquebus barrels were lifted, the slow matches set in place beside the touch-holes.

Their Indian allies kept them from sight of the enemy. The Algonquins were naked except for breechclouts. The warriors' faces were expressionless beneath the war-paint designs. Some were bright red, with blue noses and black eyebrows. There were red, black and blue stripes that reached from the ears to the mouth. Others were made of a single wide black stripe that went ear to ear, around the eyes, and were finished with three stripes on each cheek.

4

Samuel de Champlain

The Hurons and the Montagnais gripped bows, to which were fitted flint-tipped arrows. Their war clubs held along the striking surface the bones and tusks of animals. The shields they carried were round, made of wood. The stone scalping knives swung on sinew lanyards against their chests.

The Iroquois warriors were paint-daubed, and wore stiff turban-like buckskin caps crested with feathers. Their armor was woven of reeds and sticks, and beneath it they wore doeskin kilts and thigh-length leggings. They marched in regular order out from the barricade and over the smooth grassy ground above the beach.

They were strong and tall men. There was for a moment almost no sound along the lake. Squirrels chittered in the forest, a duck clacked in the shallows and the rest was the harsh rapid breathing of the men, and the rustle moccasin leather made upon the grass. Champlain counted 200 Mohawk warriors. They outnumbered his allies by more than three to one. He wrote of that fight:

> They came slowly to meet us with a gravity and calm which I admired; and at their head were three chiefs. Our Indians likewise advanced in similar order, and told me that those who had the three big plumes were the chiefs, and that there were only these three, whom you could recognize by these plumes, which were larger than those of their companions; and I was to do what I could to kill them. I promised them to do all in my power, and told them I was very sorry they could not understand me, so that I might direct their method of attacking the enemy, all of whom undoubtedly we should thus defeat; but that there was no help for it, and that I was very glad to show them, as soon as the engagement began, the courage and readiness which were in me.

The Algonquin warriors began to call loudly to Champlain. They had run forward and then stopped, divided themselves in two groups so he could pass between them. He went ahead of them, alone, slowly marching.

6

> I marched on until I was within some thirty yards of the enemy, who as soon as they caught sight of me halted and gazed at me and I at

them. When I saw them make a move to draw their bows upon us, I took aim with my arquebus and shot straight at one of the three chiefs, and with this shot two fell to the ground, and one of their companions was wounded who died thereof a little later. I had put four bullets into my arquebus.

As soon as our people saw this shot so favorable for them, they began to shout so loudly that one could not have heard it thunder, and meanwhile the arrows flew thick on both sides. The Iroquois were much astonished that two men should have been killed so quickly, although they were provided with shields made of cotton thread woven together with wood, which were proof against their arrows. This frightened them greatly.

Champlain battles the Iroquois with the aid of the Algonquin warriors and two Normans.

While Champlain reloaded, one of the Norman arquebusiers fired from a concealed position. The Mohawks lost their courage. They had never before been under fire from weapons like these. They did not even defend the barricade and ran in panic into the forest. "Whither," Champlain wrote, "I pursued them and laid low still more of them. Our Indians also killed several and took ten or twelve prisoners. Of our Indians fifteen or sixteen were wounded with arrows, but these were quickly healed."

The Algonquin canoes, on the trip back to the St. Lawrence, were deep-laden with Mohawk corn, armor and weapons. But this was the beginning of a war that was to continue in various forms of violence for two hundred years. Champlain had won a temporary victory, no more.

The Iroquois raids continued, and increased in intensity. Most of them were directed against the Hurons. These were a handsome and very intelligent tribe, cousins of the Iroquois who had broken away and settled at the southeastern corner of Georgian Bay. The great lake where they lived was named for them, and they came to control it. They grew rich as traders.

The Hurons created early in the seventeenth century an intricate system of barter that used birchbark canoes to move cargo along the rivers and lakes through the northern forests. They went west each spring to keep a rendezvous with the hunting Indians who came from Lake Superior and the regions beyond it. Ojibways, Chippewas, Potawatomis, Sauks, Foxes, Illinois, Menominees and Dakotas dealt with them.

They sold corn, tobacco and fish. They bought furs, and sheets of soft copper that were from surface mines on the Keweenaw peninsula of Superior. Then they started east to meet the French.

That was the real journey. It meant 1,000 miles of paddling and about fifty portages eastward. The furs were packed in bales, chosen from prime beaver, with some sable, marten and mink. Buckskins covered the loads against spray and rain. But a warrior who stepped carelessly as he boarded a canoe would put his foot right through the hull, and the craft was just as easily wrecked by contact with a snag, a rock or a hidden log in a boiling river rapids.

The Hurons were among the very best canoemen on the continent.

They built their own craft, following the traditions of centuries. Their big work canoe carried ten warriors and several hundred pounds of cargo.

A canoe could be built in about two weeks. Squaws were adept at the work and helped the men. Whenever it was possible, a single sheet of birchbark was taken from a tree. This was stretched out on the ground with stones to hold it. Two false gunwales were laid upon the bark, and the workers bent up the sides and set a series of stakes. The hull design was given a slight outward flare, and the bow and stern were canted, with short curves.

The main rails of the gunwale were set so that one was outside, the other inside the bark. These were secured at intervals with spruce roots or basswood fibers. Cedar pieces were bent into shape for the bow and stern, covered with bark and sewn in place with spruce roots. The thwarts were sewn and mortised to the inside gunwale rail.

The hull was lined with thin cedar strips, laid lengthwise, and secured between the bark and the ribs. The ribs were also made of cedar, and firmly placed under the gunwales by a wooden mallet. The final job was the caulking. Fir or spruce pitch was spread on the outside seams, and over the lower bow and stern sections. The gum from which the pitch was taken was masticated by squaws and young boys and girls, then heated until it was fully liquid. It was applied by sticks plucked ablaze from a fire, and hardened as it cooled.

Clan totems—a wolf, a turtle, a heron—were painted on the bow. A repair kit of spare birchbark, pitch and spruce roots was carried in every cargo canoe, along with a bark bailing scoop. Paddles were made of various woods, and often locust was used. The blades were narrow and long, the tips of the blades painted red, with feathers around the throats of the handles.

The easiest of the three routes to the French settlements was the southernmost. This was across Lake Nipissing, down the Ottawa River to a set of bad rapids, and then down the St. Lawrence to Tadoussac. The middle route swung at Mattawa and went through a number of lakes to the St. Maurice River, and down that to Trois Rivières, where it joined the St. Lawrence. The northernmost route included passage across Lake Mattagami, only a little more than 100 miles from Hudson Bay, then over

9

a very difficult portage to streams that led to Lake St. John, the Saguenay River, and Tadoussac.

The Hurons traded constantly along all of their routes. They bought from the nomad Indians of the far north anything of value. French goods, cloth, knives, hatchets, awls and articles made by the more civilized Indian tribes were exchanged for furs and walrus- and whale-bone tools. Despite their lack of enthusiasm for the Hurons, barter that came from them entered the territory of the Five Nations.

Iroquois squaws used walrus tusks as scrapers to work on deerskins. These were from Hudson Bay, had been picked up by Huron traders around Lake Mattagami. Fine-textured smooth red pipestone that when carved into a bowl and fitted with a long reed stem became a ceremonial calumet was eagerly sought by Five Nations warriors. The pipestone was mined in Minnesota, and the sources controlled by people of Sioux stock who dealt with the Hurons. It was bought through intermediaries, and sold to the Five Nations for a high price.

The Five Nations warriors had a liking, too, for Algonquin canoes, so much handier than their ungainly elm-slab craft. They exchanged their famous five-colored corn for the canoes. The dealing was done by intermediaries, people of the Erie tribe, or the Petun. But the Five Nations knew that the profit really went to the Hurons.

The Huron trading parties traversed two and three thousand miles a year, returned home in the fall with new supplies of French goods. They were the richest of any Indian people, and the Iroquois came to regard them with brooding envy that was about to burst into frightful mass hatred. They raided the Hurons along the trade routes, and sold the looted French merchandise at considerably reduced prices.

The Huron chiefs complained to the French. The raiding was a menace to all French affairs in Canada. It had begun to reduce the east-west movement of trade goods and furs, the great source of wealth. Champlain was convinced in 1615 that he should take action against the Iroquois. He joined a force of 500 Huron braves at a rendezvous on Georgian Bay.

Their objective was the Onondaga town on a pond south of Lake Oneida. It was one of the main Iroquois settlements, and known to be fortified. Champlain recognized that if it could be taken, French power would be very much strengthened and probably peace arranged with the Five Nations. He had been given reports of Iroquois dealing with the Dutch at Fort Nassau on the Hudson. That must be stopped. The Dutch were shrewd traders, and sold cheaper and better goods than the French could offer.

The members of the Huron war party feasted, boasted, danced and were finally ready to leave. Champlain had with him fourteen Frenchmen, all of them carrying arquebuses. He counted greatly on their skill with the weapons to take the Onondaga stronghold. He had been promised many more warriors than were mustered here.

The force moved south and east from Georgian Bay in canoes. Champlain was again impressed by the Hurons' handling of the craft. The steersmen at the stern and the bowmen used longer paddles than the other warriors, and they alone changed the course. A steersman was in practically full command, only obeyed a signal from the bowman in extreme emergency, when running through rapids or where an unseen rock or a submerged log presented sudden danger.

The paddle stroke maintained by a crew was steady, smooth. The blades hardly lifted from the water in the forward motion. The backward swing was finished with a quick but always balanced flick of the wrist. The pace could be lifted to forty strokes a minute when a canoe was running in rough water or was confronted by a stiff headwind.

Champlain sat motionless amidships in the canoe he rode. He watched the Hurons, studying all of their actions. Frenchmen would do this work in the future, he realized, and must be better than the Indians at it. Canoe traffic was absolutely essential to the fur trade, with the French in command.

The war party moved through magnificent country, the trees in the valleys and along the ridges splashed with the red, the orange and gold of autumn. Moose stood ruminant among the lily pads of the many lakes they crossed. Elk and deer were at the water's edge to drink. Raccoon scooped up fish, and back among the groves of immense trees bear gathered nuts and berries.

When one of the numerous portages was made, Champlain insisted upon hauling a full share. He was a stockily built man, and his usual load was three of the cumbersome arquebuses, powder and shot

11

Champlain's plan of the Fort of the Iroquois.

boxes, his own personal gear, and part of the gear that belonged to his younger companions. They joined the Hurons in carrying the canoes.

Both they and the Hurons had respect for Champlain's strength. The arquebus was so heavily constructed that a man could not hold the barrel horizontal long enough to aim it unless given support. An iron rod was attached to the underside of the barrel, and used as a rest before each shot was fired.

12

The route taken to the Onondaga town started with a hard portage. It was over the watershed that divided Lake Huron from Lake Ontario. Then the party kept on east to a series of lakes, down the Otanabee River, across another lake, and down the Trent River to the Bay of Quinte on Lake Ontario.

They had fifty miles of open water crossing Ontario, reached the south shore under the bluff at Stony Point. This was Iroquois country. They hid their canoes and kept on with great caution, south along the lake shore to the Salmon River, where they turned inland. The march was made in single file, without sound, each man stepping exactly upon the footprints of the man ahead of him. But the party was seen, and the alarm was given.

There was no need for concealment. Champlain and the other Frenchmen exposed themselves alongside the Hurons and in broad day-light began a furious fusillade with their arquebuses. They killed several Onondagas who stood and fired volleys of arrows at them. Then the Onondagas picked up their dead and moved into the town, and the big heavily barred gate in the stockade was shut against the attackers. The enemy here, Champlain recognized, understood the effect of the French fire power.

The assault lasted some hours, and Champlain was infuriated by the reckless behavior of his Huron allies. They foolishly exposed them-selves in front of the stockade. He tried to get them back, beyond arrow range, and as a result was struck twice. An arrow severely tore the tendons of a knee, and another pierced his lower leg. He was immediately aware that the battle was lost.

Champlain left the site of the battle carried like a papoose. He and the rest of the wounded were moved in rough harnesses made of hickory frames with seats projecting at right angles. These were secured to the backs of warriors. They walked so burdened along the narrow forest trails, forded rivers.

The weather was very cold, with snow flurries. The footing was treacherous. Champlain suffered excruciating pain. His wounded knee was inflamed and badly bandaged. He could not walk, though, and kept silent, lost in despair over the defeat.

When the party reached Lake Ontario, the canoes were found

intact. Champlain asked at once for one. He wanted to go to the St. Louis Rapids on the St. Lawrence, he said. It was only a four- or five-day trip. But the Huron chiefs refused. They told him that they could not spare the men.

Champlain said that he had four volunteers who would handle the canoe. The chiefs again refused. They could not spare a canoe, they said.

Champlain accepted the rebuff. He returned to Georgian Bay with the Hurons, spent the winter there, 1,200 miles from his head-quarters at Quebec. He had plenty of time to contemplate the results of the defeat by the Onondagas.

A great deal of his prestige had been stripped from him because of that. The Hurons had eagerly looked forward to winning with the help of the French fire power. Now the Hurons distrusted him, and the Onondagas had shown that in a closely fought action a quick-fired arrow was just as effective as the slow-firing arquebus.

Champlain returned to Quebec in the spring, a considerable amount of his confidence restored. The Hurons were good hosts, treated him and his companions well. His wounds healed. While he sat with the chiefs in their lodges, they drew for him on a buffalo hide the location of the lakes to the west, and the Shining Mountains, and the sea beyond. That must be the South Sea, he reckoned, and across it was China and the greatest wealth anywhere in the world.

France would win, he believed. She would hold her place on this continent, get ready to drive out the Dutch at Fort Nassau and Nieuw Amsterdam, and the English in Virginia. Then an expedition which he might well lead would start west, keep going to the Shining Mountains and across the sea, and take possession of all that wealth.

But Champlain's dream was so obsessive it thrust from his thinking the consequences of the battle fought at the Onondaga town. Their magnitude escaped him. He did not realize that what had happened in front of the rude stockade had irrevocably changed the destiny of French occupation of North America. The struggle was to go on for more than a century, although it was already impossible for France to win.

14

The Onondaga town was held sacred among the Five Nations of the Iroquois. During the summer of 1615, shortly before Champlain's abortive attack, Mohawk warriors of the Five Nations confederation had gone to Fort Nassau. They traded beaver skins for muskets with the Dutchmen who had established the settlement on the Hudson at the site of Albany. The Dutchmen were unwilling to let the Algonquins of the neighbor tribes have the weapons. It was all right for the Mohawks, though. They came from a remote valley and needed a substantial inducement to bring in their pelts.

Back along the Mohawk, the word was passed among the Five Nations. Deputations of warriors led by chiefs thoroughly examined the new weapons, tested and fired them. There was a systematic collection of beaver skins, and loaded canoes were sent to Fort Nassau.

The celebrants in the various towns listened to a common shout from their orators when the guns were received: "Let the French rest in death!"

The Five Nations were prosperous. But soon after the Dutch arrived, the warriors began to talk about the shortage of beaver. The best furs came from further west. The Mohawk Valley was not a natural breeding ground for the animals. An average of 4,000 pelts a year had been delivered at first at Fort Nassau, and that rapidly lessened. There were by the 1640s no more beaver along the Mohawk or the Genesee.

The fur trade had accustomed the people to a new set of values. A warrior's finest possessions were his musket, his steel hatchet and his scalping knife. His squaw used steel awls and needles; her cooking was done in an iron pot. She sewed bright-colored stroud cloth instead of buckskin, which shrank when wet and when frozen stiffened, loudly rattled, then cracked. Both men's and women's clothing were decorated with ribbons and with crystal beads. They had small mirrors in which to admire themselves.

The Confederate Lords of the Five Nations met at the Onondaga town. They talked of the Great Binding Law which held them together in peace and gave them unity of purpose. This was fortunate, because they had no furs, and must either loot furs directly from other Indians or force those others to trade through them as middlemen. Various speakers mentioned the Hurons.

The Hurons were cousins of the Iroquois. They were also the wealthiest of all Indians, although their home territory was poor in both

15

furs and agriculture. The Hurons made themselves rich by trading, and through their friendship with the French. They had landed eighty canoe-loads of furs in 1646 at Montreal. But the French had not yet given them guns.

It was recalled by the Confederate Lords that emissaries had been sent several times during the last few years to suggest that the Huron cousins expand their trade to include the Five Nations. The unchanging answer was flat refusal. This was not a cousinly gesture; it was not even friendly. The Hurons should be considered as enemies of the Five Nations.

War was planned. The former raiding parties composed of a few warriors out for scalps and glory were not to be used. Their effect would not alter the course of the fur trade. The Five Nations would send armies of more than 1,000 men, armed with muskets. The purpose of the war was the absolute annihilation of tribes handling the fur trade, or conquest and tribute.

The first attack was made at dawn in March 1649 upon a Huron village whose people had lived peacefully for decades. The Iroquois force of 1,000 warriors showed no mercy. Squaws and children were burned in their cabins. Two French Jesuit missionaries were tortured, one for fifteen hours. The final toll was 300 dead.

The Five Nations forgot the meaning of peace. They became dedicated to war, delighted in carnage, torture and cannibalism. Squaws who had danced happily at husking bees tore the hearts from captives, seared armpits, ripped out genitals and screamed in laughter when the captives writhed.

It took thirty-eight years to destroy the Huron nation. They were reduced from 30,000 people to 300 stuttering, stumbling beggars herded by French missionaries onto a small island in Georgian Bay. The Erie nation was long extinct, gone in 1654, the so-called Neutral Nation was obliterated by 1651, and in 1653 the Susquehannocks of Pennsylvania were finished.

The war continued with intermittent, ineffectual truces for fifty years. During it, the shores of Lake Huron where thousands of Indians had lived were empty. There were years when not a single canoe-load of furs reached Montreal from the west. The Indians of the entire

Great Lakes area refused to work for the French. They feared the Iroquois and the torture that could be made to last for three days.

An Iroquois force had attacked Montreal, and the big French trading post at Trois Rivières was struck several times. Remnants of the Hurons wandered benumbed west to Wisconsin, where they were joined by other fugitive tribes from the Ottawa River Valley, the Ohio, and southern Michigan. Fear of the Five Nations was epidemic.

The Confederate Lords at the height of their power exerted terror upon the nomad tribes around Hudson Bay, and upon the Cherokees, the Creeks and the Choctaws in the forests at the southern end of the Piedmont. Riding their canoes proudly alone, Iroquois tribute-gatherers came down the streams in New England and in the Ohio country, and asked for and received payment from warriors they called their "children."

The French were glad to make a treaty November 5, 1653, with them, although fully aware that it would not last. The Iroquois had obliterated or absorbed eleven tribes, and believed themselves all-powerful.

## 2

---

IT WAS WHEN AN AUTUMN GALE BROUGHT HEAVY snow that the Dutch at Fort Orange began to feel isolated. Then the Hudson froze. Communication with Nieuw Amsterdam, almost 150 miles away to the south, was stopped. Bleak, deep despair caught the settlers and the garrison.

There were in the 1640s several hundred of them, depending on the size of the garrison and the number of civilians who had decided to leave on the last ship before the river froze. Fear sent the civilians away, or, as they said it, common sense. They did not mention the possibility of Iroquois attack.

The first fort here, named Nassau, was built in 1614 on an island in the river. That was abandoned and the new one, the name changed, was built in 1617 on the west bank, at the site of Albany. It was strongly constructed, supplied with cannon, and located on the slope of the hill above the sharp river bank.

But in the early easy days of trade with the Iroquois, a village spread around the fort on the hillside. The settlers lived there. It was called Beverwyck, in honor of the beaver. Looking back, life in the village only a few years before seemed very happy.

The Iroquois who came to trade in 1634 asked for a big beaver skin four handsbreadths of wampum and four of duffel cloth. They got their price because the West India Company traders knew that the French were offering the same amount of wampum for a pelt, and six handsbreadths of cloth. Some of the people in the western Iroquois towns had bought French goods, shirts, coats and razors, through long-range barter.

But the Iroquois understood that the Mohawk Valley was their trade channel. It meant weeks of paddling and portages by way of Lake Oneida and the Oneida River to Lake Ontario, then east again down the St. Lawrence to reach Montreal. That route was through enemy country. The route to Fort Orange was shorter, safer and through the land of brother nations, sworn to obey the Great Binding Law.

Some of the people paddled down the Hudson from the mouth of the Mohawk, nine miles above the fort. Others emerged from the forest trails, the warriors ahead, the trade muskets conspicuously lifted, the squaws carrying the packs of beaver skins. But even the *royaneh*, the tribal nobles, lost a little dignity, stared, poked and were profoundly curious as they moved through the village.

The French lived far away, and from the beginning were enemies; the Iroquois had seen only a few of them. But here they could stand and watch a man who worked black metal and with fire made it turn red, take another shape. They could pat a horse on the haunch as it passed in the narrow street, and look at cows, see them give milk. Pigs were everywhere; their meat, roasted, was better than beaver tail.

The broad-doored house near the fort was the tavern, where the rum, the beer, the brandy were sold. The owner would sell to Indians. But if he was caught, he was made to pay a heavy fine. So he charged a lot, almost a guilder, for a small, very sour-smelling leather cup full of rum.

A warrior got just as much pleasure over at the bakeshop, and the squaws were delighted. They had no flour and no sweetening like the stuff the Dutch made. Dignified sachems danced on one foot and then the other as they ate buns right out of the oven.

Holding onto a sugar-sticky bun or a piece of gingerbread, the Indians left the bakeshop. The warriors stood for hours, part-hidden in shadow, and studied the fort. They wanted to know about the long buff coats the soldiers wore, and the steel body armor worn by the officers, and the halberds, the half-pikes, the silver-plated rapiers.

Most of the squaws watched the white women at work in the houses. Some few shyly advanced into a dooryard and touched the flowers. The houses were of a storey-and-a-half construction, the roofs sloping low. The dooryards were shallow; houses were built close together here on the edge of the forest. But the Dutch women raised a number of flowers, roses, tulips and lilies among them.

The Indian women, craning, could see the floor of the main room of a house, and the glint of pewter and a piece of silver. They did not understand the operation of the spinning wheels being worked, but they recognized the purpose. The squaws in the Iroquois towns already sewed with steel needles.

They had learned a great deal more. Scissors were used to cut cloth. There were iron cooking pots. The longhouses were built with steel-bladed axes. Warriors bought iron hinges and nails, knew how to handle a hammer.

The Mohawk warriors owned in 1642 more than 400 muskets. The Oneidas had their share, and the rest of the Five Nations. They asked as late as 1641 only one Dutch clay pipe for a deerskin. Then, within three years, the Fort Orange traders sharply complained. The warriors insisted that a deerskin was worth seven guilders.

The beaver were gone from the Mohawk Valley and the Genesee, the Iroquois said. Now the deer were almost finished, and had started to move to the hunting grounds of the Algonquins. This, the Dutch realized, would lead inevitably to war between the Iroquois and the Algonquins.

The Dutch sought no part of it. Their purpose here was trade. Letters were sent from Fort Orange to the Director General of the company, a merchant named Willem Kiefft who made his headquarters at Nieuw Amsterdam. He was severely criticized for his brutal treatment

20

of wandering bands of Indians who had been forced by the discontented, belligerent Mohawks into the lower Hudson River Valley. Other letters were sent to their High Mightinesses, the lords of the States General of the Netherlands.

The States General was the legislative body that represented the most liberal and progressive country in Europe. It was the philosophy of their High Mightinesses that the Mohawk Valley and all the Iroquois lands belonged to the Dutch preserve that extended from Virginia to the St. Lawrence. They called the Mohawk people Maquas, and the other members of the Five Nations were known as Sinnekens. A distinction was made in the case of the tribes that dealt with the French; they were simply "French Indians." The collective name for Indians of any category was *wilden*—savages.

Orders were given by the States General to develop the fur trade, agriculture and settlement. The factor who was in command at Fort Orange was also told to be industrious in "conversion to Lutheranism." Dominant through all of the thinking of their High Mightinesses, though, was the extreme importance of the Dutch West Indies Company's possession of Fort Orange.

The French owned nothing like it. Fort Orange, on the smooth-flowing Hudson only a few miles from the juncture with the Mohawk, might not be the gateway to the route which led to China. But it was the source of immediate and tremendous wealth.

West from the Hudson, along the Mohawk, then west again across the lakes and the plains country, and in the vastness of the unexplored regions beyond, lived Stone Age people. The Christian culture of the white man had already made contact with the Stone Age culture of the Indians at several places in America. Not at Fort Orange, though, with a valley like the Mohawk lying open to the forests and rivers and lakes where the beaver were to be found by the million.

Let the French and the Iroquois and the Algonquins fight, the people at Fort Orange told themselves. It opened the door still more for the Dutch. The *wilden* could not hold the Mohawk Valley forever. The Dutch were too smart and too stubborn to be kept out. The *wilden* should be swept aside so that white men—Dutchmen—could pass to the west and greater fortune.

The soldiers of the garrison force, the factor, the company traders and clerks were Dutchmen. But they were not the fat-bottomed, block-headed kind described in popular fable. They were lean, hard and vigorous. A number of the soldiers had served duty at the Dutch colony in Brazil, and the senior officers were veterans of the Lowland wars at home. Most of the settlers in Beverwyck were French-speaking Walloons. The free traders, a group that was not very highly regarded by the factor, were Irishmen, Swedes, Germans, Danes and Englishmen.

They were nearly all illiterate, and the majority quite intelligent. The factor considered them to be tough, careless about company regulations and the law, brave when it suited their fancy, and cruel. A report sent to the States General complained about the lack of settlers, of men willing to farm or take up a craft. But there were too many "petty traders who swarm hither with great industry, reap immense profit and exhaust the country without adding anything to its population or security."

The free traders were called, more or less in derision, *bosch-lopers*. That meant forest-runners, and the greater part of the year they were absent from Beverwyck. But they spent the severe winter months in the village.

The entire settlement, garrison, company clerks and sick folks, turned out on the river bank when the ice started to break in the spring. The dominie offered a prayer of thanksgiving. Then, having waited that long, the *bosch-lopers* went down the bank to their canoes.

They lifted the canoes from the racks, examined the seams, the bow and stern pieces, the thwarts and gunwales, the thin cedar strips that lined the hull. These were fine and light Algonquin craft made of St. Lawrence birchbark. A man risked his life and all he owned aboard one. He should make certain of it here and now, in every possible way.

The *bosch-lopers* left as soon as the big, rough ice chunks were out of the river. They ranged the country north and east of the Hudson for hundreds of miles, and southwest as far as the Delaware, close to the Swedish settlements. They were the first American frontiersmen.

2 2 Moving singly, the men who headed north went to Lake George and Lake Champlain and to the Winooski. They portaged around the Winooski Falls and reached the Connecticut. It took them in broadly

sprawled loops past beautiful, verdant intervales to the Dutch post at the site of Hartford.

This was called Fort Good Hope. The people there had another name for the river. It was to them "Fresh River." Salmon were caught in large quantities by the Indian tribes that lived on tidewater, down at the river mouth. They bartered the smoked fish along with sealskins and beaver pelts at Fort Good Hope. But trade was not good. A lot of it was going to the New England settlements or was lost to the Englishmen who came up the river in sailing craft loaded with goods.

The *bosch-lopers* did not stay long at Fort Good Hope. They renewed the trade articles they needed. Then they went back to the river and the forest. Keeping to themselves, working as separate agents, they met many tribes.

They were generally well received in the Indian villages. They no longer wore anything except the vestiges of European clothing. Their

A birch canoe poled against a rapid stream.

shirts were buckskin, and their feet were in moccasins instead of stiff, clumsy boots. Trousers were of duffel cloth; it dried quicker than buckskin and was more comfortable. Sealskin caps were chosen by some men, but most of them were former soldiers and liked more formal headgear. They sported beaver hats, broad-brimmed, looped up at the side, and decorated with silver or gold lace. The crowns bore dents and gashes from overhanging branches; the lace was tarnished by rain, repeated river wettings and campfire smoke. But the original hat was just as fine as that worn by a High Mightiness in Amsterdam.

The men spent a great part of their time alone on the forest rivers. They were extremely skillful canoe-handlers and hunters. It was necessary for them to know how to tickle a trout at the bottom of a rock-edged pool, fashion a snare for rabbit or squirrel, bring down a plump, noisy partridge with a single musket shot. There was no other way to exist. Rations purchased from the Indians took up cargo space in the canoe, and that was too precious, kept for the stowage of either trade goods or the slowly increased packs of beaver pelts.

A *bosch-loper* knew that where mast, acorns and various kinds of nuts gathered on the forest floor, squirrels were to be found. Deer paths were a yard or so wide, and the animals often showed themselves there, were an easy target. Young foxes and wolves tumbled around at play, and could be picked off with a snap shot. Otters disported themselves loudly on mud slides along the river bank. Fat, keen-eyed beaver whacked the water with their broad tails in the ponds they had made behind felled trees, and the sound severely tempted a *bosch-loper*. A single musket ball might mean a very fine pelt.

But the Indian villages were several days' canoework from each other. There were always portages, rapids, falls and rocky stretches where the utmost care must be taken. Summer would soon become fall, and in early November the trading season was finished. Several ambitious *bosch-lopers* stayed in the forest beyond that time, and their skeletons were discovered in the spring, the bones scattered by wolves around a tumbled lean-to hut, a rotting canoe and a pile of mildewed, worthless beaver pelts.

A veteran *bosch-loper* rarely interrupted his voyage to hunt or fish. He camped without fire, his supper a handful of leached corn picked up at the last Indian village and carried in a birchbark container. His shelter was the careened canoe. He slept with his musket in his hand, loaded and primed. When he reached the first portage in the morning, he took time to gather the small, bright blue whortleberries that grew along the way, and wild grapes, big rough-shelled black walnuts, chestnuts and beachnuts.

When he approached an Indian village, he moved with caution. He was usually seen by hunters, or warriors who tended the fish weirs, or by squaws in the corn patches. Then he sat up straight in the canoe and fired a couple of shots in salute. The chief met him at the landing place, dressed in his finest feather or black-squirrelskin mantle and ready to talk about gifts. Behind the chief were the warriors, solemn and silent, but also anxious about gifts, and in back of them, unfailingly clamorous, were the squaws, the children and the dogs.

A *bosch-loper* returning to Fort Orange in the fall met at some of the Mahican villages Frenchmen who were there also for trade. They were amiable enough, and with personal histories that were quite similar. But the French attitude towards the Indians was subtly different, and they traded in another fashion than the men from Fort Orange.

The Frenchmen called themselves *coureurs de bois*—forest-runners —the exact equivalent of the Dutch term. They wore full Indian clothing, though, and spoke the various tribal dialects fluently, mingled in absolute freedom with the people, proposed to spend the winter in the villages. They already had squaws, wigwams and in-laws.

The *bosch-lopers* stayed away from the Frenchmen as much as possible. They were both here for the same thing, and the Frenchmen had arrived first. Canoe brigades carrying thousands of pounds of prime beaver would move out of this country next summer headed for the St. Lawrence and the annual trade fair at Trois Rivières. They would be led by the *coureurs de bois* and return with Jesuit missionaries as companions.

Christianity was a great help to French trade. Sieur de Champlain had known it, encouraged the missionaries and worked closely with them. Jesuits had gone into Huron country and broken up the trade negotiations between the Hurons and the Iroquois. If the Hurons and the Iroquois got together, trade would go to Fort Orange—not Montreal. Dutch goods were better, cheaper.

The French sent their missionaries everywhere, even among the Mohawks. Père Jogues was a little skinny man, a mystic and a scholar. Maybe he sought death because of his beliefs. But when Jogues was brought to Fort Orange by a Mohawk fishing party in 1643 he made veteran soldiers weep. His hands, his back, nearly all his body had been seared, twisted, scarred, mutilated. The Dutch had paid 300 gold livres to buy him from the Mohawks, then there was trouble getting him aboard ship for Nieuw Amsterdam. The Mohawks came looking for him. And later he went back to Mohawk country, sent from Montreal, and got a tomahawk in his skull.

The *bosch-loper* spent a sleepless night in the Mahican village. There was not much left in his trade pack, and most of that he gave away as gifts. He noticed that the warriors carried French muskets, and the chief wore a ruffled shirt. The squaws had loose wrap-around smocks and skirts of French cloth of inferior quality, and mirrors, beads, needles, awls.

With dawn, the *bosch-loper* was on his way to Fort Orange. He moved fast. His cargo of beaver was valuable, and he saw no reason why it should become part of the Mahicans' shipment next summer to the Trois Rivières trade fair.

The familiar quadrangle of the stockade at Fort Orange appeared unchanged as the *bosch-loper* climbed to it from the canoe landing. He shouted to old comrades, was greeted by the sentries, bought the first round of drinks for everybody in the tavern. Then he took his furs to the company store, established a price for them and came back and drank some more.

He found great dissatisfaction among the other free traders. There were too many regulations in effect, they told him, and named the most galling. It was forbidden to run up the hill to meet Indians entering the settlement to trade. No resident of Beverwyck—no white man—could keep Indians overnight in his house. Children were forbidden to play with Indians, nor could they trade with them.

The *bosch-loper* who had lived unbrokenly for the last seven months in the deep forest felt an irksome restraint put upon him at Fort Orange. He very much missed his freedom. This place was no longer part of the frontier. It was owned by a wealthy patroon, a gold and diamond merchant who lived in Amsterdam. The patroon wanted to build a town here, put up a mill, start farms, raise cattle.

The Dutch West Indies Company owned only the site of the fort and the land right outside it. The patroon owned all of the land on both sides of the river from Barren Island, eleven miles below the fort, to the mouth of the Mohawk, nine miles above, and the inland boundaries had not been set.

The name of the patroon was Kiliaen Van Rensselaer. He was a *jonkheer*, a nobleman of the Province of Guelderland, and one of the original Lords Directors of the Dutch West Indies Company and a member also of the Amsterdam Chamber in the Assembly. His agent here was Herr Brandt Arendt Van Schlectenhorst, who bore the title of Director of the Colony of Rensselaerswyck.

The early settlers mocked Van Schlectenhorst with the nickname of "Gray Thief." Still, he was powerful. He had built houses between the fort and the river bank, openly defied tough old Peter Stuyvesant, the governor, refused to take them down or move them. His gunner on Barren Island had challenged the sloop *Good Hope* when she was bound for Nieuw Amsterdam, fired a round through her mainsail as a warning to lower her flag in salute to Rensselaerswyck.

The patroon was about to take over the river. When that happened, the *bosch-lopers* should leave and find another, where men could live free.

## ))) 3 )))

CAPTAIN GOUVERT LOOCKERMANS WAS AT THE tiller of the sloop *Good Hope* during the exchange of shouts and shots off Barren Island. He was a veteran sailor, a smuggler and Indian fighter, fully representative of the disgruntled faction at Beverwyck. The order to lower his colors was given in one word: "Strike!"

That was shouted out over the river by Nicolas Coorn, who served Jonkheer Van Rensselaer as quartermaster in command of the fort on the island. Loockermans shouted back, "For whom?"

"For the right of Rensselaerswyck!"

"I'll strike for no one," Loockermans told him, "except the Prince of Orange and the man I work for."

Then Coorn fired the cannon. The ball cut a gap in the mainsail above Loockermans' head, struck away a shroud, a halyard and a gasket. Loockermans reached aft and lifted from the taffrail socket the staff that held the flag of the Prince of Orange. He brandished it and shouted, "Fire, you dogs! And the devil take you!"

28

Kiliaen Van Rensselaer

Coorn fired again, but wind and current were with *Good Hope*. The shot went wild. A Mohawk warrior in temporary employment at the fort was seemingly irked by the bad gunnery. He had been issued a musket, and he took the sloop as his target. That shot just missed Loockermans; afterwards, the vessel was out of range downriver.

Loockermans reported the incident upon arrival at Nieuw Amsterdam and when he got back to Fort Orange. There was very little done, although court action was begun against Coorn. That was delayed repeatedly by Van Schlectenhorst in obedience to orders from the patroon in Amsterdam.

It was not difficult for Van Rensselaer to handle his affairs while more than 3,000 miles away from Fort Orange. He was very wealthy, ranked high among the High Mightinesses, and wielded great influence with cynicism and cunning. He had written Willem Kieft, the director general of the New Netherland colony, as early as 1639 about the treatment of people he sent forth from Holland as settlers on his Rensselaerswyck land:

> I would not like to have my people get too wise and figure out their master's profit, especially in matters in which they themselves are somewhat interested. These I would rather keep a secret between the company and myself. I shall then be able to trade with my people and to satisfy them.

Kiliaen Van Rensselaer never took enough time from his Amsterdam counting-house to inspect the Hudson River property he had quite illegally secured. He left to men like Van Schlectenhorst and Coorn the details of robbing the tenants at the commissary he maintained at Rensselaerswyck. A sly, smooth-spoken man, Bastiaen Jansen Crol, had been entrusted with the land deals, and was extraordinarily successful.

Crol was a layman who had talked himself into the good favor of the West India Company and assumed the capacity of Comforter of the Sick. This had enabled him on the voyage out from Holland to perform baptisms and also marriages. Along the upper Hudson, and in the Council at Nieuw Amsterdam, he glibly served Van Rensselaer; the patroon paid him well.

All of the tremendous land seizure on the part of Van Rensselaer and the concomitant flouting of the law were made possible by the vote on June 7, 1629, of the Assembly of the XIX, ratified by their High Mightinesses of the States General of the Netherlands. They accepted for the West India Company a charter whose sixth article specified:

> The Patroons, by virtue of their power, shall and may be permitted, at such places as they shall settle their colonies,* to extend their limits four miles (sixteen English miles) along the shore, that is, on one side of a navigable river, or two miles (eight English miles) on each side of a river, and so far into the country as the situation of the occupiers will permit; provided and conditioned that the Company keep to themselves the lands lying and remaining between the limits of the colonies, to dispose thereof, when, and at such time, as they shall think proper, in such manner that no person shall be allowed to come within seven or eight miles of them without their consent, unless the situation of the land thereabout were such, that the Commander and Council for good reasons, should order otherwise.

But such broad and vague distribution was not enough for Van Rensselaer and the other patroons who had holdings lower on the river. They wanted and got more land. A new Charter of Freedom and Exemptions was approved on June 19, 1640, in their favor. It was revised on May 24, 1650, and gave them still further rights.

Crol gained for his master through various shrewd purchases an enormous domain. It extended on both sides of the Hudson for approximately twenty-four miles north and south, and forty-eight miles east and west. The property included most of present-day Albany, Rensselaer and Columbia counties.

The patroon was intensely proud of what had been done in his name. A ship's manifest listed among the items he sent out early from Holland "a silver-plated rapier with baldric and a black hat with plume." Those were to be presented to Rutger hendrixsz van Soest in his capacity as "officer and Schout of Rensselaerswyck." Four black hats "with

3 1

* Colony, in the Dutch sense of the word, means estate, or plantation.

Pencil sketch of the Manor in Rensselaerswyck, Albany, N.Y.

silver bands" were on the same manifest, "to be presented in my name to the following persons, whom I have designated as schepens and councillor of Rensselaerswyck."

The men were mentioned in relation to the importance of their duties, and told to preserve a spirit of wholesome amity. Van Rensselaer's feelings for the settlers were somewhat different. He wrote about them, "Those in the colony, even if I were not their lord, need me here [in Amsterdam] more than I need them there, for who will supply their necessities if I do not? Who will furnish them the money if I do not?"

He shipped as part of the necessities "one brandy still, weighing 115 pounds." His interest in the settlers' welfare went beyond brandy to religion. He wrote to Arendt Van Corlaer:

In the box is a wooden model of a small church; please use diligence in erecting it at the least cost, if the building of the farmhouses does not prevent it. I have at Craloo a farm house of that shape, which is 60 feet wide. This church would be but 48 feet wide, so that it ought not to cost so very much. However, the upper structure is somewhat heavier and a storey higher. It is my definite intention that this church be put opposite Castle Island, north of the small grove and south of the farm of Gerrit de reux, deceased, not far from the small grove on a small hill, near or on the bank of the river. Cornelis Theunissen would perhaps rather have it on the west side of the river, but I am firmly resolved to have it on the east side, at the aforesaid spot. Near the church ought to be built also a dwelling for the minister and one for the sexton.

Having shown his amazingly thorough knowledge of Rensselaerswyck, and who was the master of it, he wrote to Pieter Cornelissen to "cause the people to assemble every Sunday, to train them in the commandments, the psalms, the reading of the Holy Scriptures and Christian authors, in modesty, love and decency."

Kiliaen Van Rensselaer died in 1647, and was not greatly mourned at either Rensselaerswyck or Fort Orange. He was succeeded as patroon by his son Johannes, who was not yet of age. Herr Van Schlectenhorst was appointed to direct the affairs of the colony. He was strict, hard-willed and penurious. The dissident minority element among the settlers and the *bosch-lopers* and the men who sailed the Hudson River sloops were unanimous in their dislike of him.

Men were needed at Rensselaerswyck to work as masons, carpenters, brick burners, stone and lime breakers. But very few of the unemployed took the jobs. The rest chose to go into the forest as *bosch-lopers,* accept the risks to be found there or serve aboard the river sloops whenever the chance offered. They wanted to get away from Rensselaerswyck as soon and as far as possible.

The men who worked aboard the sloops came to love the river life. There were still large regions of wilderness between Fort Orange and Nieuw Amsterdam. When a sloop finished her loading of beaver pelts and deerskins and shoved off downstream, she was due for a passage of at least a week, maybe ten days, before she reached Manhattan Island.

33

She sailed alone usually, and had the river to herself. Meantime, under the command of a captain like Gouvert Lookermans, a very great deal was to be learned, and every day something new.

The sloops the Dutchmen sailed in the Hudson River trade were heavily built, and broad-beamed. The sterns were high, with ornamental taffrails. The mast was stepped well forward and the boom was generally about ninety feet long, although average overall measurement for a boat was seventy feet.

They were fitted with a huge mainsail and a small jib, often set double topsails. Sailcloth was made from hemp. Standing and running gear were Baltic hemp, coarse stuff with an uncertain breaking strain, and carefully spliced, served and tarred. The tiller was long, reached well inboard, and the rudder was large, bound with iron for strength and as a safeguard against spring ice, drifting logs and belatedly seen snags.

The earliest vessels on the river were European-built. Some of those were *Gilded Otter*, *Broken Heart*, *Seven Stars*, *Bachelor's Delight*, *Glowing Oven* and *Angel Gabriel*. The craft put into service later, and made in local yards, were given more prosaic names. They were cargo-haulers, and passenger traffic was secondary. The money was in beaver and deerskins bound for Nieuw Amsterdam, and hogs, butter, brandy, rum and Indian goods headed upriver.

Passengers shared the crew's quarters, and ate the same food. The sloops provided the only form of regular conveyance in New Netherland. Ashore, the easiest route from Nieuw Amsterdam to Fort Orange was along the east bank. It was known as the Beaver Path, could be negotiated if necessary by a man on horseback, was nowhere suitable for wheeled traffic. Sloop passengers, if so minded, brought their own bedding, food and liquor. They seldom complained.

But all river men were forbidden by court order to sail from Fort Orange without permission and a rigid inspection of their vessels. This was put into effect after a veteran sloop master, Jacob Klomp, was caught in 1654 trading with the Indians at Catskill. He had sold them a large iron kettle, which, as proof that it would not leak, he filled with brandy. The court fined him 250 guilders for his disregard of the law;

still, other masters and crew members kept on selling brandy, rum and even beer to the Indians until they were apprehended.

Klomp, a profane and rugged man, remained active as a sloop master for some years. He traded, but within the law. Captain David de Vries was a sloop master who went early into the trade with the Indians on the river, then retired. He cruised the breadth of Tappan Zee in 1640 and bartered for fine pelts. He put his sloop at anchor and allowed the warriors aboard a few at a time from their canoes. His crew stood by, armed, watched the warriors and the nearest stretch of shore from which attack might come.

A sloop downbound from Fort Orange negotiated first a notorious pair of mud banks called the Upper and Lower Slaughs. There were a number of other shoals and bars near them, and from the Highlands a treacherous west wind whipped with the speed and motion of a tornado. This was a whirly-willy, and had dismasted vessels, capsized them and drowned their crews.

The master of a sloop kept a sharp lookout when abreast of the somber mass of the Highlands. Strange gusts, cat's-paws and squalls were common along the same reach of water. The crew did not relax until clear from it.

Then the men off watch often talked about the river. They were not quite aware that it occupied a very large part of their lives. But they knew the Indians called the valley Ontiora, which meant "mountains of the sky." The Katzberg Mountains were called that because of the panthers that screamed there at night, and the thunder so often heard was made by lightning storms playing among the bleak ridges. The Indians said that all animals and birds, any living thing that drank from the river, belonged to it. They were citizens of the river, too, like the tribes.

But that concept was difficult for the crew of a sloop to comprehend. Their lives were counted in tides, so many ebbs, so many flows, and each ebb brought them closer to Nieuw Amsterdam. The men who had never been there before questioned the old-timers at great length about it. When they reached it, they would have before them the wideness of the entire world, they realized, and not just the river, the fort, and Rensselaerswyck.

A river-boat crew tried hard to catch wind and tide right and tie up at Nieuw Amsterdam during daylight. All hands were excited by the traffic in the lower river, and off Spuyten Duyvil the captain went into the cabin and came out wearing a ruffled shirt and his best hat. Then he took the helm and occasionally pointed out the sights.

The sloop sailed among gundalows loaded with brick, tile, plaster, firewood, corn and hay. Hagboats and pinks and snows and brigs maneuvered dangerously close with wherries, skiffs and sailing ferries all headed for the East River wharves and wanting to tie up before dark. The shore scene could still be appreciated, though.

Windmills swung their latticed sails high and slow. The gilt weathervanes on the thicket of church steeples shone against the afternoon sky. Above the parapet on Fort William, the semaphore arms moved; a ship was coming in from seaward. That was the gallows on the stretch of common outside the city wall.

The wall was palisaded and sodded. The sentries on duty at the gate wore buff jackets and carried halberds. The officers wore body armor. They were armed with swords or rapiers.

Most of the houses were built of pale brick. The gabled ends faced the streets. The roofs were made in crow steps right to the top. That was so the chimney sweeps could get up, step by step. There were trees and gardens around many of the houses, tulip-trees and chestnuts and maples and elms. But the city had a sour, nasty smell. A lot of people died here each summer from fever.

The crew off a sloop went ashore at the water gate next to the Battery. The taverns were close, and the crew seldom went any further. Talk in the taverns was with men wearing gold earrings and pistols in their belts, and men who had sailed ships to Java, around the Cape of Good Hope.

The men with the earrings said they had served as Brothers of the Coast—buccaneers—on the Spanish Main. The money they spent here was Spanish loot. They were going back for more. The other men had stories about black, frizzle-headed pygmies, and lions, and palaces in Java where the rajah's throne was made of solid gold. They had touched at Brazil and Curaçao along the way, and now were bound for Holland.

The crew from the Fort Orange sloop listened, silent and awed, then bought another round of drinks. But they went back aboard their own vessel when the taverns closed. They loved the river, would spend their lives on it, and nowhere else.

Homeward-bound for Fort Orange, a sloop sailed on the incoming tide. The captain kept a rough log for departure and arrival times, and a cargo tally sheet. But he had long ago memorized the tides.

High water at Sandy Hook meant the same at Tarrytown around two-thirty in the afternoon, an hour later at West Point, about five-twenty at Poughkeepsie, seven-forty at Hudson, and a bit after ten-twenty at the Fort Orange wharf. Westerlies were the prevailing winds off Manhattan, and a sloop sailed for home rap-full, with all sails filled, and not quite close-hauled. The captain drove hard; he had plenty of cargo, and upstream he would almost certainly be set back by headwinds.

The crew cleared the decks of port litter, rigged the hose, started the pump and washed down fore and aft. Gulls still screamed in flight over the mast truck, but most of them soon left in pursuit of fish. There was the gush and clunk of the pump, the swish of the men's swabs along the deck planks, and the small fine sound of the wind in the sails and the rigging. Far up on the westerly bank, where the Palisades lifted their

Sloops sailed
up the Hudson
past the Palisades.

jagged, enormous buttresses, an eagle flew out from a cave beneath Great Chip Rock.

The last of the gulls disappeared. All the birds along the river were motionless, their song stopped. Rabbits and squirrels made a scampering run for cover. But the eagle passed, leaving magnificent shadow, and once more the birds sang.

The river was the brilliant floor of a vault of sunlight during summer. The crests of the trees were luminous. Where the sloop's wake spread astern, bubbles were phosphorescent, and the froth a white that gleamed against the surrounding surface blue. A haze was often over the water, particularly in afternoon. When the wind or the current was wrong and the sloop anchored, the men who went swimming made aureoles around them with each stroke.

Ashore, once past the Palisades, the banks were verdant. Here were daisies, buttercups, blue vervain, tiger lilies, pink and white clover, lupines, yellow wood sorrel. Ferns grew almost as tall as a man, and there were elder blossoms, budding sumac, grapevines along the tree branches, honeysuckle and wild roses clinging to the boulders.

Fish of half a dozen kinds were caught while the boat was at anchor, and in the spring the shad offered roe. A fire was made in a sandbox on the main deck with the sail furled and the boom hauled over out of the way of sparks. The meal was eaten fast if the wind changed. A veteran captain who knew the river well kept going after dark.

He drove the sloop hard across the choppy width of Tappan Zee, tacked back and forth to set his course beyond, his landmark the peak of Hook Mountain. Then he held Haverstraw broad on the port hand, usually picked up a favorable westerly there, and pointed for Sailmakers' Reach, the Crescent, and Hoge's, Vorsen, Fisher's and Clover. The last reaches seemed the longest. The crew was always happy to drop sail at the wharf below the fort, secure the mooring lines and get ashore.

The men in the Beverwyck tavern wanted to hear the news from Nieuw Amsterdam. They were interested, too, in the stories about the buccaneers, the Cape of Good Hope pygmies and the rajah's golden throne in Java. But their own news occupied most of the conversation.

The patroon had taken over this end of the river, lock, stock and foresight. Unless a man worked for Van Rensselaer or went along with the orders given by the overseers, he was put in jail on some easily arranged charge and his wife and children starved. There was no way out. The patroon owned too much land, and the fort was stuck in it like a fly in honey—very sticky honey.

The system was wrong and could only be set straight in Holland. There, a man would run up against their High Mightinesses, the Van Rensselaers' close cronies, and the people who had started the patroon system. Asking them for help would bring more trouble. If there was to be a fight, the patroon was sure to win.

The first structure the patroon built on his land was a fort. It was put up in 1642, and Van Schlectenhorst, the tough, shrewd man who had been appointed Director of Rensselaerswyck was in charge of the work. The materials for it were sent out from Holland aboard the ship *De Houttyn*, each brick, tile and slate checked. Inscriptions were already on the cornerstones, one in honor of the patroon, which read "K.V.R. 1642 ANNO DOMINI." A stone in the opposite wall honored the dominie, "DO MEGAPOLENSIS."

His Reverence, Dominie Johannes Megapolensis, had arrived with his family in the same ship to take over the duties of spiritual adviser to the colony. He was needed if not appreciated. The Rensselaerswyck settlers, who now numbered several hundred, were close to open rebellion against the patroon's practices and the law as enforced by Van Schlectenhorst and sheriffs either in his pay or afraid of him.

The settlers had been promised a great deal by Van Rensselaer's agents before sailing from Holland. A letter of instruction was given to Megapolensis which specified the details. Van Rensselaer hoped that the dominie could be of secular help in the colony, restrain and pacify the settlers. The letter stated:

> Each farmer must take with him at least two servants and one boy who understands farming, and himself equip them; the patroon, on his part, provides their board till they arrive in New Netherland at the Island of *manhatans* and on their arrival in the colony causes them to be provided upon condition of repayment with grain for eating and sowing and with a suitable site on which to establish their farm,

where the patroon will once and for all have a good house with [hay] barrack and barn built for them, which according to the custom of that country are usually placed near the river, the waters of which flow by clear and fresh and full of fish.

The patroon causes them also to be provided once with a wagon and plough and what else is needed for farming, the same to be kept in repair and replaced by the farmer; he will further assign them 30 or 40 morgens* of land toward the interior, consisting of beautiful woods filled with excellent game, such as deer, turkeys and all sorts of nourishing fowls. He also turns over to them on each farm, from the surplus of animals in the colony, four horses and four cows, of which they are to have half the increase, the other half to be paid to the patroon in money or in kind.

The fault in this was that a farmer could never own the land he worked. It belonged in perpetuity to the patroon and to the patroon's heirs. A Rensselaerswyck tenant was forced to give each year a share of his crops and his increase of livestock to the owner of the land, and the fact became the greatest instrument of injustice in the entire history of the Hudson Valley.

Cornelis Van Tienhoven, secretary in 1650 to Peter Stuyvesant who then served as director general of New Netherland, was openly scornful about the tenant problem. He dared write home to their High Mightinesses that in Rensselaerswyck "no one down to the present time can possess a foot of land of his own but is obliged to take upon rent all the land which he cultivates."

The land was rich and fine for farming. Men raised on it abundant crops of corn, hay, squash, pumpkins and many other vegetables, and, as the trees grew and the vines were cultivated, apples, pears and grapes. They worked all day long in the corn rows, their families faithfully behind them with hoes. Their boys drove the teams that pulled the huge wains in haying time. They stood on the wains or in the cramped, hot darkness of the barn lofts and pitched off the load with furious haste when a rain squall threatened. They hurried to get in the other crops before frost came along, and to plant in the spring as soon as it was out of the ground.

41

* Morgen: approximately two acres.

They did not have much time to go fishing or hunting. The best they could do was to stop work for a moment on a fair day and look out over the river where a sloop showed her topsails at a bend. The forest meant more work, scrub to be cleared, and Indians, wolves, bears and lynx.

The fort the patroon built was on the eastern bank of the river, across from Fort Orange. It was called Crailo after a country estate the patroon owned in Holland. The site was called Greenbush, and the tenants gathered there on rent days in a long file of carts and wagons filled with produce.

The fort was three storeys high, with firing slits in the walls at the ground-floor level. The walls were brick; the roof was made of slate. Crailo was supposedly built to keep its people safe from Indian raids. Some of the tavern talk over in Beverwyck, though, was that the patroon used it as a refuge. He could hide there from his tenants.

The patroon was young Johannes Van Rensselaer, Kiliaen's son, and he held fiercely to every bit of land his father had claimed. The Greenbush grant was 1,800 acres. The grant alongside it to the southward on the same bank of the river, known as the Claverack tract, was more than 60,000 acres. That had not been surveyed, and nobody could reckon the full extent of it.

There was a bad epidemic of smallpox in the early spring of 1663, and a number of people in Rensselaerswyck, Beverwyck and Fort Orange died. The river overflowed when the ice jam broke with the spring thaw and earthquake tremors passed through the valley. Predictions of worse happenings were made. Then, the following year, a British squadron came up the Narrows and anchored off Nieuw Amsterdam.

The director general, Peter Stuyvesant, was told to surrender. The British squadron was only five ships, but the city's defenses were weak. Stuyvesant obeyed.

The British took over for James, Duke of York, and brother of Charles II of England. The city was given the name of the duke, became New York. The river, which the Dutch had called the River of Prince Mauritius, was changed to Hudson. The first British governor of the colony, Colonel Richard Nicolls, sailed north on a tour of inspection of the upper reaches.

Van Rensselaer and the other Dutch landowners with big estates were apprehensive. The name of the town of Rondout was changed to Kingston, and Beverwyck became Albany. Land titles could be changed as rapidly, and the estates declared British property, put up for public sale.

But Colonel Nicolls was affable, and perfectly willing to leave the land-tenure system untouched. He wanted to secure the friendship and support of the patroons, retain them as prominent figures in the colony. His only orders, he told the worried group that met him in Albany, were to remove the trade restrictions, the duties and taxes imposed by the West India Company. The valley would surely profit from that action, the patroons realized, and offered the colonel immediate, warm expressions of loyalty.

The Rensselaerswyck tenant farmers had been able to dream briefly of a better existence in which they owned land. But British rule of the colony left them as much as ever in the patroon's debt, forced to buy at his commissary, sell for the prices he offered, stand trial in the court where he was the judge. Young unmarried men and boys in their teens who were big enough to handle a musket slipped away and joined the *bosch-lopers* in the forest. Others found jobs aboard the river boats, or entered into deals as smugglers. They acted as intermediaries between the river men and the *bosch-lopers*.

The British occupation of the colony had shown them how easily loyalty could be shifted. They were supposed to take orders from the same master, work in the same way. But the patroon swore allegiance to Charles II; he was now a loyal British subject.

They did not owe any allegiance to the patroon or to the British. All the patroon and the British wanted was to make money. The patroon had his system, and the British shared in it. But there was money, too, in smuggling.

The runaway farmers from Rensselaerswyck hid in the copses along the river bank near the rendezvous points they kept with the sloop crews. A dark night was best, although sometimes they worked when the moon was high and a sloop was visible a mile or so away on the river, her jib shivering as she slowly breasted the current.

A skiff was rowed from the sloop to the shore. The man at the oars and the man in the stern were armed. It carried a neatly stowed load of Indian trade goods, blankets, cloth, powder shot, hatchets, all the usual trinkets. Those were of English manufacture, and better made and cheaper than what the French merchants at Montreal could supply. English merchants in New York were the source, bought the goods wholesale in London.

This lot when put ashore and paid for was moved next in packs the smugglers carried on their backs. They skirted the settlements at Rensselaerswyck, kept to the northward through deep forest. Their rendezvous point with the *bosch-lopers* was usually along the headwaters of the Hudson where canoes were concealed.

The *bosch-lopers* paid for the goods, put the load in a canoe and went north. They met at the foot of Lake George *coureurs de bois* who had come down the Richelieu and then Lake Champlain for the express purpose of buying the goods. French-speaking Walloons among the Hudson River men talked with the *coureurs de bois*. The two groups camped together for the night.

They agreed that the Iroquois would soon know about this. Some of the warriors were certain to find traces of the smugglers, catch up with a group. Torture and the stake were to be expected afterward. The Iroquois, particularly the Mohawks, were growing rich by barter for furs with the western tribes. Cheaper goods would ruin it, and without the western trade the Five Nations were beggars, even the deer gone from their land.

The gamble was worth the chance of Iroquois torture, though. Both the *bosch-lopers* and the Frenchmen understood that. It was time the Five Nations were pushed out of the Mohawk Valley. They were the last force to block free passage to the west. The Algonquins were firmly under French control, could be handled any way the big merchants at Montreal wanted. The western tribes lacked a leader, were not strong. The country beyond the Mohawk was wide open, and filled with prime pelts, copper, iron, all kinds of wealth.

*Bosch-lopers* and *coureurs de bois* tapped out their pipes. Ashes were tossed across the campfire. The men slept deeply, side by side. They trusted each other, at least for this night, held by a common dream.

44

## ))) 4 (((

THE BRITISH REGIME BROUGHT ONLY ONE UNCOM-
mon man to Albany. He was young, red-headed and attractive,
and of proud Scottish descent. He was also more avaricious and ambitious
than any man yet to reach the place, came to it in the fall of 1674 from
Boston. When he had landed in Boston he was almost penniless. But he
used his wits, some letters of introduction and his father's reputation to
finance himself with a small sum of borrowed money.

His father was the Reverend John Livingston, a Presbyterian
minister who had been forced to leave Scotland in 1663 because he opposed
the Episcopalian tendencies of the Stuart Restoration. Reverend Livingston became the pastor of a congregation of Scottish refugees in Rotterdam. He sent back for his wife, one of his daughters, and Robert, his
youngest son. Robert grew up in Rotterdam, was as fluent in Dutch as in
English, acquired a thorough knowledge of the shrewdest European
business practices in a Rotterdam counting-house.

Robert Livingston was twenty when he got to Albany. The Province of New York had just come back under the British flag after a short period of repossession by the Dutch. The Duke of York was again the proprietor of the colony, and Livingston was exceptionally useful to the duke's agents. They were in the middle of complicated deals with the Dutch burghers and with the Iroquois, whose interpreters were Dutch-speaking. Livingston was kept busy as a "linguister," learned the inner operations of the provincial government, and gathered a considerable fund of information on local affairs.

There were, he found, a number of land purchases, trade opportunities and social alignments which would be profitable to a man who, although very young and a recent arrival, clearly foresaw the future of the colony. A salient fact in his calculations was that during a single year an average of a million pounds of beaver pelts moved through Albany to New York and the markets overseas.

Sir Edmund Andros, the governor of the colony, came to Albany in 1675, and Livingston took great care to be of service to him. When he left, Livingston had been appointed to the secretaryship of the Board of Indian Commissioners for the colony and the clerkship of the Albany General Court. The combined salary for the two offices was 400 guilders, and within two years this was raised to 600 guilders.

Livingston had also secured the right to take a commission of four per cent on the taxes he collected in the Albany area. He was aware that the tax collector's job would not add to his popularity. But he was not immediately interested in maintaining it. He was occupied with what he believed to be much more important and imperative matters.

Without the distortion of national prejudice or emotional involvement of any sort, he recognized the immensity of the struggle that had begun to veer back and forth violently once more between Quebec and Albany. They were both vital in the struggle because of their strategic locations on major rivers, and whoever owned them would in time win control of the continent. The French understood this, but were not able to make use of their knowledge. The smartest men sent as administrators or soldiers to the New World were severely hampered by religious issues and court politics.

The course of North American destiny was reasonably obvious. It would be resolved by trade, not war, not missions and the planting of flags and crucifixes. The effect of the smugglers' trade upon the Montreal merchants and the haughty but not so wealthy warriors of the Five Nations was proof of that.

Both *bosch-lopers* based in Albany and *coureurs de bois* who sailed the Canadian rivers had entered the trade. Many of the leading citizens in Montreal eagerly bought the English goods. They corresponded with Albany and New York merchants, asked for specific items. Entire sloop-loads of merchandise were sent upstream from New York. The original smugglers, somewhat surprised, were offered high pay to work in broad daylight and transfer cargo to the French canoe fleets on Lake George. The only clandestine part of the operation was that the Iroquois had not been officially informed about it.

The Iroquois killed some of the smugglers, then made very strong representations at Albany. The trade with the western tribes belonged to them, they said. The French should not be allowed to handle it. Robert Livingston, as secretary of the Board of Indian Commissioners, listened to the Iroquois with care, and reported to his superiors. Smuggling was drastically reduced, and again the Iroquois set out along the Mohawk in canoes loaded with goods and headed west.

The Iroquois were, Robert Livingston realized, just as much middle-men as the members of any commercial guild in England, Holland or France. The splendid buckskins, the rituals, the great personal dignity and courage meant very little. The Iroquois worked for a wholesale mer-chandise organization that was directed from London by way of New York and Albany. When they fought the Hurons, their enemies were being paid by another set of wholesalers whose main office was in Paris.

The French had made a determined effort to stop competition when they came down from Canada in 1666 after the Mohawks. A famous soldier, the Marquis de Tracy, led 600 veterans of the Carignan-Salières regiment, 300 militia and a collection of 100 Indians willing to enter Mohawk country. Marquis de Tracy had a splendid record of victories in the Turkish wars and a campaign in the West Indies. The Carignan-Salières regiment was to be permanently stationed in Canada, the men given wives and land. 47

But the force did not distinguish itself. It sailed along Lake Champlain in a fleet of 300 *batteaux*, went ashore at the site of Fort William Henry and started into the wilderness to the westward. The Algonquin scouts were afraid of Mohawk ambush, and moved so slowly the main force never established contact. The Carignan-Salières men, wearing corselets, carrying halberds and arquebuses, sorely floundered. They remained hungry, though, and exhausted their provisions.

Marquis de Tracy led them finally into a couple of Mohawk towns deserted by the inhabitants. The order was passed to burn the longhouses and the corn cribs, but to take enough corn to get back to Canada. This campaign was being abandoned.

The Five Nations were quite circumspect in their relations with the French afterwards, though. They concentrated on the destruction of the Hurons and the other tribes that opposed them, and expanded their Great Lakes trade. Now, in 1675, they saw the French as their principal enemy, and they were ready to return to war. They were convinced that their wealth, their land and their prestige would be lost if they allowed the French to push further west.

Robert Livingston used his position with the Board of Indian Commissioners to gather all possible knowledge about the French penetration. The old Iroquois route to the St. Lawrence was guarded by forts along the Richelieu and at the head of Lake Champlain, and those were held by large garrisons. The Iroquois were cut off there. And out west, they were confronted by another formidable force.

Well-armed parties of *coureurs de bois*, and explorers commissioned by the king, and resolute, tireless missionaries had moved into the Great Lakes region. There was a French trading post at Michilimackinac, at the straits which led to the southernmost lake and the enormous river called Mississippi. A ceremony had been held at a falls called Sault Sainte Marie in 1671 where a French nobleman in spangled court uniform took possession of the entire west of North America in the name of Louis XIV. The ceremony was witnessed by the chiefs of fourteen tribes, and the fleur-de-lis flag was raised, and a cross. Then a post was built and trading started.

48    The Iroquois had a number of very valid reasons why they should go to war against the French. But, Robert Livingston recognized, this time it would not just be Indian fighting and hit-and-run raids on

In a Canadian farmhouse.

isolated forts and towns. New France had become too solidly populated for that, and the war would undoubtedly engage regular French and English troops. Albany was a primary target in any large-scale French campaign, and even if the English succeeded in defending it, the fur trade would be very badly disrupted. That meant the end of the flow of wealth into the town. Beaver was still the mainstay of all trade.

But land in this beautiful fertile valley along the Hudson held permanent value. Right from the beginning, old Kiliaen Van Rensselaer had favored farms rather than furs. Now his sons were the richest men in the valley. They owned an almost unbelievably vast estate, and operated it with ruthless, feudal simplicity. They were literally the masters of all they surveyed.

Livingston came from an ancient Scottish family. He knew about the various forms of Highland clan procedure and the inherited rights and privileges of the lairds. Here on the Hudson, he came to admire the patroons. His sense of cupidity, his compulsive desire for wealth were so great that he keenly envied them.

The Van Rensselaers took one-third of a tenant's crops, and income from hunting licenses, and fees for grinding corn and wheat. They conducted their own courts, used torture when they thought it necessary

49

to get confession. Their homes, their yachts, their carriages and horses were magnificent. Some of their women, unless they became too fat, were beautiful.

Robert Livingston's consuming ambition was to live like a patroon, own as much wealth. He devoted all of his considerable intelligence, his forceful nature and wit and charm to it. The entire patroon class stood ready to refuse him entrance, he realized. The *jonkheers* during his first few months at Albany had made it clear that they did not accept him as their social equal.

The Van Rensselaers, the Van Courtlands, the Van der Doncks, the Schuylers, the Melyns, the Philipses had consolidated their wealth and their power along the river by constant intermarriage. They remained aloof, very nearly invulnerable. There was, though, Livingston knew, a way to join the patroons. That was by marriage among them, preferably to a woman who belonged to the wealthiest of their families.

It had become traditional at Albany that the town clerk should perform the same duty for the Van Rensselaer family. The town was the patroon's unofficial capital. The patroonship stretched out all around it, nearly fifty miles long from east to west and fully forty wide at its greatest width from north to south. Livingston was appointed to serve as secretary of Rensselaerswyck in 1675 at a salary of 200 guilders a year. The appointment was made by Dominie Nicolaes Van Rensselaer, the manager of the patroonship.

Livingston approached his ambition gradually, and worked with tremendous diligence at his three jobs. Those, when created, had been intended as work for a quiet young man who could write a legible hand, cipher accurately and keep a neat set of ledgers. Livingston greatly increased their range, and took profit from them.

He taught himself law so that he could serve in the capacity of a paid consultant in the General Court which employed him as salaried clerk. His duties as secretary to the Board of Indian Commissioners gave him an insight into Iroquois activity which he found to be of substantial help in his private endeavor as a fur trader. He was awarded the contract to supply the garrison with provisions. His idea of what was a sufficient ration did not appeal to the troops, and Scots among the force stopped him in the street. They took the trouble to tell him that it was his kind which brought Scotland a bad name.

Livingston disregarded the insults. They meant little to him, and he had become accustomed to them. He was growing wealthy, and that was what mattered. That and the fact that Dominie Nicolaes Van Rensselaer was ill and about to die.

A story that was never fully confirmed but which formed a part of Albany folklore was passed around the town after Van Rensselaer's death. It told how Robert Livingston, in response to an urgent request, boarded the family yacht at anchor in the river off Albany. He went to take the last will and testament of the patroon as his faithful secretary. But Nicolaes had called himself "Nicolaes the Prophet" ever since he had correctly forecast that Charles Stuart would one day sit upon his father's throne.

Now, aboard the yacht, Nicolaes reared up in the bunk. He shouted at Livingston to get out of his sight. "Anyone but you," he said, "for you will marry my widow!"

The Prophet died a few hours after Livingston left the boat. Livingston began at once to woo and win Van Rensselaer's widow. Her name was Alida. She was twenty-two, blonde and quite pretty. She was not only the heiress to the Van Rensselaer wealth, but born a Schuyler, closely related to the Van Courtlands. Her connections extended to all of the patroon families along the river.

Livingston was bony-faced, with a long nose and a big jaw. He was not among Alida Van Rensselaer's most prepossessing suitors. But he was wily and persistent, could exhibit great charm. He explained to her with care the handling of her estate. He made her understand the details of the will left behind by Nicolaes.

Alida wore her hair massed high on her forehead, with a ringlet that reached down to each shoulder. Her gowns were of brocaded silk, and low-cut. She and Livingston walked in the back garden at Crailo in fair weather when he came to call, the lilac hedge a fragrant barrier around them. There were other matters to consider that had nothing to do with the Prophet.

Livingston married Alida fourteen months after Nicolaes died. He was welcomed more or less graciously by the patroons. Then he took over the direction of Rensselaerswyck. But he did not let that interfere with the enlargement of his own fortune.

When he was free at Albany, he moved up and down the river to the various Van Rensselaer holdings aboard the family yacht. It was a sturdy Hudson-built sloop, but with Javanese-teak panelling in the main cabin, a big rattan chair on the poop for Alida's comfort, and a striped awning for the hot summer days. Alida was pregnant a great deal of the time. Livingston made most of his inspection tours alone.

He became familiar with the operation of the several gristmills on the estate and the revenues they brought, improved the efficiency of the windmills that turned the grindstones. Overseers answered his searching questions or were dismissed. He knew all of the work done at the boatyard, the carriage shop, the grain-houses and the sawmill. He often inspected the out-kitchen, the smokehouse, the dyeing-room, the fowl yard, the hothouse and the root cellar. The work performed by the Negro slave girls who churned, knitted, sewed, and carded and spun wool was checked. He looked into the slave quarters near the stables, and with Alida visited the Greenbush dominie and occasionally went to church.

But he did not maintain his role of pro-tem patroon very long. There were highly jealous and capable Van Rensselaer men to take over the management as majority owners of the property. Livingston collected Alida's belongings and they went across the river to Albany to live.

Albany received its charter in 1686 from Governor Thomas Dongan, a hearty and bluff Irishman. He was exposed to the best of the Livingston charm, and saw that Livingston was assigned further lucrative offices. These were clerk of the peace and clerk of Common Pleas, and soon afterwards Livingston was appointed to the posts of sub-collector of the excise and receiver of the quitrents for Albany County.

It was the practice of the time for the provincial government to borrow needed funds in advance of taxes from men able to make a loan of considerable size. Governor Dongan went to Livingston, and by 1686 he was £3,000 in Livingston's debt. He had already been of major assistance to his Scottish friend in some real-estate negotiation.

When popular dislike of Livingston reached the point where he

52

was forced from public office for his multifarious acts of self-aggrandizement, he was perhaps unduly called a thief, and a rogue. But two royal governors, in soberly contemplated reports to the home government, had nothing to say about him that was pleasant. Benjamin Fletcher stated that Livingston's "whole thirst" was for wealth. Livingston, the governor said, never spent sixpence without expecting twelvepence back. He summed up Livingston's character in a rather critical way: "His beginning being a little Bookkeeper he has screwed himself into one of the most desirable estates in the province."

Governor Bellomont wrote that as a purveyor of supplies to the military, Livingston had been a failure, but Livingston had "pinched an estate out of the poor soldiers' bellies." Bellomont held the rare reputation of being incorruptible, although he was once Livingston's personal friend.

The greatest triumph for Livingston was the acquisition of this estate. He schemed very hard to get it. He started out by claiming a portion of the Van Rensselaer properties as his wife's guardian. The action was bitterly contested but finally settled by a cash payment.

Then, with the permission of Governor Andros, he bought in 1683 a tract of 2,000 acres from the Wappinger Indians. The land was on the east bank of the river, some forty miles below Albany and where the Roeliff Jansen Kill flowed into the Hudson. He paid 300 guilders' worth of wampum, guns, powder and miscellaneous trade goods for it. Governor Dongan sanctioned the purchase and on November 4, 1684, granted a royal patent.

Governor Dongan again approved of his friend's ventures when the next year he granted a royal patent to Livingston for 600 acres of Indian land located along the Massachusetts border. Livingston described this tract as "lying upon ye same [Roeliff Jansen] Kill called by the Indians Tachkanic behind Patkook about Two or 3 hund: acres." He bought it with wampum and truck goods that cost him 600 guilders.

Livingston was issued on July 22, 1686, a royal patent that brought the two parcels of land together in what was to be known as Livingston Manor, "with full power and authority at all times for ever hereafter in the same Lordship and Manor one Court Leet and one Court Baron to hold and keep." * The annual quitrent to the Crown was twenty-eight shillings.

Either Livingston's geography was faulty, though, or Governor Dongan was exceptionally generous. The two pieces of property were in no sense contiguous. Livingston had increased, without expense to himself, 2,600 acres until they became 160,000 acres. The trick was in the application for patent and the phrase that read, "about Two or 3 hund: acres."

His original purchase was on the Hudson. The second piece of property was many miles inland, further to the east, and in between were 157,400 acres which had never been bought and which, by law, still belonged to the Indian people who lived or hunted there.

Livingston kept the estate. He hung onto it and to his various official assignments during the period of the Leisler revolt in 1688 that swept a torrent of popular resentment of the royal government through the Hudson Valley. He was still in possession in 1690 when the French put into effect their "Grand Plan" of attack.

That was the familiar pincers-movement attempt which always seemed simple when laid out on a map thousands of miles away from the St. Lawrence, the Richelieu and the Hudson. His courtiers had at last convinced Louis XIV that resistance to French power should be destroyed in North America. Attacks against Manhattan Island would be made by land and sea. Two warships dispatched from La Rochelle could proceed without serious delay to New York, bombard it into submission. Their crews would make "happy junction" there with the French land force that had driven south from the St. Lawrence along the Hudson.

The land force was ordered to give everlasting chastisement to the Five Nations. Prisoners were to be taken from among the Dutch and English, for ransom later at huge sums. Rensselaerswyck and the other estates would be occupied, the people worked as slaves. Count de Frontenac had indicated to the king how much wealth was being lost through the diversion of beaver trade to Albany. There was also a dream which Louis XIV refused to relinquish. He looked forward to having Iroquois

54

* A Court Leet had jurisdiction over crimes committed within the manor; a Court Baron had jurisdiction in civil actions arising within the manor.

braves, in uniform, at the oars of his galley as it carried him along the Seine.

Robert Livingston held himself in readiness at Albany for the French attack. But there had been a number of abortive assault plans, and this became another. The warships never arrived from La Rochelle to bombard New York. The land force dwindled to a combined French-Indian group that made a single raid upon the outpost village of Schenectady, near Albany. It ended in a bloody, terrible massacre at dawn in the middle of February, 1690, with some recently "Christianized" Mohawks as volunteer raiders.

The failure of the Grand Plan did not bring peace. Sporadic fighting continued, and war parties raided back and forth in fierce reprisal. But a Dutch interpreter and *bosch-loper* named Arnout Cornelius Viele had gone west through the Appalachian range in 1682 and explored the Ohio. During the next eight years, working with several Albany traders and aided by French deserters, he almost succeeded in the diversion of the Great Lakes fur trade from Montreal to the Hudson. Anglo-Dutch expeditions went up the Lakes as far as Michilimackinac and bartered there with the regional tribes.

The terrible massacre at Schenectady in the winter of 1690 stopped this. Frontenac had returned from France and was in command in Canada. The Iroquois who the year before had perpetrated awful atrocities at La Chine, a settlement on the St. Lawrence near Montreal, kept pretty much to their home territory. They had a great deal of respect for Frontenac as a soldier.

The heavy-handed treatment of the Shawnees by the Iroquois had also brought a new source of wealth to Albany. The Shawnees who lived in the beautiful Ohio Valley were rebellious against the Iroquois' and the Five Nations' method of exacting tribute. Representatives of their tribe appeared at Albany and said they wanted to establish trade on their own account.

Viele was sent out in 1692 to the Ohio to investigate the possibilities. He came back two years later followed by a fur-laden brigade of Shawnees. His description of the route he had taken was vague.

Robert Livingston could never establish whether Viele crossed from the Mohawk to the Delaware and from that to the Susquehanna.

55

There was an alternate route that went directly from the Mohawk to the Susquehanna, and then by a short portage to the tributaries of the Allegheny and down it to the Shawnee villages on the Ohio.

But Livingston was not allowed to consider the possibilities of the Shawnee trade at any length. People in Albany were insistent; they wanted him ejected from office for malfeasance. He had taken too much too fast. He was accused in 1695 of misappropriation of the public funds and threatened with the sequestration of his property.

Livingston left Albany. He went to London and presented his case before the Lords of Trade and the Privy Council. His powers of logic and rhetoric were fully used, and he was acquitted of any wrong-doing. This encouraged him. He pointed out to the members of the board of trade and the council the supreme importance of Indian affairs at Albany. It was too much of a responsibility for the town clerk to give correct care to those and conduct his other duties. A separate official should be appointed to handle the Indian work.

Livingston argued the proposition so well that he was awarded several jobs. He was given a royal patent that confirmed him in his town clerkship and the other offices he had held. Then he was appointed as secretary for Indian Affairs. If he was aware of any confusion in the thinking of the Lords of Trade or the Privy Council he said nothing about it, and sailed for home.

His enemies in Albany were not satisfied, though, when he came back in 1696 and tried to take office as Indian Affairs secretary. They said the job had been created to enrich the man who occupied it. He was suspended from it by their action, and stopped from being paid. All of the property that he owned was sequestered, and he eventually lost his various offices until only that of town clerk was left.

He waited, and Bellomont became governor, and then Lord Cornbury. But Cornbury was a poor governor, only made matters worse for Livingston. It was time once more, Livingston decided, that he appear in London and plead his case.

He sailed in 1703 and did not return for five years. But then he carried a patent from Queen Anne that established him in all of his duties, including that as secretary for Indian Affairs. His right to hold them was never again challenged.

The men who disliked or distrusted him finally gave up their opposition. He became speaker of the provincial assembly in 1718 and was kept in the office until 1725, when he decided to retire. Livingston Manor prospered under his management. His marriage with Alida was quite happy. She bore him nine children, three of whom died in infancy.

## ))) 5 (((

IT WAS THE FRENCH CAPACITY TO DREAM AND THEN relate dream to reality, or at least make daily compromise with it, that led them to great explorations in North America. The early French were just as bold in their concepts as the Spanish who sought across the desert the fabulous cities of Cibola and El Dorado, and more so than the Englishmen who sailed among the icebergs, the vast tidal currents and fogs off Labrador searching for the Northwest Passage.

During his last years at Quebec, embittered, profoundly frustrated, and afflicted by old wounds, Samuel de Champlain was still credulous. He believed in the quite obviously impossible. Champlain accepted as fact a story told by Sieur de Prevert, a Saint-Malo shipowner. Prevert had been along the Nova Scotian Coast, and described the sorry condition of the Micmacs, the local tribe.

A monster called Gougou lived there, the shipowner said. Gougou occupied a cliffside lair and satisfied its hunger by eating Micmacs, con-

58

sumed alive. The monster was twice as tall as a ship's mast; when it was hungry, it made evil hissing sounds. Sieur de Prevert had been close enough to the lair to hear Gougou about to go out and catch a Micmac.

But the learned, often brilliant Jesuit and Recollect missionaries in New France preached a literal Heaven, and Hell. It was not illogical for Champlain to associate Gougou with the Devil. He had been told the story in 1603 and continued to give it credence.

When he made a trip west in 1613, he found circumstances that confirmed his belief in mysterious powers, if not in the underworld itself. He stayed for a time among the Algonquins whose village was on Allumette Island in the Ottawa River. They maintained a cemetery where they honored their dead with elaborate tombs. These were painted red and yellow, and bore sculptured portraits of the deceased.

The cult of the dead was very important to the Allumette people. Their *shamans* held long conversations with the departed. Indians who passed the island were asked to pay tribute as a form of gift for the dead. They did not refuse, Champlain noticed, and paid without objection. All of the people of this region lived in very intimate contact with the spirit world.

When he went further west in 1615, he stayed among the Nipissings, the Sorcerers, of Algonquin stock. They were famous for their supernatural abilities, and were treated with great respect by the neighboring tribes. Many of them talked on intimate terms with the Devil. They possessed the power to cast spells and inflict diseases upon people they did not like.

Champlain listened, and believed. The tribe was prosperous, numbered about 800 people who lived in stout bark-walled lodges. The warriors were very successful traders. Those who served as buyers for the tribe made the journey on snowshoes in the depth of winter to Sault Sainte Marie. They bartered their European trade goods for the furs brought by warriors who came from the Lake Superior and Lake Michigan tribes. Then, with the opening of the rivers in the spring, a party of Nipissing traders undertook the forty-day journey to Hudson Bay and bartered for furs. Nipissings visited the Hurons at Georgian Bay in the fall, and sold dried fish from their home lake for corn. They were too busy trading much of the year to plant crops.

Champlain, back at his Habitation in Quebec which he had so laboriously built, pondered these and many other matters. He was aware that some of the late arrivals among the colonists mocked the name of La Chine, given the rapids at Montreal. The rapids lay at the head of navigation in the St. Lawrence, and beyond them to the west the wilderness stretched, and became the unknown. La Chine, of course, meant China, and the recent colonists were amused by the idea that here was the entrance to the Northwest Passage that gave forth to the South Sea and the everlasting splendor of Chinese wealth.

It had been Champlain's experience as a young man, though, to stand on a ridge in a jungle-clearing at Panama and look out at the South Sea. He was to believe for all of his life in the Northwest Passage, and his agents had orders to seek constantly for it in the western wilderness. He was mistaken in that part of his dream, but he was not a fool. When he wrote about Panama in his book, *Bref Discours*, he prophesied the building of a canal across the narrow isthmus. "The voyage to the South Sea," he wrote, "would be shortened by more than 1500 leagues."

Towards the end of his life, when from 1633 to 1635 he ruled the colony as royal governor, he had only a dozen or so regular soldiers under his command. But as early as 1611, his agent, Etienne Brulé, had gone to spend the winter with the Hurons at Georgian Bay, to learn Indian speech and ways. Before Champlain's death, Frenchmen were west of Lake Michigan and along the shores of Lake Superior. Frenchmen had gone down the Mississippi to the Gulf of Mexico before the end of the seventeenth century.

The English, meantime, had advanced much more slowly westward. Their frontier in 1700 lay upon the Allegheny ridges.

The final effort for Champlain was to build the trading post at Trois Rivières. He died the next year, in 1635, but the settlement was firmly established. The squat, heavily walled cabins flanked the chapel within the stockade on the north bank of the St. Lawrence, and right past the stockade wall was absolute wilderness.

It was only the great river which penetrated that, cutting an avenue through the forest, winding westward. Champlain, the cartographer, the navigator and soldier and explorer, saw the majesty of the river in his mind as he stretched sleepless on his narrow bed in the Habita-

60

tion. When pain bothered him until he was forced to walk the room to find relief, he stopped at his desk and looked at the map he had made in 1632 and profusely illustrated. The actual landmarks represented there restored memories, clarified them, put them in order.

He had spent twenty-one years along this river. It was easy to get confused; there were so many memories. And the pain entered in, and all of the fragments of personal sensations and old emotions that did not really matter. He stood at the window, the breeze upon him off the heights of Lévis filled with the tang of evergreens, and from the dovecote above, persistent and soft, the talk of the birds. He listened, though, to the river. The river was always in his thought.

He came to it first in June 1603 aboard a twelve-ton pinnace built in France. The forest was verdant, the river shimmering with sun. He was entranced, and awed. Jacques Cartier had made a very great discovery, Champlain realized.

When the pinnace reached the Quebec narrows and trimmed sail for the passage there, he remarked how beautiful the country was. Fruit trees and grapevines grew in profusion. There were oaks, cypresses, birches, firs and aspens. The soil seemed good for cultivation.

The head of tidewater was at Trois Rivières. Where the broad St. Maurice flowed from the north into the St. Lawrence was a good site for a fortified post, Champlain recognized. The Algonquin braves who accompanied the French swung to the north alongside a high-rushing rapids past Trois Rivières, and said they took the route because of fear of Iroquois attack anywhere further south. Champlain wrote in his journal, "If this river were inhabited we might make friends with the Iroquois and with the other savages, or at the very least under protection of the said settlement the said savages might come freely without fear or danger."

A wide lake was above the rapids, and the Frenchmen called it Lac Pierre. With the pinnace at anchor among some small islands, Champlain took the longboat and some of the Algonquins as guides. They entered a river which flowed into the St. Lawrence from the south. The Algonquins were uneasy; they spoke of it as the River of the Iroquois,* 61

* The French soon called this river Richelieu.

said it led to enemy country. Champlain turned back from it at a set of rapids, kept on westward up the St. Lawrence.

The country here was thickly forested, and the trees were maple, beech, white cedar, oak, poplar, ash and aspen. There were also a few pines and firs, and butternuts and chestnuts. Champlain noticed strawberries, and raspberries, currants, gooseberries and wild cherries. But the river held his attention more than the shore. He was at the site of the future city of Montreal.

He gave the order to anchor the pinnace in the lee of a small island near the northern bank. Then he and his companions contemplated the turbulence of the river as it hurled towards the sea. These were the famous La Chine Rapids, and beyond them, Champlain knew, he would move only by birchbark canoe that could be carried over portages. He wrote about the rapids in careful detail, aware of their importance:

> I assure you I never saw any torrent of water pour over with such force as this does, although it is not very high. It descends as it were step by step; and wherever it falls from small height, it boils up extraordinarily, owing to the force and speed of the water as it passes through the said rapid, which may be a league in length. There are many rocks out in the stream, and about the middle are very long narrow islands, where the current runs both beside the islands that are towards the south, and also to the north; and it is so dangerous, that it is beyond the power of any man to pass with any boat, however small it may be.
>
> We went by land through the woods, to see the end of the rapid, which is a league away, and there we saw no more rocks or falls, but the water runs with the utmost possible swiftness; and this current extends for three or four leagues, so that it is vain to imagine that any boats could be conveyed past the same rapids.

Champlain lacked the time to continue upriver beyond La Chine. But he carefully questioned the Algonquins about the country to the westward. His pervasive dream influenced what they told him. He gathered from their stories that 400 leagues further west was an endless body of water. So he wrote in his journal, "Without doubt, from their account, this can be nothing else than the South Sea, the sun setting where it does."

He returned, seeking the South Sea, in late May 1613 and continued his western exploration. With two canoes and an Indian guide, he left Quebec and proceeded up the St. Lawrence. The party unpacked their gear and provisions at La Chine, made the long and terribly fatiguing portage around the rapids. Then they paddled into placid reaches where the work was easy and they could sing and relax. But they came to a narrows where the water roared in warning. Champlain wrote about that:

> Here we had much labor, for so great is the swiftness of the current that it makes a dreadful noise, and, falling from level to level, produces everywhere such a white foam that no water at all is seen. This rapid is strewn with rocks and in it here and there are some islands covered with pines and white cedars. It was here we had much difficulty, for being unable to portage our canoes on account of the thickness of the woods, we had to track them, and in pulling mine I nearly lost my life.

Tracking a canoe meant to haul it along the bank by a rope attached to the bow. It meant also that the man who hauled was forced to scramble through underbrush, over rocks, wade, cling to tree trunks for support, and grab fast for anything handy when his sodden moccasins betrayed his footing, or a loose stone rolled, or a sudden buffet of the current caught him or the canoe. Champlain's craft swung broadside in a whirlpool.

He was very lucky, and fell between two rocks. Otherwise, the canoe would have dragged him out from shore, into the swirl of the current. The hauling rope was twisted around his hand; he could not let go, and it nearly cut off his fingers.

The loaded canoe, carrying provisions, blankets, personal gear, weapons and Champlain's astrolabe, weighed at least 1,000 pounds. Broadside-to, with the current thrust, it exerted enormous force. He took all of the weight, the shock and pain, and held onto the rope although his hand might momentarily be severed.

He was a religious man, and cried aloud to God for help. It so happened that the canoe entered a back eddy, and Champlain was able to pull the craft to him. Then the Indian guide came along the bank and relieved him of some of the strain. But Champlain had already saved the canoe.

He took care to write in his journal his reason for wanting to hang onto the canoe. Without it, they would have been forced to stay there in that bleak wilderness circumstance and wait for a wandering band of Indians to come along the river. This, he said, was "a poor prospect for those who had nothing to eat" and were not used to such fatigue. The Frenchmen who accompanied him were almost lost several times, but they also escaped without serious injury.

These rapids came to be known as Chute à Blondeau, and Champlain's bravery was almost forgotten. But he thought little of it. He considered it as something to be expected by a man who made his life on the river.

Champlain was the first great *voyageur*, the prototype of all the superbly strong, immeasurably daring and forever restless Frenchmen who followed him along the rivers into the North American wilderness.

Hunger and fatigue, danger and illness and wounds were kept under harsh control by fortitude. When the party he led in 1613 got beyond the Chute à Blondeau they found easy paddling. But then they met Indians who showed a lot of surprise.

The river was bad below, the Indians said, and worse above. They tried to dissuade Champlain from going further. He hired a guide, though, a husky warrior who was obviously a good paddler. Champlain divided here the strong Frenchmen in his party from the not-so-strong, sent the weaker contingent back downriver.

The winter dress of the *voyageur* was a coat of buff with fur collar and trim, embroidered light doeskin lapels and belted with a red sash, fringed and garnished buff trousers and moccasins.

He kept on to the westward. The country was fine, with good soil and open woods. He reached the site of Ottawa on June 4th, where the Rideau flowed in from the south and the Gatineau from the north. The Ottawa River fell wildly in descent, and Champlain named the falls La Chaudière—"The Boiler." There was a long portage around it, and many more, as the Indians had warned, where falls blocked the upper reaches.

Champlain persisted. The party entered a long lake he called Lac de Chats. Red cedars grew on the islands in the lake, and Champlain went ashore on one. He built and reared up, supported by stones, a high cross adorned with the arms of France.

But the portage work was so cruel that even Champlain stumbled gasping under the loads, exhausted. The Frenchmen cached most of their food, took off all of their superfluous clothing. They went to a seven-mile carry over high, rough, heavily wooded ground with mosquitoes in thick wreaths around their heads. Their eyelids puffed until the men could barely see; sweat streaked through the masks of crushed mosquitoes on their cheeks.

Champlain drove the men forward, and drove himself. They came to a pond and dropped their loads on the bank, once more had their hands free. When they were finished swatting mosquitoes, they made a smudge fire, sat down around it. But the party had not eaten in twenty-four hours. The men got to their feet, spread nets in the pond and caught fish for a meal.

The country through which they passed the next day was the most difficult they encountered on any of the portages. A violent wind storm had smashed across the forest and left an enormous, jagged tangle of pine trees flung in mazed heaps. Champlain wrote about the area, "which is no small inconvenience; for one must go now over and now under these trees." It was during this portage that he lost his cherished astrolabe, the navigation instrument he used to establish latitude and longitude. But he accepted the loss as he had accepted so much else, and the party came out on calm Muskrat Lake, and the men were greeted by friendly, greatly impressed Indians.

These were Algonquin people who lived by agriculture and fishing. Their chief, Nibachis, gave Champlain and his men a big meal of fish. Then he lent them a guide and two canoes, sent them on over an easy

65

portage to the Ottawa River. Here they were in the country of the Allumette tribe, also of Algonquin stock.

The Allumette chief was shrewd, one-eyed, and named Tessouat. He remembered Champlain from a meeting ten years before on the lower St. Lawrence and greeted him with delight. It was on Tessouat's stronghold island in the middle of the Ottawa River that Champlain saw the elaborate carvings which adorned the tribal tombs, and noticed the way Tessouat exacted toll from all travelers using the river.

But at the Allumette town Champlain suffered the most severe disappointment of his career. He had brought along on the expedition a young Frenchman named Nicolas du Vignau, who had spent a considerable amount of time among the Algonquins of this region and afterwards reported to Champlain his discovery of a salt-water sea. Now, confronted by Tessouat and other senior warriors, and closely questioned by Champlain, he admitted that he had lied. The warriors wanted to kill Du Vignau. They told Champlain, "Give him to us, and we promise you he will tell no more lies."

Champlain was shaken by terrible anger. His abiding dream of a passage to the South Sea was almost completely destroyed. Still, he could not bring himself to give Du Vignau to the warriors. They would keep "the liar" alive for hours, perhaps days, while they tortured him. Champlain wrote in his journal:

> And because they were all howling to get at him, and their children still more loudly, I forbade them to do him any harm and made them also keep their children from doing so, inasmuch as I wished to bring him back to the Rapids to show him to those gentlemen to whom he was to bring salt water; and I said that when I got there, I should consider what was to be done with him.

Champlain decided to turn back, go east. There was no more purpose in continuing west in search of a salt-water sea whose existence had become very dubious. He built a tall cross of white-cedar timber, and decorated it himself with the fleur-de-lis device of France while the local

66  tomb sculptors stood and keenly watched. Then he raised the cross on the river bank, said goodbye to Tessouat and his other friends among the tribe and on June 10th started towards Quebec.

Tessouat made parting quite pleasant, though, and sent along forty canoes well filled with furs. The Allumette guides took the flotilla through a series of very bad rapids and avoided the difficult overland route. When the flotilla reached the Chaudière Falls on the Ottawa, the canoes gathered alongside the bank and were secured. Champlain witnessed a ritual Indian observance unlike anything he had seen before.

The warriors assembled near a large rock that had been fantastically carved by wind and weather to resemble the head of a man, and a pair of stump arms upraised. They explained to Champlain that this was a powerful divinity. One of their chiefs who had accompanied the fleet took up a collection of tobacco from the canoe crews. It was piled on a wooden plate, and the warriors danced around it and sang a song in honor of the divinity.

Then, Champlain wrote, one of the chiefs made a speech, "pointing out that for years they have been accustomed to make such an offering, and that thereby they received protection from their enemies; and that otherwise misfortune would happen to them, as the devil persuades them. When he has finished, the orator takes the plate and throws the tobacco into the middle of the boiling water, and all together utter a loud whoop. These poor people are so superstitious that they would not think they could have a safe journey, unless they had performed this ceremony there."

The flotilla came safely through the Chaudière, the spray a white, drenching splatter over the gunwales, the bottom ribs of the canoes quivering with the impact of the whirlpool waves. Champlain sat very still; he trusted the Allumette paddlers much more than the rock divinity.

It was the time of the annual trade fair when the flotilla reached the St. Louis Rapids on the lower river. Champlain found the merchants eager and ready, their rough, sailcloth-covered booths set up on the beach below the rapids. The French had not yet begun the barter practice of brandy for furs. But the merchants had cheated the tribes at the last fair, and some of the Algonquins were wary, and sullen.

Champlain supervised the trading. He made a lengthy speech. A great banquet of boiled fish, roasted venison, bear meat and caribou, and squash, succotash and beans was served to the warriors. They ate, happily hiccoughed, stretched out on the beach beside their canoes and slept. Then,

67

with dawn, they gathered again at the booths and sold what was left of their pelts. The chiefs made grandiloquent expressions of gratitude and amity to Champlain, went aboard their craft and pushed off for home. None of them had been cheated, Champlain knew, and the season had been profitable.

Champlain went back to the Habitation at Quebec and began to prepare for winter. He would not be here this year. He was going home to France. But the brief Canadian summer was almost over, and winter was the bleak, the terrible enemy to be feared more than Iroquois raiders coming out of the snowy dark or Englishmen who entered the river from seaward in their well-armed vessels.

Cold threatened a man as soon as he ventured outside to hunt, or help a neighbor. It acted slowly, was subtle, and did not bring much pain, only drowsiness to a man too tired to drag any further on snowshoes through the forest drifts or over the ice hummocks of the river. Women who sat at the hearthside saw milk freeze in jugs close to a blazing fire. They went to beds that never seemed to respond to bodily warmth, and many of them died there from various ailments caused by the cold. Winter along the St. Lawrence was often death itself.

Looking back now in this, the last winter of his life, Champlain knew that he would die soon. A paralytic stroke had afflicted him in October 1635 and he was confined to his pallet in the governor's chamber of the fort. His mind remained clear a good deal of the time, and he recalled his young wife, Hélène, and her unhappy sojourn here at Quebec. It was eleven years ago; she had become a shadowy figure, and belonged to his memories of France, where she had taken holy orders.

The Canadian memories were much more sharp. He remembered men like Tessouat greeting him, paint-streaked, smeared with rancid bear grease, yet dignified. Their shouts echoed over the water, "*Ho, ho, ho!*" Their powerful arms clasped him and made his paddle-sore muscles contract. Then they fed him, and afterwards they talked, told him of rivers, lakes, other rivers. They used a paint stick and a deerskin to make a map. "*Hari co,*" they said, "yes, out there—there is the endless water."

68

But the western water was not endless, Champlain knew. No man had come back yet from that region with any story to substantiate it.

Poor, lying Du Vignau had seen Lake Huron, that was all. Champlain was content to think about what was proven, and real. Too much of his life had been spent in dreaming.

Still, he told himself, the Iroquois could be defeated, and he had written Cardinal Richelieu in Paris and explained the details of the campaign. After his death, Richelieu could send some other officer out here to conduct it, break the Five Nations forever. A corps of 120 rangers, picked veterans able to live in the forest and eat Indian food, would be used along with three or four thousand Algonquin and Montagnais allies.

The campaign would start with a sudden assault upon an Iroquois town. Grenades, bombs, mines would destroy the stockade, and from *cavaliers*, the same sort of platform built for the attack on the Onondaga town, sharpshooters could drive away the defenders from the parapets. There were only five Iroquois towns of any consequence. They would be razed, burned to the ground in a few days. Then a general peace would be arranged among all the victims and enemies of the Iroquois.

Champlain knew the language of the letter word by word. His appeal to the cardinal was eloquent; Richelieu was the king's all-powerful adviser:

> If this peace is made we shall enjoy every advantage. Possessing the interior, we shall drive out our enemies, both English and Dutch, and force them to retire to their coasts. By taking from them the commerce with the Iroquois, we shall constrain them to abandon everything. We shall render ourselves absolute masters of these peoples in a year or two, and that will spread the practice of religion and incredibly increase trade. The country is rich in mines of copper, iron, steel, brass, silver, and other minerals. Monseigneur, the cost of 120 men is little to His Majesty, and the enterprise as honorable as can be imagined, and all is for the glory of God, to whom I pray to give you increase in the prosperity of your days, etc.

There was no answer to that letter in Champlain's lifetime. The plan of campaign, though, was based in fact, and went well beyond dream. During the summer of 1633, the Hurons gathered their courage and an enormous quantity of furs. They ran the Iroquois gantlet without

Quebec—The Intendant's Palace.

trouble and came east, down the rivers to Quebec. The flotilla contained 140 canoes, each filled with prime beaver pelts. It meant a fortune on the Paris market.

But as his thought ranged back and forth, Champlain was forced to remember how he had been captured here by the English, and all of New France easily seized. It was on July 20, 1629, and by a fleet of only three ships. Those were a flyboat of nearly 100 tons and carrying ten cannon, and a pair of forty-ton cutters both armed with six guns. They were commanded by Louis and Thomas Kirke, who were Scots, but French-speaking.

The surrender ceremony was performed with the utmost punctilio. The garrison was starving, and the troops and the few civilians left alive

QUEBEC, *The Capital of* NEW-FRANCE, *a Bishoprick, and Seat of the Soverain Court.*

The Citadel. 2. the Castle. | 7. Cathedral of Our Lady. | 11. St. Charles River. | 14. The Bishop's House. 15. The
Magazine. 4. y. Recolets. | 8. The Palace 9. y. Seminary. | 12. The Common Hospital. | Parish Church of the Lower Town.
Ursulines. 6. Jesuits. 7. | 10. The Hôtel Dieu. | 13. The Hermitage of the Recolets. | 16. The Upper Town y. y. Lower Town.
| | | 18. The Platform & Battery of Cannon
| | | 19. The Isle of Orleans. 20. Point Levi.

after the winter looked upon the Kirkes as saviors. The French coat-of-arms was stripped from the stockade, though, and replaced with the English emblem. Louis Kirke, the new commander, hoisted the St. George ensign on the flagstaff halyards; his troops paraded to their drums; salutes were fired. Then Champlain and nearly all of the French people were put aboard ship and taken as prisoners to England.

71

Champlain could not erase that memory. England had relinquished Canada in 1632, given it back to France after just three years of occupancy. Still, Champlain held the knowledge that the attack might be repeated. He had been too long around ships, the sea, the rivers, to fail to recognize the danger. There was nothing to stop an enemy fleet from entering the St. Lawrence and blockading the settlements until the French surrendered or starved.

It was in his thought on Christmas Eve. He was sixty-eight, and extremely tired. He listened to the bells of the midnight mass as *Te Deum* was celebrated in Notre-Dame de la Recouvrance. Then, at the fort, cannon were fired three times as a signal of victory. He loved this colony very much, and perhaps, with this victory, it would be safe.

He died on Christmas Day. Veteran soldiers wept as they mourned him. Indian warriors came from far away to give him tribute. Samuel de Champlain was a great man.

## )}} 6 {{{

THE MEN KNOWN AS *coureurs de bois* CAME AFTER
Champlain. These were the profoundly lonely, the wanderers,
the forever curious and unsatisfied. They found in the North American
wilderness the same thing a sailor found on the sea—each day a new horizon beyond which wealth might be lodged, and Cathay finally reached,
but, if no more, the unknown. Many of them were of peasant origin, had
served as artisans, or as soldiers or sailors or farm hands when they arrived
in Canada. Some were of noble birth, or members of the ruling class of
landowners.

They shared a common heritage. They were almost completely of
Norman stock. Their direct forebears were Vikings, the Northmen for
whom Normandy was named. It was very probable that an *habitant*
working a field in the July heat of the lower St. Lawrence Valley knew
little about his ancestry. His mind was not excited by the recognition that
Northmen had founded colonies by power of conquest in Russia, Sicily,

Great Britain, Ireland and France. He had not heard the stories of the great sea journeys in the dragon-bowed ships whose names were *Reindeer of the Breeze, Horse of the Gull's Trace* and *Lion of the Waves*.

He set a bright red woolen cap slanted on the side of his head, though, and he preferred to go barefoot rather than use the wooden clogs worn by his Breton neighbors. He was not by nature a farmer. What he wanted on his feet was a pair of buckskin moccasins, fringed, with colored porcupine-quill decorations on the insteps. His hands should hold an ash paddle instead of this spade. He was going to join the *coureurs de bois*, enter the forest, sail the rivers and the lakes, live among the tribes.

During Champlain's time and afterwards, the Canadian fur trade was a monopoly of the very powerful Company of New France, or of the Crown itself. A limited number of trading licenses was issued, usually no more than twenty-five a year. These were assigned to *bourgeois*, men who dealt in barter with the Indians for furs. But the licenses were granted with the consent of the proprietors of the seigneuries, the huge estates along the lower St. Lawrence and in the Richelieu Valley, and who were favorites at court, known to the king.

The trading privileges were part of the feudal system France had rigidly installed in the New World. The men who owned thousands of acres of fertile river-bottom land did not enter personally into the fur trade. But through shares in the Company of New France they were well paid for their investment. They did not particularly care whether a newly arrived peasant became a farmer or joined the *coureurs de bois*.

A man who had come out from France with the hope of farming the land generally could buy only a miserable piece sold at a high price by the owner of a seigneury. He paid in Quebec Province the *dime*, the tax that took a twenty-sixth of all his crops. Most pioneer families lived in slab-wall cabins with thatched roofs. The demands of their work kept a family too busy to make tables and chairs. They used the butts of logs, and slept on piles of reeds. During the long months of winter, they brought the cattle into the single room with them to save the animals from being killed by wolves, bears or the cold.

74      If a man failed at his own farming venture, he could get work at one of the seigneuries as a hired hand. The conditions there were more feudal than the worst of what was still endured in France. He had gained

nothing by leaving home. And although the Catholic Church owned immense amounts of property and sought laborers, they could never take for themselves any of the land they worked.

There was a similarity of experience between the early Hudson River Valley immigrant and the Canadian peasant employed on a St. Lawrence seigneury. They both suffered severe inequities. The motivation to quit work, get away and be free and independent was fully as great. Still, the *bosch-loper* bore only small resemblance to the *coureur de bois*.

Despite his transgressions, his drunken brawling and gambling and loose living, the *bosch-loper* was welcomed at Fort Orange. He was an accepted part of the community, and when sober even went to Lutheran service on Sunday. The government looked to him as a source of profit, and very essential in the fur trade and all of the commerce along the river.

But in Canada, for a number of years, almost into the eighteenth century, to call a man a *coureur de bois* meant that he was an outlaw. This was mainly due to the influence of the Catholic Church. The Recollect and Jesuit missionaries understood right at the beginning that Canada must have an agricultural economy to survive, and that the fur trade was not enough to support it.

The first Canadian census was taken during the winter of 1666–67, with everybody present in the settlements to be counted. It showed a population of 3,125, with the addition of 1,200 troops. There were 100 priests and nuns. There were also, surprisingly for such a small

*A Coureur de Bois*

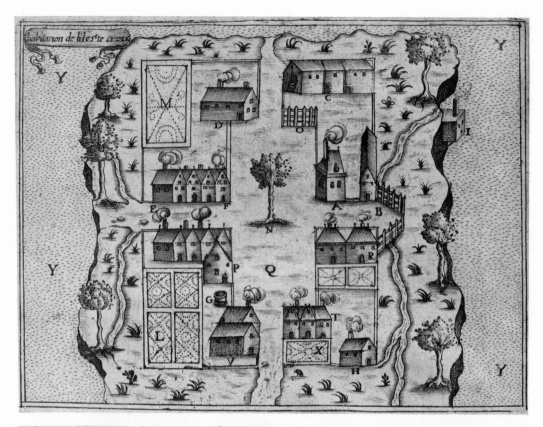

Champlain's drawing of the settlement on the island of Sainte Croix.

number of people, thirty-six carpenters, thirty tailors, nine millers and three locksmiths. The rest of the settlers were officials, a few proprietors of the seigneuries and their tenants, and the formidable muster of *coureurs de bois*.

76

There were only three settled districts: Quebec, Trois Rivières and Montreal, then known as Ville-Marie. Quebec held the most people, but the town itself, founded fifty-eight years before, had less than 600 inhabitants. The king's representative, the Intendant, was named Jean Talon, and had taken great care with the census. He knew what was happening in the English possessions.

Virginia, after a very bad start, had become populous. More than 80,000 people were in New England. The English had just taken the Hudson River Valley away from the Dutch, threatened to extend their fur trade along the Mohawk to the Great Lakes.

So here in Canada men should marry and settle down on the land, become *habitants* and have big families. Their wives should be French, and not of Indian blood. The Church absolutely refused to perform mixed marriages. The missionaries understood the lure of the forest and of the handsome, easy-smiling Indian girls who belonged to the river tribes. French blood should not be debased with the infusion of savage strains, the Jesuits insisted to Talon. Most of the tribes were still infidels, some outright cannibals. Paganism must be stopped.

The Intendant sent to France and arranged for shipments of suitable girls to Canada. He passed a regulation that kept out of the forest any man who remained a bachelor fifteen days after the arrival of one of these shipments. There were a number of marriages as a result. Men got married, though, and then immediately went back to the fur trade, remained *coureurs de bois*. Others evaded marriage entirely, and they were the real outlaws.

They spent practically all of their time in the forest, rarely came to Quebec or Trois Rivières. With the rest, the quasi-married and the men who had given up family responsibility of any sort, they numbered more than 1,000, stayed away from the settlements and outside the law.

They formed a new American type, and were much more daring and far-ranging than the *bosch-lopers*. Those men operated with Fort Orange as a base, kept pretty much to the Hudson, the Mohawk and the Connecticut, went no further north than Lake Champlain. The *coureurs de bois* went anywhere they could paddle, push or pull a canoe. They were the greatest river men in history.

They or their immediate successors, the *voyageurs*, reached the Arctic Ocean at Hudson Bay, hunted whale in birchbark canoes. The range of mountains in Wyoming known as the Grand Tetons—"the

77

Big Tits"—was named by them. They sailed the Wisconsin, the Illinois, and the Ohio, built Fort Duquesne, which was later Pittsburgh, went down the Mississippi to the Passes and the Gulf of Mexico. The names they gave as discoverers remain on hundreds of landmarks across more than half of North America. They traversed the Rockies, hauling their precious birchbark canoes in sledgelike cradles. Then they went on, down the western slope, to the Pacific.

Some of their number were on every principal river west of the Appalachians. They knew intimately the villages of the main Indian tribes, traded, married and lived among them. For over 200 years, they roamed the waterways of the continent almost as they wished, and they held in their heads geographical knowledge which no man has since matched.

The dangers and privations they surmounted were incredible. Many of them—countless, because no accurate record of their voyaging was ever made—lost their lives in action against various human enemies, or at Indian torture stakes, or in a sudden winter blizzard, alongside a capsized canoe in a rapids, or dashed against a rock in some precipitous falls.

They were incessantly daring, gambled their lives against enormous odds. When time pressed them, and they had a valuable cargo of furs to deliver, or it was a question of pride that involved first arrival, they would keep moving throughout the night, ride white-water rapids in moonlight, maintain a pace of 100 miles of progress within twenty-four hours.

The degrees of risk presented by the proximity of the huge white Arctic bear, the timber wolf, the sly-moving water moccasin and the seemingly clumsy alligators of the Mississippi delta were fully calculated. These men, like all frontiersmen, told greatly embellished stories when they returned from the wilderness. But the events of their daily lives belonged in legend. They were in themselves the sources of history.

The first voyage for a novice river man was a cruel and very nearly insupportable experience. The best of the early French missionaries, men already inured to privation and rough living, and imbued with a religious faith that was often of enormous help when courage, stamina and strength were practically exhausted, found themselves a useless burden in a canoe. The journey west into the wilderness along the St. Law-

7 8

rence, then the connecting lakes and portages and the other rivers to the Great Lakes, was most difficult for men like them whose lack of skill kept them from using a paddle.

They sat in a craft that was deeply loaded and extremely cranky. The Indians of the crew that handled it had explicitly warned their pas-sengers not to shift position in any way once the canoe was out in the stream. So the white men sat hunched on a narrow thwart while their necks, backs, buttocks, thighs, lower legs and feet began to ache, then throb. The position they had been ordered to hold made them bend forward, heads lowered, or they would be repeatedly jolted by a paddle. This brought their faces within inches of the Indians who sat forward of them.

The Indians were half-naked in the summer heat. They sweated as they paddled. The odor of their sweat was almost overwhelmingly foul to the white men. But, the white men knew, their own bodily exudation was equally repulsive to the Indians. They restrained the im-pulse to cover their faces, express some protest or even a word or so that would lessen tension. There was nothing to be done except wait for the next portage. Then it would be necessary to move fast and get to a place on the bank and urinate before the portage work started.

The portages were more de-manding for the novice white men

A Canadian *voyageur* on snowshoes.

than any part of the canoe journey. They felt their real futility when the Indians began to carry the various trade packs, the other gear, the weapons and the canoes overland, sometimes across portages that extended for miles. It was all the white men could do to stand upright and walk.

The packs, covered with tightly lashed deerskin or canvas, weighed at least ninety pounds apiece. Several trips were needed to lug the entire lot of cargo from one end of the portage to the other. A sixteen-foot birchbark canoe weighed approximately 1,000 pounds, and two or perhaps three men would carry it, their number dependent on the terrain to be crossed.

Some portage trails were through reasonably open country, where the forest trees grew wide apart and the underbrush was not thick. Others went close to the edges of steep cliffs, or through swamps and bogs where the mosquitoes were a frightful menace, and into boulder-littered ravines where a misstep might permanently injure a canoe hull. The worst led into the kind of region that Champlain encountered near Muskrat Lake. Storm had devastated the forest; snapped tree trunks and inextricably entwined branches formed weird, immense barriers.

The Indians accepted the dangers of the river instead of trying to hew, climb and haul out of a stretch like that. They went into the water in great disregard of their safety and the speed of the current, and dragged the canoes upstream by hand, wading alongside the craft at the bow.

Current betrayed them by an abrupt shift of direction. A sodden moccasin skidded on bottom pebbles. The rapids-worn shoulder of a rock was slippery, failed to give sufficient purchase. A gust of breeze thrust suddenly into the river gap over the wall of the forest, struck and swung the canoe beyond the warriors' control. The Indians floundered, reached out to catch the canoe, missed, and submerged. Broad red backs showed in the pale, fast water. A scalp lock, still stiff and bright with moisture beads, rose above the surface and disappeared.

The canoe swerved perilously, thrown by the current. Then it emerged from the rapids and fetched up, bow pointed to shore, in a quiet eddy. Warriors shouted and went running along the bank. They splashed through the shallows to get to the craft and secure it. Green withes and grapevines were plaited to make rough rope, and the passage was tried again, the canoe tracked close to the bank. But there were men who had gashes on their arms and legs, struggled bloody and limping upstream.

The missionaries in their long, full-skirted habits were a great vexation to their canoe-mates. They got back aboard the craft dripping water, shedding sand or mud. Their open-topped sandals had exposed ankles and insteps to brambles, fallen branches and mosquitoes. They bled profusely, and because they were not yet immunized to the sting of the North American mosquitoes their faces were so badly swollen that their eyes were puffed almost shut. They had stumbled half-blind over the portage trails, climbed clumsy and in acute agony aboard the canoe. Their Indian companions grunted at them with unconcealed dislike.

The Indians knew each river reach and the shores of the lakes and ponds in accurate detail. They possessed marvelous powers of memory, were able to recall exactly the food caches they had made on the downstream passage. Some of these, the novices saw, were hundreds of yards inland, hidden among the roots of trees, buried under moss at the sides of boulders and beneath smooth expanses of windswept beach sand. The caches held birchbark cartons of leached corn, the Indian staple.

When darkness began to spread from the forest shadows and obscure the river, the Indians made camp for the night. A good campsite with a beach and dry wood close was sought in the last hour or so of paddling. Troll lines, baited with frog skins, had been trailed astern, and some fish were already caught. Men set nets along the beach, too, once the party was ashore. Every man had his established duty, performed it without orders or delay.

One went to gather wood. He laid it carefully, then bent down with his fire-making apparatus. This was a small hardwood bow which fitted into a hole in a piece of soft wood and was rapidly revolved to create friction, and heat. Small, shredded bits of tinder were set ablaze by the heat, and the fire was started.

The cook filled his kettle with water dipped from the stream and hung it over the fire on a Y-shaped piece of sapling. He laid an animal skin on the ground, used that as a base to pound the leached corn with flat stones. The result was the famous Indian mush called *sagamité*. But the first Frenchmen to taste it, even the missionaries, gave it another name.

81

Everything that had been on the animal skin when the cook started pounding was tossed into the kettle to boil. Common ingredients were dirt, refuse, cinders and ash from the fire, and stray insects. Water flies seemed to be particularly esteemed as flavoring. Fish or meat were put in the kettle entire, the entrails considered a delicacy.

The Frenchmen in the party had a short time after supper to repair the damages of the day's journey and to enjoy the sunset. They treated their injuries, bathed their swollen faces, dried their clothing at the fire. A hush was on the forest and the river.

The vast, all-pervasive beauty of the wilderness enwrapped the men. They were conscious of the spell, and for the most part sat in absolute silence. The sky where the sun had passed below the forest rim was gold and russet and saffron and hyacinth, then blue and purple and black. The crests of the ripples were no longer flecked with light. Fish still leaped for flies, dropped heavily back, but the cascades they made were unseen. Stars were out; Venus was clear above the western horizon. The campfire embers were ruddy, but thick with ash.

The cook tossed the contents of the kettle onto the embers. The Indians were getting ready for sleep. They lay closely, side by side, under the small pine-bough shelter one of the warriors had built. The Frenchmen stretched out near them, but where they would not disturb the warriors during the night. Repose was hard for the Frenchmen, and sleep almost impossible.

The unaccustomed diet, the long hours in wet clothing, and exposure here on the damp ground with only a cloak for covering and a rock for a pillow kept the Frenchmen awake. They rose four or five times a night to relieve themselves. When they stretched out again, they were bothered by cramps, their bites and bruises, and visions of the next day's journey. The ordeal frightened them.

An Indian canoe party was ruthless in its determination to continue the journey. Frère Brebeuf, one of the first Frenchmen to make a journey west with the Indians, witnessed the bad fortune of an Algonquin warrior who had burned himself at a campfire. His tribesmen executed him without warning or debate; he might be an inconvenience in the canoe for the rest of the journey.

But some of the senior warriors, aware of the novices' distress, lent them bear robes or reed mats to ease the night hours. They showed the white men various balms and ointments and poultices for the insect bites. During a portage, they indicated how to walk, carry and haul with the least possible strain. They very gradually taught the French, and the newcomers at the completion of a month-long voyage had become wilderness veterans, were ready to serve as river men.

The white men began to call the Ottawa River *La Grande Rivière*. Upbound, from Montreal, they named the landmarks, stubbornly using French designations instead of the Algonquin. Among those were Portage du Fort, and the Culbute Channel, Paquette Rapids and Les Joachim Rapids. The word *culbute* meant a somersault, and *paquette* was a trade pack, the name given for one lost from a canoe in the wild piece of water off Allumette Island. And Allumette in itself meant a match, because of the island's shape, or the fires the tribe kept alight there at night.

Beyond, further west, was the Mattawa River, and then the ponds and portages that led into Lake Nipissing. Here the Sorcerers lived, and from their lake the French River flowed into Lake Huron. It joined the lake and formed a shallow harbor off Bustard Island. This was a part of Georgian Bay, and Huron country. A canoe party headed west paid homage in gifts to the Hurons, then kept a south-southwest course past huge Manitoulin Island, turned northwest towards Bois Blanc and the Straits of Mackinac. There Champlain's *mer douce*—the sweet-water sea that the Indians called Huron—met Lake Michigan.

During the summer of 1624, Champlain had succeeded in arranging peace between the Iroquois and the Montagnais, and the first evidences of the wealth to be made from the river trade were seen at Quebec. A flotilla of thirty-five Iroquois canoes loaded with prime furs arrived, bringing also young Etienne Brulé, and Brother Gabriel Sagard, a Recollect missionary. The two Frenchmen had spent the winter among the Hurons and were on very friendly terms with them.

Brulé was husky and sharp-witted, and Champlain's personal choice for a man to live with the inland tribes. He gave a report of tremendous importance to Champlain. Brulé said that he had gone past Lake Huron to what he described as "some great rapids," which were actually Sault Sainte Marie. Then he had reached "another enormous inland ocean," which was to take the name of Lake Superior.

Brother Gabriel Sagard made his own report to Champlain in privacy. He confirmed what Brulé said about the great falls, and another inland sea. There were, he told Champlain, accounts the inland tribes repeated about strange civilized races, "far to the west, near the Chinese Sea." Then he added a note of warning, and discord.

He said that Brulé and the other interpreters had agreed among themselves not to teach the native languages to the clergy. They were *coureurs de bois*, after all, and had the tendencies of outlaws. It was their intention to keep the forest for themselves, increase the fur trade at the cost of agriculture and a settled, civilized life.

Champlain pointed out that Brulé had proven himself very brave, witnessed and survived awful torture when a young boy and held a captive by Indian enemies who later adopted him. Brother Gabriel agreed to that; he knew Brulé's story. But, he insisted, Brulé was dissolute and unreliable, was destined to meet harm at the hands of the warriors.

The Huron girls, who began their sex lives at the age of eleven, fascinated Brulé. He lavished his trade goods upon them, bid for their favors in competition with the warriors. The Hurons, Brother Gabriel said, were too proud to let Brulé continue his success as a lover for any lengthy period of time.

Champlain, who had a young wife, was tolerant, and refused to speak to Brulé. He was also influenced by the fact that Brother Gabriel showed definite signs of close contact with "the savages." The gaunt, extremely pious missionary had spent the winter in a Huron lodge filled with warriors, squaws, children and dogs. During the unbroken weeks when he could not get outdoors he experienced a considerable change of viewpoint.

He had taken on as a relief from his boredom and revulsion the training of a mascot. This was a muskrat. The smart little beast was with him when he arrived at Quebec. It was his constant companion, slept every night in the wide sleeve of his habit.

Brother Gabriel wanted to make a gesture of repayment to his Huron hosts of the winter. He invited them to a banquet in the Recollect convent. He gave them various presents, and to the captain of the canoe that had brought him from Georgian Bay he offered a big house cat.

The warriors had never before seen an animal of the species. Brother Gabriel wrote in description of the encounter:

84

This good Captain thought the cat had a rational mind, seeing that when he was called, he would come and play with one, and so he conjectured that the cat understood French perfectly. After admiring this animal, he asked us to tell the cat that he should let himself be carried home to his country, and that he would love the cat like his own son. "Oh, Gabriel!" he cried, "he will have plenty to live on at home! You say that he is very fond of mice, and we have any amount of them. So let him come freely to us!" So saying, he tried to embrace the cat; but that wicked creature, who did not understand his way of caressing, immediately thrust out all his claws and made him let go quicker than he had clasped him.

"Ho, ho, ho!" said the good man. "So that's the way he treats me! *Ongaron ortischat!* He's ugly, he's bad! Speak to him!" Finally, having got the cat with a great deal of trouble into a birchbark box, he carried him off in his arms to the canoe, and fed him through a little hole with bread that he had received at our convent.

But when he tried to give the cat some *sagamité*, to his despair the cat escaped and flew up on a tree and they could not get him down again. And as for calling him down, nobody home (*personne à la maison*); he didn't understand any Huron, and they didn't know how to call a cat in French, and so they were forced to turn their backs on him and leave him in the tree, very unhappy at losing him, and the cat very worried about who was going to feed him in the future.

It was without doubt the first tragedy of its kind along the Canadian rivers. Brother Gabriel mourned the animal when later informed of the parting by the Huron canoe captain. But Gabriel felt a small sense of satisfaction when news was brought to Quebec of Etienne Brulé's death. The tough *coureur de bois* had been killed by a Huron brave in a fight over possession of a squaw.

Jean Nicolet was more circumspect. He went west in 1634 from Quebec carrying, carefully packed, a damask Chinese robe and a mandarin's cap. He had orders to present himself to the Emperor of China as an official French emissary. The orders, issued by Champlain, specifically stated that he should meet "the people of the sea."

Some of the officials who stayed within the walls of the fort at Quebec laughed afterwards about the misconception Nicolet held. When his Huron paddlers set the canoe close alongshore off Green Bay, Wisconsin, he took the lashings from the pack, got out the rumpled robe and the little round cap with the velvet button on top. Then he stood up in the bow, quite a feat in a moving canoe. He was ready to step onto the beach and be greeted by the Emperor.

The people on the beach were naked Winnebagoes. They were fish-eaters, and they stunk. The remains of their last meal and thousands of other meals were scattered on the beach. They belched politely when Nicolet stepped from the canoe. Nicolet soon recovered his poise, and talked with them through an interpreter. The bay where he landed was afterwards called Stinking Bay, and he charted it as part of the work of exploration he had begun. Somewhere, somewhere further west, he might find Cathay.

Jean Nicolet had a very clear understanding, though, of the importance of the St. Lawrence and the waterways system that spread forth westward from it into the wilderness. He knew that the St. Lawrence was the only entrance to the Ohio territory, from which the English were barred by the Appalachians. He explored Green Bay, and the Fox River Valley, and went on, possibly as far as the upper Mississippi.

He spent a considerable length of time among the Sacs, got to know them well. They were big men, the tallest and the best-natured of the western Great Lakes tribes. The warriors painted their faces black. Hair rose above their shaved heads in a sort of crest. That was stiffened with clay and painted bright red; it resembled a horse's mane. They wore buckskin leggins and, after Nicolet had introduced them to French trade goods, red belt cloths. Their bare upper bodies were greased, and around their necks they hung a rawhide lanyard. It was attached to their favorite item of barter, a heavy-bladed scalping knife. They carried under their left arms bags made from the whole skin of a bird or small animal. The contents of the "plunder bag" were usually a pipe, tobacco, fire-making gear, an awl for canoe repair work, and a mirror for inspection of the latest facial adornment.

Nicolet did not find the Sac body odor offensive. It was to him a sweet smell that was a compound of resin, wood smoke, grass, fur, and rancid bear and fish oil. The Sacs lived on the Fox River, below Green Bay. Their town was situated where the land ran smoothly back for half a mile from the gravel river bed in neat terraces. A long chain of hills was in the distance. The terraces and the hills were wooded, with small groves of maples, elms and birches, verdant grassland in between them and the river.

Brant, ducks and geese rose in huge, darkening clouds from the river surface as a canoe approached the town beach. There were continuous thumpings of wings against water, and the slur and whisper of the wet, feathered bodies in flight. Huge sturgeon ranged over the gravel at the bottom of the river, and above them, near the surface, were trout and whitefish.

The Sac squaws kept their field gardens beside the river. They grew beans, melons, pumpkins and the inevitable corn in long rows. The houses were on the second and third terraces above the river. Nicolet counted more than ninety structures.

The houses resembled New England barns, with holes in the roof for smoke exit. They were built of hewn planks and beams, covered with bark. A shedlike shelter was in front of each door, and the people sat there in good weather. Spears and poles were thrust into the ground in front of the houses, and some bore scalps. The children went naked except in the bitter winter months, and everywhere, snarling, quarreling, barking, and resentful of the white man's strange smell, were hundreds of half-trained wolf dogs.

An average of five families lived in one of the houses. Tree-trunk fires were maintained in pits dug along the dirt floors and kept the dwellings reasonably warm, if often filled with smoke. The main council house where the chief and the senior warriors met was 150 feet long, with broad fire pits near the center. Nicolet was tremendously impressed.

The Sacs had fought against both the Hurons and the Iroquois, kept their independence as a tribe. The Sacs traded to the westward, with the sloven Winnebagoes, the easy-going Pawnees, the Ottawas, the Chippewas, Menominees, Iowas, Illinois and Sioux. The presence of Sioux warriors in the Sac town drew Nicolet's particular interest. He was still thinking of Cathay, and the Sioux talked of the Shining Mountains beyond which the sun set, and "the white Indians to the south."

Nicolet attempted to disentangle fact from fable, hearsay, common Indian boasting. His knowledge of the various Indian dialects was not at all complete, and he suffered from poor translation. But he was convinced that here was the center of the continent, and that the massive rivers he had seen and the greater rivers still to be followed westward and southward would make France the richest of all nations. The Sac chief was certainly not the Emperor of China. But he took profit from trade routes that stretched for thousands of miles. Nicolet had already been along the Wisconsin where on a flatland close to the much larger river the tribes met in an annual gathering to barter.

That other river, called by several names but commonly the Mississippi, was supposed to flow into some southern sea. The "white Indians," who were of the Mandan tribe, Nicolet learned, lived along the Mississippi, and many clans of the Sioux. They came north to trade for copper from Lake Superior, and the red stone used to make their treasured ceremonial pipes, and furs which did not grow plentifully in their country.

Some of them, who came from far away, carried worn sword blades, a broken spur as ornament, and knives. They had been in contact with the Spaniards along the Gulf of Mexico, Nicolet realized. He paid extreme attention to the Sac chief before he started his return trip to Quebec. He wanted to be as accurate as possible in his report of this region and these people. They held at present the key to the continent.

The chief wore leggins that were fringed with black hair, the scalp locks of enemies he had taken. A band of scalp-lock hair was stitched over the shoulders of his buckskin shirt, reached in a deep V-form on his back and chest. The necklace around his throat was made of huge bear claws. He wore broad silver bracelets above his elbows. His leggins were fastened below the knees with blue-, red- and black-bead garters, with tabs a foot long hanging from them, and swaying as he walked. There was colored porcupine embroidery on his moccasins, and the tops were turned over in loose cuffs where small brass bells were set. Those tinkled a musical punctuation for each step the chief made.

The bells, Jean Nicolet guessed, had probably been passed west in barter by the Sorcerer tribe, and were of French manufacture. But the silver bracelets were of much different origin; they must have come north with the people who paddled and tracked and portaged along that mysterious and mighty river which flowed into the Gulf of Mexico. There was no silver in the region here, nor even rumors of its existence. The stuff the chief wore had been turned out by Indians who worked for the Spaniards in the settlements thousands of miles away.

The Sac chief's hair swept his shoulders, was glossy and wavy. He

88

bedizened himself on formal occasions with a facial-paint design in which his eyes peered forth from white discs, his chin and lips were blue, and the background color was vermilion. The *shaman*, the tribal priest, was almost as flamboyant. He wore a buckskin vest that was intricately decorated with beadwork, and he carried an enormous medicine bag made of a number of black hawkskins sewn together. Both he and the chief owned calumets, the bowls and stems carefully carved and festooned with strings of beads and eagle feathers. They smoked the favorite summer mixture of *killikinnic*, leaf tobacco to which powdered wintergreen was added.

There was another phase of Sac life that greatly interested Nicolet. This was the tribe's insatiable desire to gamble. Various games of chance with animal bones or colored pebbles were played almost constantly by many of the warriors, beaver pelts, bows, arrow quivers, tomahawks and canoes put up as wagers. He had also met on the eastern rivers during his trip here entire clans of more than 100 people moving by canoe to attend a lacrosse match. The Sacs were local champions, and took on all comers.

There were 300 braves to a side in a match. The braves wore as uniform a strip of cloth in front and a horse tail in back, otherwise were naked. The lacrosse bat, made of an ash pole and a rawhide net with a hook-shaped outer point, was sometimes used for more than catching or hurling the hard, horse-hide-covered ball. Warriors who had been outwitted or outrun often smacked an opponent with the hooked end of the bat, aiming for the eye socket. Fights were common, and long. The goals were a third of a mile apart, and the first team to score 100 goals won.

Lacrosse match—invented by the North American Indians.

Jean Nicolet saw blood flow copiously over the Sac greensward. Thousands of spectators lined the playing field. Fights occurred among them, mainly between Sacs and neighbor Foxes, with squaws engaged as well as warriors. The amount of betting was fantastic. Losers paid off to the extent of fifty ponies, or twenty Pawnee slaves; piles of bearskins, beaded coats, tobacco pouches, belts, spears, bows and other weapons were exchanged.

A people as rash and as wealthy as this, Nicolet decided, would respond in a very satisfactory way to French trinkets and more worthwhile trade goods. Beaver was plentiful along the Wisconsin, and the voyage from Trois Rivières to Stinking Bay not too difficult for French-led canoe brigades. It was time he started for Trois Rivières and Quebec to make his report.

One of the greatest explorers in North American history, Médart Chouart, Sieur de Groseillers, was the next Frenchman to reach Green Bay. He came there in 1654, and noticed the wide expanses of lake shallows where wild rice grew, affording the Indians both a fine cereal crop and a variety of birds to be cooked with the rice. But, much more important than the happy combination of feeding grounds for Indians and wild fowl, he corroborated Nicolet's statement about contacts with the Spanish. There were in the Sac and Fox towns a number of warriors who had knives and beads; they had dealt in barter for those articles that unmistakably had a source in the Spanish settlements.

Groseillers heard also the stories of the Mississippi and the Missouri. He knew that inevitably the Spaniards would come up the Mississippi, establish forts and trading posts along it and along the Missouri. He sat during the winter nights beside the slow-burning logs in the fire pits of the Sac council house while a warrior drew with a paint stick upon smoothly stretched buckskin a map of the Long River, the Mississippi.

He memorized that map. He believed the details to be reliable. Frenchmen should get into the vast regions it indicated, claim them for the king. There was an empire which could be taken by a few hundred soldiers moved by canoe transport and stationed close to the main Indian towns and trading centers.

90

But he stayed on among the Sacs, gathering wealth for himself in the slow, accepted fashion of daily barter. He picked the best beaver, marten and otter skins, and only when the last of his trade goods were gone, in 1656, went back to Trois Rivières. He kept his knowledge from the local commandant, who, although the king's representative, was busy as a fur trader on a very personal basis.

Groseillers went west again in the spring, as soon as the rivers were navigable. He took with him as his partner his much younger brother-in-law, Pierre-Esprit Radisson, who was already an Indian-country veteran. They were headed for what was to be known as *le pays en haut*—The High Country—that stretched north and west from Lake Superior. It had only been touched by Etienne Brulé, whose reports were fragmentary and vague, but told of an enormous amount of wealth in fur-bearing animals.

The pair of Frenchmen, gaunt, hard, in splendid shape after the weeks of upstream work from Trois Rivières to Georgian Bay, entered Lake Huron alone. Their sixteen-foot canoe, built by Montagnais braves during the winter at Trois Rivières, was freshly daubed with resin and as watertight as birchbark could be made. Their long-barreled flintlock muskets lay propped against thwarts within immediate reach and tomahawks were in their belts, knives with heavy five-inch blades were pendant from throat lanyards.

They trusted nobody, and this, around them, was complete wilderness. Any human being, any animal must be regarded as an enemy until proof could be established otherwise. They paddled without sound, keeping the momentum of the canoe's passage unbroken. When they took their paddles from the water at a single word from Groseillers, it was to drift with the wind, and smoke a pipeful of *killikinnic* in the Indian style.

But their pipes were not red-stone calumets. They were of French-made clay, and much less valuable. Hundreds of pipes like them were in the trade packs stowed amidships, along with the rest of the knickknacks and the more substantial goods which should bring 1,000 per cent profit on the partners' investment. The partners counted on a considerable stay among the tribes, had deeply loaded the canoe. It was arduous labor at the paddles.

Noon, with the sun hot and high for those latitudes, they let the canoe drift once more and took time to eat. The food was kept in a

91

birchbark container. It was pemmican, the Indian river man's variation of corn mush, and just as satisfying, although eaten in greasy, grayish cakes. The stuff was lean meat pounded into a paste by Indian squaws and mixed with suet and crushed, dried berries. It contained an immense amount of energy, and to the educated taste was quite palatable.

Groseillers and Radisson ate, sat back to get the ache out of their backs and shoulders, had a smoke, then picked up the paddles. The country inshore was changing, and became a direct challenge to them. The broad open waters and sandy beaches of the lower region near Georgian Bay were gone. This was suddenly a new landscape, bold, and stark, and broken. It was the southern rim of the great Laurentian Shield which lay in a semicircle around Hudson Bay.

The weary pair of men bent over the paddles knew nothing of the composition of the Laurentian Shield, or of the existence of Hudson Bay. But the bleak outcroppings of stone, the rough shore littered with boulders startled them, gave warning of what they would meet further north, in Lake Superior and beyond. Groseillers had come this way on his voyage to Green Bay, made the traverse through the Straits of Mackinac into Lake Michigan. He told his partner that not all of the country ahead was the same. Then he turned the canoe for shore and a site for the night's camp.

The pair kept on across Lake Huron, swung north past the Straits of Mackinac towards the St. Marys River. This was at the head of the lake, and they moved from it into deep forest country where on the river banks bear, elk, caribou and moose stared at them. The wild-surging falls, the Sault Sainte Marie—which later took the name of Soo— were above, and made a long portage necessary. But the two men knew that they were in the wealthiest fur-bearing region on the continent, and that with any luck their personal fortunes were made.

They followed the headwaters of the St. Marys to Lake Superior and decided to go no further before winter. The brief summer was gone; there was scum ice in the river and along the lake shore. This was Menominee country, and they spent the long and terrible months with the tribe. The Menominees spoke of it as "the starving time."

The tribe exhausted all of the food supply, even the village dogs. Rations were reduced to bark stripped from trees and eaten in stewed or powdered form. Beaver hides were the only edible item. Many people died, and the corpses were stacked like cordwood outside the lodges.

Groseillers and Radisson put their canoe in the water with the spring thaw, though. They kept on north, and met the Crees, the tribe that ranged across a large part of the wilderness past Lake Superior. Trade goods were exchanged for almost unbelievably fine pelts. The partners were elated. They had met through the Crees several clans of the Sioux. These were the Dakotas, and their tribal group was the most formidable and powerful among the northern Indians.

Dakota chiefs treated on terms of warm friendship with the partners. They invited Groseillers and Radisson to enter their territory when the Frenchmen had more trade goods available. This was a good meeting place, here at the Grand Portage, which connected ten miles beyond with Pigeon River. The river led to others that flowed north, the Dakotas said, and finally into salt water.

The partners guessed that the salt water must be Hudson Bay, and part of the Arctic Ocean. They realized that a canoe route could be established between Montreal, almost 4,000 miles away, and Grand Portage. Trading posts would be needed in between, for fur storage and provisions, and to give rest to the canoe crews. The distance was tremendous, but so were the profits to be made. The High Country was wide open.

Groseillers and Radisson spent two years in the High Country. One man remained at Grand Portage while his partner went inland along the meandering system of lakes, ponds and rivers through the flat, treeless muskeg. They collected an enormous amount of furs, bought canoes, hired paddlers from among the local tribes, and pushed off for Montreal.

There were 360 canoes in the flotilla. It was the largest ever assembled on the Great Lakes. The Indians sang as they paddled, mournful and low-pitched chants that passed from canoe to canoe until the sound became huge and water fowl took flight, frightened.

The flotilla reached Montreal in the fall of 1660, at a time of financial crisis for the colony. The governor, the Intendant, and all of the lesser officials assembled to greet Groseillers and Radisson. A tax was estimated for the cargo of furs, and in its final form was presented as 24,000 gold pounds, equivalent to half a million dollars.

The partners thought this rather exorbitant, and so informed both the governor and the Intendant. During his youth, when he was fifteen, Radisson had been captured by the Iroquois. He had escaped and been recaptured, and put to the torture. It was relatively mild; a red-hot sword was thrust through his foot, his fingernails were extracted, and a small boy tried unsuccessfully to saw off a thumb. He was saved by a Mohawk family who wanted to adopt him, and with whom he later lived until his eventual escape.

He had not forgotten the experience. Now he proposed to his partner that they scalp the governor, the Intendant, and several of the other officials. Groseillers, an older and a calmer man, restrained Radisson and advised a patient approach to the problem. But that got them nothing, and they sailed from Montreal for France, took their grievances to the court of the Sun King, Louis XIV, at Versailles.

They were just another pair of importunate, stubborn colonials at Versailles, and the High Country had no meaning. So they went across to England finally, and were given an audience by Prince Rupert. He was a cousin of the English king, and was known to have intense curiosity about all northwestern exploration.

Prince Rupert listened to the High Country story, then arranged for King Charles to hear it. The king was fascinated, and Rupert undertook a concrete plan of action. Groseillers and Radisson had not been missed at Versailles; the courtiers there thought nothing of the men's disappearance. So Rupert worked unhindered. He formed in London the group that was to become the Hudson's Bay Company. It hired Groseillers and Radisson. They sailed from England in June 1668 aboard a pair of sturdily built ketches, *Nonsuch* and *Eaglet*, bound for Hudson Bay.

News of their departure was sent to Versailles by the French ambassador in London, and counter-action taken three years later. The Sun King had decided to secure his holdings in New France, and proclaim himself master of a region whose vastness he barely understood. He had sent, though, as his personal deputy to New France one of the most ornate of the court favorites. That man was Simon François Daumont, Sieur de Saint Lusson, and his actual title was Commissioner sub-delegate of my Lord the Intendant of France.

94

A treaty with the chiefs or the representatives of seventeen tribes was to be signed. The site chosen was alongside the rapids at Sault Sainte Marie, where a mission and a trading post had been built inside a stockade. The ceremony of signing was held in fine weather, in June 1671, and Sieur de Saint Lusson appeared in his finest court costume. He wanted to gain the admiration of the assembled chiefs, who wore brass rings, coils of copper wire, strings of shells, bear-claw necklaces and rows of brass amulets in addition to fur mantles, gaily decorated buckskins, and face and body paint.

The costume De Lusson wore had been brought west from Montreal in sealed cases aboard the canoe he rode as passenger. He appeared through the stockade gate with a splendid, wide-brimmed beaver hat under his arm. It had a white ostrich plume which attracted the chiefs' glances. His wig was powdered, curled. He had a short coat, and long breeches of brilliant velvet. His stockings and his slippers were silk, and the slippers were set with silver buckles. A small ceremonial sword in a gold scabbard was at his hip. There was lace at his throat and wrists. When he had saluted the company, a prayer was said, hymns sung. The treaty was read in sonorous French phrases that were completely unintelligible to the chiefs.

They represented Crees, whose hunting took them from Lake Nipigon to the Hayes River and Hudson Bay; and Assiniboins, who came from Lake Winnipeg; and Sacs, Foxes, Winnebagoes, Menominees, and Illinois, and Chippewas. They stepped forward when it was indicated they do so and signed the treaty. Their signatures were their clan symbols: an elk, a fox, a deer, a sturgeon, a beaver, a bear. They knew almost as little about the real value of the territory they relinquished as the Sun King himself.

But the Hudson's Bay Company was firmly established. It had held a similar ceremony on the southern shore of the bay, conducted September 1, 1670, by the governor of the company. A metal plate was nailed to a tree to prove possession. The governor made a short speech in which he announced that he took over in the name of Charles II of England all of the rivers of Canada that lay east of the Continental Divide and that did not flow into the Atlantic, the Arctic, the St. Lawrence River or the Great Lakes, and all the land they drained, and all the beaver, and all the Indian tribes which would trade beaver for goods.

New France was being threatened from both north and south. Three months after Sieur de Saint Lusson succeeded with the treaty signing at Sault Sainte Marie, English settlers began to cross the Alleghenies. They were not migrant hunters, or traders. They were farmer folk, pushed forth by the population increase in Virginia. From the Blue Ridge, the men looked over treetops at the glint of rivers. Those were in French territory. But the men on the ridge would go westward along them, wherever they led.

## 7

---

FEVER, DESPAIR AND HOMESICKNESS KEPT THE SET-
tlers close to Jamestown after the founding in 1607 of the
Virginia colony. None of them except Captain John Smith, an indomitable
man under almost any circumstances, moved more than a few miles from
the lopsided stockade on the marshy and malarial bank of the James River.
A twelve-year-old English boy named Henry Spelman was the first to
explore the headwaters of the James, the Potomac and the other broad-
flowing rivers that entered the Chesapeake from the wilderness.

Henry was the son of Sir Henry Spelman, an historian and scholar
at Oxford University. He ran away from home in 1609, and reached
Plymouth, sneaked aboard a ship bound for Virginia. Her name was
*Unity*, part of a nine-ship flotilla commanded by Vice Admiral Sir
Christopher Newport. *Unity* and the rest of the ships carried capacity
cargo, a lot of it stowed on deck, and 500 men, women and children.

Captain John Smith

Henry was able to keep hidden until the vessels were out of Cawsand Bay and it was too late for him to be sent ashore.

John Smith took a great liking to Henry in Virginia. He arranged for Henry and another English boy to stay among the Potomac tribe. Henry became a close friend of Pocahontas, who was a year or so older. He got to know her father well, Powhatan, the dour and deeply concerned sachem, who foresaw with the vision not given to many of his people their extinction by the white men. Henry, because of his presence among the tribe, was able to warn the Jamestown colonists when an Indian raid was planned.

John Smith wrote about this: "Pokahantas the King's daughter saved a boy called Henry Spilman, that lived many yeeres after, by her meanes, amongst the Patawomekes."

Despite constant danger from warriors belonging to tribes not known to him, Henry stayed in Indian country. He served the colony as a scout, then interpreter. But he came more and more rarely to Jamestown. He lacked the sense of respect that Sir George Yeardley, the governor, thought necessary. Sir George had him brought up on charges before the Virginia Assembly.

The members of the Assembly could not take Sir George's accusation very seriously, and only stripped Henry of the rank of captain of the troop of militia. They declared that his further punishment was to be "condemned to perform seven years service to the Colony in the nature of Interpreter to the Governour."

When he heard the sentence, Henry muttered "certaine words." These were in English, and addressed both to Sir George and the Assembly. He returned seldom to Jamestown after his trial in 1619, and never to act as interpreter for the governor.

He was the first English frontiersman, and the rivers and the regions to which they led fascinated him. He kept a record of what he saw; he was in his way an historian, and his early education at Oxford, his father's influence, and the scholarly environment of his home were not wasted.

Henry Spelman told of Indians who hunted deer along the tributary rivers of the Chesapeake in fall. They set fire to the woods, drove the animals by flame and smoke and loud cries into the water. Other warriors waited there in the bark or dugout canoes the tribes used, and easily killed the deer with spears and arrows. When tribe fought tribe, he crouched in the long grass and watched the "chiefest men" get their skulls knocked in from blows of deerhorn tom-

Crafted from a single log, the dugout canoe was universally used by the primitive American and quickly adopted by the frontiersman.

ahawks, and scalped with knives whose blades were sharpened reed splinters.

The invaders of the Chesapeake were Iroquois. They rode down the tributary rivers into the bay in canoes which Spelman described as hog troughs. Some of these clumsy craft carried as many as forty warriors. The survivors went promptly aboard after combat and started back towards the Mohawk. A valuable exchange of information about Iroquois fighting methods could have been made between the young, keen-eyed Englishman and Samuel de Champlain.

But Spelman was only aware in a partial fashion of the Frenchman's dreams of imperial expansion. His own objectives were local, and immediate. He wanted to explore all of Chesapeake Bay, then go on further from the coast, probably up the Susquehanna. He did not care much about a route to Cathay, or the South Sea, although he knew that the copper bracelets Powhatan wore came from a great distance, and through repeated barter. First the Chesapeake trade should be secured, he told himself, and took a small vessel loaded with trade goods up the Potomac River.

This was late in 1622, with the leaves off the trees and the chance of ambush small. He was with Captain Henry Fleet, another frontier trader, and a crew of twenty-six men. The vessel carried broadside and bow and stern cannon, and Spelman felt reasonably safe. He put the ship at anchor off the present site of Washington and went ashore to trade with some of the Anacostan tribe who lived in the area.

He and his companions who climbed the bank from the ship's boat were ambushed. His head was severed from the body and tossed onto the

bank, rolled into the river. Canoes filled with warriors appeared from the underbrush and an attack was made on the ship. The men aboard her beat the warriors back, heaved in the anchor, and maneuvered the ship downstream into the Chesapeake, returned at once to Jamestown.

Henry Spelman was more or less of a shadowy figure in Jamestown. Men there were occupied with the tobacco trade and the profits to be made on the London market. The frontier was a source of deerskins and a few hundred furs a year, no more. Spelman was the young fellow who had once provoked Sir George Yeardley by his surly behavior, and preferred life—and death—among the savages. But, in England, Captain John Smith heard of Spelman's death and made careful record of it. Smith, of all the Virginia settlers, had known Henry Spelman the best, understood what he had done for the colony, and for England.

A young London doctor, Henry Woodward, was the next Englishman to find frontier life to his liking. He followed Henry Spelman into the wilderness in 1665, arrived on the coast with the advance party of the expedition sent from Barbados to colonize Carolina. Woodward was immediately responsive to the lure of the forest and life among the Indians. He belonged by family background, tradition and training to the upper middle class that had emerged during Tudor rule in England. But he ignored these factors, or pushed them far from his consciousness.

He became the first English squaw-man of record. John Rolfe had married Pocahontas in a formal Church of England ceremony held in 1614 in Jamestown. When Dr. Woodward took a squaw into his tepee, he had no intention of matrimony, and the buxom middle-aged woman of the Kusso tribe did not expect it. She looked for sexual satisfaction

A large dugout canoe found in Great Dismal Swamp, N.C.

certainly, because she was healthy and a widow, but she was also very lonely. Her son had gone away with the English—Dr. Woodward's former companions—as a hostage. Dr. Woodward replaced him in the tribe. The arrangement was an early form of exchange scholarship.

The Indian youth who had volunteered to join the English was the Kusso chief's nephew. Dr. Woodward had in his turn volunteered to stay with the tribe, and the chief and the senior warriors appreciated the fact. Woodward was well treated and progressing steadily with his Kusso vocabulary and knowledge of Indian ways until a detachment of Spanish troops raided the village. Woodward was lucky to remain alive, and was put in solitary confinement in the Spanish military prison at St. Augustine.

He spent some months there until an English pirate, Captain Searles, raided the Spanish post. Dr. Woodward was released, but the pirates needed a surgeon aboard their vessel. This time, there was nothing voluntary about Woodward's service. He stayed on the ship for almost two years, and was forced to recall all that he had learned of the *Treatise on Gunshot*. Then, caught by a West Indian hurricane, the ship was hurled ashore in wrecked condition on the island of Nevis in the Leeward Group. A ship bound for Carolina had taken refuge in the lee of the island, and Woodward hurriedly boarded her. It was 1669 when he got back to Carolina.

The capital of the colony had been established at the juncture of the Ashley and Cooper Rivers and was known as Charles Town. Malaria took great annual toll among the settlers; there were frequent Spanish raids from Florida, and the local Indians, the Kussos and the Westos, were no longer friendly. They picked off any small or poorly armed groups of Englishmen who ventured inland along the rivers. The population of Charles Town in 1672 was less than 400, and the people had given up hope of any substantial assistance from the Lords Proprietors in London.

But Dr. Woodward persisted. He went into the interior, and in buckskin clothing, alone in a dugout canoe, explored the tidal rivers. He sensed the wealth that could be drawn from this region with its rich estuarial soil, ready access to the sea and almost innumerable waterways. He wanted to go on also further west, and explore the range of hills that lay blue, faintly visible within the river haze over the crests of the palmettos, the live-oaks and the cypresses and pines. When he was first here, his old friends, the Kussos, had told him of western tribes who dealt in furs and copper bracelets and red-stone pipes. Those tribes came from beyond the hills, and a range of mountains, "where the sun lived" and there were great rivers.

The Kussos had proven themselves treacherous in 1671, and Dr. Woodward had talked with captives who admitted the tribe was secretly allied with the Spanish. Woodward felt no sympathy. He had seen during his enforced pirate service in the Caribbean how Spaniards treated Indians. Their cruelty was complete; Indians were unredeemable infidels, and fit only for the stake, the lash and slavery. Spanish provincial governors in Santo Domingo worked native slaves without food until the people collapsed and died of hunger.

So Woodward took part deliberately in the war against the Kussos. He stood on the palmetto-log wharf in Charles Town and saw warriors he had not long ago called friends sold into slavery, and along with them their squaws and their children. They were bound for Barbados, where the equatorial sun, sadistic overseers and competition with recently imported African slaves would kill them inside a couple of months.

Dr. Woodward and the other supposedly enlightened men of the colony lived according to a double standard. They had resisted with fierce indignation the conditions of slavery which had caused the deaths of thousands of whites on Barbados. These people were red-skinned, and savages; they had conspired with the Spaniards. They were sold for nominal sums to shipmasters or the agents of Barbadian planters.

This, in 1671, was the beginning of the Carolina slave trade.

Dr. Woodward had served with such efficiency that in 1674 he was appointed Indian agent by Governor Joseph West. His specific orders were to "open trade with the Westos." They were a tribe that lived east of the lower Savannah River, and Woodward approached them from the coast. He sailed alongshore in a big dugout canoe, entered Port Royal Sound and went with an Indian guide through the inner waterways, past Hilton Head Island to the mouth of the Savannah. He was in hostile Indian country, and moved across a route often used by Spanish raiding parties.

But he was not halted or attacked. He took the tide and went up the winding, silt-clogged river among canebrakes where a multitude of wildfowl squawked, screamed, flapped and dived. He and his guide left the river as soon as possible. It was too exposed, and they could easily be ambushed.

Woodward found his way further upstream to the Westos. He spent months with the tribe and exerted all of his diplomatic skill. He secured large amounts of furs and deerskins for the Charles Town market, and also dealt in slaves. The slaves were Indians captured by the Westos, a warlike people who raided often among the Yemassees and the Kiowas, seized husky young male and female prisoners. These, when bought by Woodward, were marched in coffles under Westo guard to the Savannah. Then they were transferred to canoes and sent down to the mouth of the river where vessels from Charles Town waited.

The Westos reached the decision in April 1680 that they wanted no more traffic with the white men. They had exhausted all credulity. The white men were their deadly enemies. It needed very little imagination to place themselves among the next contingents of Barbados-bound slaves. Dr. Woodward took to the forest and made his way alone over back trails to Charles Town.

He was one of the leaders of the English campaign of pacification. He led detachments in canoes, wherries and pinnaces up the Savannah, the Broad, the Coosawhatchie and the branches of the Edisto. The English soldiers were armed with muskets and wore body armor; the boats carried culverins that hurled murderous charges of small shot at close range. The Westo villages were destroyed and before the end of the year enough warriors were killed to make the survivors plead for peace.

The Westos were convinced that they should cooperate in trade with the western tribes. The Indians who lived in the Piedmont region still listened to English blandishments and were willing to barter beaver pelts and the actually much more valuable deerskins for the usual trade goods at the usual vastly inflated prices. The deerskins shipped down the Savannah after pack trains had brought the bales to the rough riverside wharves were the greatest source of shoe and boot leather in Europe.

It had once been Dr. Woodward's ambition to go to the headwaters of the Savannah, and from them over the mountains to the western rivers of which he had heard so much. But he had become a trader, one of the governor's trusted men. Exploration was like his medicine, something that had no real part in his life. He belonged here on the Savannah, cheating Indians.

There was, though, a tremendous, constant surge of enthusiasm for further exploration. Its origin lay deep in the English spirit, went back of course to Queen Elizabeth's reign when her daring and ruthless captains had made fantastic voyages of discovery, sometimes brought her—and were able to keep for themselves—great wealth.

A Virginia governor, Alexander Spotswood, was motivated by this tradition. He made in 1716 the journey that Woodward had contemplated. He took an expedition over the Blue Ridge and with his companions stared into the magnificent valley where the vast web of the rivers stretched ashine in the westering sun. Spotswood was an extraordinary man, the most vigorous and athletic of his rank ever to serve in the colonies.

Spotswood was descended from a Scottish archbishop who had been deposed because of the independent viewpoint of his utterances but later honored by burial in Westminster Abbey. One of his grandfathers was the Earl of Montrose, who was famous for having led the outnumbered Highland clans in a series of victories in 1644 in defense of King Charles. He had gone to war himself while in his teens.

He was an officer in Marlborough's army when it made a 400-mile forced march across Austria to Blenheim to the support of Prince Eugene of Savoy. This was in August 1704, and Marshal Tallard, in command of the combined enemy army of French and Bavarians, thought his center was secured by a stretch of marsh in front of it. But Marlborough built bridges over the marsh, then sent in his cavalry.

Alexander Spotswood rode with the English cavalry. He had memories of saber and pistol fighting, knee to knee, against French dragoons. There were other memories—of French and Bavarians being thrust by the hundreds with the shift of battle into the Danube to drown.

Then, in 1709, in a thick swirl of mist and gun smoke, he fought in another great bloody battle at Malplaquet. He was by the age of twenty-eight the quartermaster general for Marlborough's army. Life in the colonies offered a change of scene from the dullness of peacetime barracks duty. So he asked for and received in 1710 the appointment as governor of Virginia.

His outstanding performance before he organized the expedition that crossed the Blue Ridge was his confrontation of the members of the House of Burgesses. It was his belief that they were obstinate when they refused to accept his proposals at once, and he described them with various oaths of a highly military but profane nature.

His opponents in the House of Burgesses were forced to admit, though, that he did a great deal to advance the colony. He brought in artisans from England, masons, wheelwrights, coach-builders and iron-workers, started local iron foundries. He was completely determined also that the passage of the "Great Mountains" should be made. The mountain range served as a wall against the expansion of the colony, and when it was traversed Virginia could establish permanently her western claims.

Governor Spotswood gathered his exploration party in late August 1716 at Germanna, on the Rapidan. Fifty men mustered in the sticky heat, the governor dressed in a green-velvet riding habit, Russian boots, and a hat with a long ostrich plume. Some of his personal friends, planters and colonial officials, were dressed in similar *cavalier* style. But if any of the two companies of rangers mustered there thought the costumes a bit strange for penetration of the Blue Ridge wilderness, nothing was said. The governor's war record was well known.

Indian guides moved out ahead of the rangers. There were servants, and hostlers to handle the pack-train mounts. A large portion of the pack load was liquid: several cases of both red and white Virginia wine, brandy, Irish *usquebaugh*, two kinds of rum, champagne, cherry punch and cider, and what was listed as "other refreshments." Samples of these were taken by Spotswood and his staff. He had with him, thoughtfully chosen, the members of several influential families—Beverlys, Brookes, Masons, Robertsons, Robinsons, Taylors and Todds. Young Ensign John Fontaine kept a faithful diary report of the venture.

Due to the sampling activities, the party got off to a slow start. The horses were shod with iron shoes for the mountain trails instead of the sandy lowlands, though, and Spotswood had a trumpeter sound the departure call. Within a day or so, the expedition was accustomed to its march formation and moved steadily forward. It was by September 2nd in the mountains. The going was rough. Plumes, broad-brimmed hats and velvet riding coats suffered. Spotswood and the other men stripped off their heavy gear. They dismounted, led their sweating, lathered, panting mounts. Reins in one hand, the other lifted to fend off back-lashing branches, they followed the guides along the ridge.

They moved through Swift Run Gap. Then, very abruptly, they looked out and down at the Shenandoah. It lay in a broad, lush wedge of valley where grass grew thick and blue-green. The Indians started down-slope into the valley, their scalp-lock feathers nodding as they loped, the rangers behind them, slower in their long deerskin smocks and trousers.

The tight little leaves of Virginia creeper were turning gold and russet on the slope, and the sumac was already scarlet. The horsemen re-mounted in the valley; the grass through which they rode was higher than the horses' heads, and they swept it aside in undulant waves. The river was clear, beautiful and cool. When men and beasts had drunk from it, Spotswood decided on a name. He called it Euphrates, which the map-makers disregarded soon afterwards in favor of the original Indian title.

The expedition camped beside the river for the night. Hunters went out into the valley and shot white-splotched deer, and tall, elusive turkeys. Wild grapes were picked from the tangle of vines around the campsite, and men collected currants in their caps, hats and helmets. Ensign Fon-taine reported in his diary:

> We had a good dinner, and after it got the men together and loaded all the arms; and we drank the King's health in champagne, and fired a volley; and the Princess in Burgundy, and fired a volley; and all the rest of the Royal Family in claret, and fired a volley. We drank the Governor's health, and fired another volley.

The next day, when the hangovers had worn off, the expedition started back towards Virginia. The same route along the James River was used. Spotswood made no attempt to open up more new country. His ambition was satisfied; he returned holding the belief that he had been within a short distance of the Great Lakes. He wrote for the official record:

> The chief aim of my expedition was to satisfy myself whether it was practical to come at the Lakes. Having on that occasion found an easy passage over that great Ridge of Mountains which were before judged

impassable, I also discovered by the relations of the Indians who frequent these parts that from the West side of one of the small mountains I saw that the Lake is very visible.

The Indians, Catawbas or Cherokees, probably lied to Spotswood. But he practiced a little self-deceit. The veteran of Blenheim and Malplaquet had from the western slope of the Blue Ridge seen no mountain that gave a view of the Great Lakes. His knowledge of geography, no matter how bad the maps of the time were, denied the fact.

Spotswood hoped to establish a trading post in the Shenandoah Valley that "would drive a wedge between the extremities of the French position." He failed in this, though, in 1724, and made no further effort. He was content to remain at Williamsburg and leave the work for other men.

Exploration of the Piedmont region had begun in 1650 when Englishmen entered it along the forks of the Roanoke. They were Captain Abraham Wood and Edward Bland, who were followed in 1671–73 by a larger expedition. The second party was led by Thomas Batts and Robert Fallam, and they penetrated the Blue Ridge along the course of the Staunton River. It brought them out of the mountains onto the westerly flowing New River. Then the Yadkin River was discovered in 1673 and explored, and a pass opened through the Carolina Blue Ridge.

Ten years after Spotswood planned his frontier post, by 1734, settlers were crossing into the Shenandoah Valley. They brought their families with them, the women on horseback and tending the pack animals, the children helping to drive the oxen and cows. The settlers moved unguarded, and took squatters' rights along the Shenandoah.

The men built lean-to cabins for the first winter before they went into the forest after game to supply the necessary meat. The women used spare muskets to kill prowling cougars, panthers and black bears who came too close at night. This was a beautiful valley, and promised the settlers much more than they had owned in the landlord-dominated Tidewater region. But fear existed here right from the beginning. Its greatest source was Indian attack, or the arrival of French troops along the frozen surface of the river that would serve the enemy as a completely open road.

The Indian threat did not hold back for long, though, the occupation of the valley by groups of settlers. They were intrepid people, willing to fight the Indians or anybody else who opposed them, and at considerable odds. There were three major pioneer groups which during the early 1700s came over the mountains from the northward and from the east.

These were Palatinate Germans with whom came some Swiss. Then Ulster Scots arrived. They were joined by English families from the Tidewater. The English had left the coastal region in a search for more land, and out of a sense of adventure.

The Germans had been driven from their original homes in the Palatinate by Catholic soldiers who served Louis XIV and took his orders. The Protestant people left Germany by the thousands. They became refugees in the classical tradition, wandered across western Europe and then to England, from England to the New World, which for them was Pennsylvania. Then, still unhappy, they left the Pennsylvania frontier and headed south, flanking the Blue Ridge. They entered the Shenandoah Valley from the southernmost range of hills in William Penn's colony, forded the Potomac near what is now Sheperdstown.

Their leader was a redoubtable man named Joist Hite and around 1726 the first German families had settled, were busy building cabins, clearing fields and getting crops in the ground. They wrote to relatives and friends overseas, and other families joined them as fast as passage money could be collected. Descriptions of the Shenandoah in summer made it seem very much like Paradise.

The Germans built their small square houses right out in the rolling prairie among the shoulder-high, blue grass. Their barns were bigger than their homes, but they had large herds. The cows, when they were brought in to be milked at dusk, stamped into the barns crimson-hocked. Their pasture was covered with wild strawberries, and the boys who herded and milked them had smeared mouths. When the milking was finished and the wooden buckets covered and put in the spring-house to keep cool, the boys headed for the river.

They went skinny-dippers from the bank. They belly-whopped, and splashed and ducked each other, dived and came up and tried to catch water bugs in their hands. Then they were called to supper, and to finish the rest of their chores.

The Ulster Scots settled mainly in the upper valley, and were a

109

Easton on the Delaware

fiercely independent lòt who for some years kept aloof from the friendly, easy-going Germans and the people of English stock. But the Scots had reason to be wary and diffident. These were the descendants of Covenanters, driven from Scotland because of their refusal to accept the tenets of the Church of England.

They had fled persecution in Dundee and, led by their Presbyterian ministers, they had marched congregation by congregation across Scotland and embarked for Ulster. There was, though, no peace for them in Ireland. Back in Scotland, because they were dissenters from the Established Church, their marriages had been declared illegal, they had been disbarred from public office, stripped of all military rank. The Irish insisted that they become Catholics. They were besieged by the Irish in Londonderry. The end of the fighting came when the Scots agreed to sail for America.

They took ship and landed at Philadelphia with an impact that shocked, then deeply vexed the Quakers. So the Scots went west, up the Delaware and to its headwaters, and on along the other frontier rivers and creeks. But the Quakers were stubborn; they profoundly disliked the Scots and Presbyterianism. Restraints were put upon the Scots with increasing severity. Their religion was threatened, and their livelihoods.

The Scots got out of Pennsylvania. They would accept no modification of their beliefs, refused to obey temporal authority. The new cabins and barns and freshly cleared fields were left. Families went south, into the total wilderness, crossed the Potomac and entered the Shenandoah Valley, and stayed.

It was almost empty when they settled there. They prospered. Their families took new land as sons and daughters married. They were so numerous that by 1738, when the first county lines were established in the valley, they sent a petition to the governor, Lord Fairfax. It read:

> For those who are of the same persuasian as the Church of Scotland to ask your favour in allowing them the liberty of their consciences, and of worshipping God in a way agreeable to the principles of their education.

Lord Fairfax made the recommendation to the House of Burgesses at Williamsburg and freedom of worship was granted the Scots. It set a precedent for Virginia. Many other minority sects were attracted to the Shenandoah Valley. There were among them Lutherans and Mennonites and Dunkards, and people of the German Reformed Church as well as the Palatinate Protestants and the Tidewater families, who were Church of England, and even some Quakers.

A considerable number of the Scots settled around Harpers Ferry, on the Potomac. They became iron-workers, built the original forges in the area. The iron they worked was sent in finished form—pots, pans and kettles—down the river in barges. Local men supplied the barge crews, and they extolled the beauties of the Shenandoah when the craft reached Tidewater.

But it took the river men who sailed the craft on the west-flowing streams to perpetuate the memory of the Shenandoah. The flatboatmen, the keelboatmen, the wanderers who had no home except in memory, sang their most haunting song about the river in its lush, mountain-held valley. Sailing-ship crews picked it up in New Orleans in the packet era, and they passed it on to the clipper-ship men who made it famous as a chantey in every major port in the world:

> *Oh, Shennydore, I long to see ye!*
> *Away, away, you rollin' river!*

## 8

---

THOMAS JEFFERSON HAD NO REAL DESIRE TO SHOOT the turkey. This was at Shadwell, in Albemarle County, Virginia, in 1753, and Thomas was ten years old. He was only obeying the orders of his father. Colonel Jefferson had told his son that at the age of ten any intelligent boy should be able to handle a musket. Then he gave Thomas a long, heavy flintlock weapon, loaded it and primed it, said that he should return with a turkey for supper.

Thomas stumbled through the forest underbrush for some time. The turkey runs were deserted; the birds had heard him coming, hundreds of yards away. It was getting dark, and he started home. But Colonel Peter Jefferson was a strict man. Thomas knew that without a turkey to present he would get no supper, and probably a severe spanking.

He passed a turkey in a pen on his homeward route. He stood and considered it. Then he took off one of his garters, tied the turkey, protesting, to the base of a tree. He steadied the barrel of the flintlock against the trunk of another, nearby tree, fired at almost point-blank range. The execution was instantaneous. Colonel Jefferson was slightly curious about the ravages the charge had made in the carcass, but Thomas got his supper, was accepted as a successful hunter.

The Albemarle County of Thomas Jefferson's youth was still frontier territory. Despite all of his absorption with books and his liking for intellectual pursuits, he was inexorably linked to the wilderness that existed a few miles to the west. Colonel Jefferson was a wealthy planter, and the lieutenant of his county. But he was also a surveyor who had gone forth and explored the wilderness regions. He helped to mark in 1746 the so-called Fairfax Line, which ran seventy-six miles straight across the Blue Ridge and determined the extent of the Fairfax family's huge grant.

Then, in 1749, with a friend and neighbor, Joshua Fry, the colonel was employed by the colony to make a more extensive survey. He and Fry ran the Virginia-North Carolina boundary more than ninety miles farther west than had been done in the famous original survey made by William Byrd of Westover. This took him deep into the wilderness, and when the survey was finished, Colonel Jefferson and his partner were commissioned to construct a map of Virginia.

Thomas Jefferson heard a great deal as a small boy about triangulation, compass error, and the translation of latitude and longitude into miles, rods and feet. But he heard more about the daily dangers of men who worked in Indian country. These excited his imagination, these and the stories of the westward-reaching rivers. Along the rivers, his father and Mr. Fry said, Virginia must expand. Her people needed space, and there was all that any settler could hope to own over the mountains, where the streams had worn gorges through the solid rock.

Colonel Jefferson died when Thomas was thirteen. He was sent the next year to board with the Reverend James Maury and attend the school the clergyman conducted. The man who sent him was Dr. Thomas Walker, a very devoted friend of his father. Dr. Walker had a strong influence upon the boy, maintained it as long as possible.

He was one of the executors of Colonel Jefferson's will, and took 113 the responsibility for Thomas's schooling. The school that the Reverend Maury ran was chosen with considerable care. There were a number of influences at work in the Tidewater country of Virginia in the middle of the eighteenth century, and those which were oriented towards an imitation of upper-class English life did not appeal to Dr. Walker.

He was a new and quite unusual frontier type, and in some ways resembled that earlier medical man on this coast, Dr. Woodward; he also bore a similarity to Henry Spelman. He was first off a doctor, with his professional education gained in England. His intellectual roots were English, and European. But he had migrated early to Virginia. He became a Piedmont region planter. He served, too, as a surveyor, and speculated in land purchase.

Dr. Walker made the original exploration of Kentucky from Virginia, and discovered the Cumberland Gap. He went in 1749 to the Holston River and East Tennessee, and on to the Clinch and Powell's Rivers, through the Cumberland Gap, to the headwaters of the Kentucky River and then back across New River and the Valley of Virginia. The march lasted from December of 1749 until July of the next year, and was historic. It was a direct incentive to westward expansion.

Dr. Walker had taken the march at the request of a land company. The year before, in 1748, he had gone with a party of "land viewers" to the Holston River and the eastern reaches of Tennessee. When he came back from his further journey, he turned over his data to Lewis Evans, a practiced cartographer. The work was published in 1755 and titled "A Map of the Middle British Colonies in America."

Dr. Walker and the Reverend Maury were close friends. They were also neighbors in Fredericksville Parish of Louisa County. The doctor often visited the school. It was small, and had been opened by the rector to help educate the sons of a few local planters and help out his limited churchly income. Dr. Walker was welcomed by the boys, particularly by Thomas Jefferson.

When school hours were over, the three sat together in the rector's study and the men talked. The long-faced, broad-browed boy remained silent, from time to time looking at the parchment maps outspread on the floor for reference, and checking for use later the name of some remote river.

114

The talk between the men was mainly of rivers and mountains. The names came to have a musical sound for Thomas Jefferson. He thrilled to

Cumberland Gap

them, as though he listened to a vast orchestral expression that represented storm sweeping, hurling over the primeval forest, and the mountain ridges, and the valleys where the rivers uncoiled like awakened snakes.

Rain pocked the rivers. The wind whipped them. Torn branches floated tossing in the current. Muskrat lodges were flooded. Birds sat huddled, disconsolate and soaked, on high limbs. Buffalo, elk and white-tail deer stared up, taut, quivering, when thunder crashed above the valleys. Then the wind fell. The rain stopped. The forest dripped, and birds began to sing, the muskrats swam back upstream to clear their lodges. The rivers gleamed with sun.

115

Thomas Jefferson, a map in front of him, placed the river names the men used. They spoke of the Rappahannock, the Chickahominy, the

Potomac, the James, the Roanoke, and of streams further away, the Santee, the Savannah, the Delaware and the Susquehanna. A design was formed; it trended westward into the interior. A man, for instance, could go from the Susquehanna and by way of the Juniata and through passes where the marching was not too hard reach the Allegheny. He could go, too, from the Cheat to the Monongahela. Both those routes would lead him to the heart of the newly explored country, the Forks of the Ohio. The French greatly coveted that, but more of that later.

There were other ways west for a settler to take. He could go from the Potomac to the Kanawha, through the mountains. Trails would soon be opened that went through Cumberland Gap and Moccasin Gap, came out on the Cumberland River, or the Tennessee. What lay beyond, in territory the French claimed west of the Ohio, was not fully determined on any of Dr. Walker's maps. He spoke of the Miami, the Wabash, the Illinois and Wisconsin and the Great Lakes waterways, but with some uncertainty. Those were like the Mississippi and the other great mysterious stream, the Missouri; few English-speaking men had yet seen them, and none had been able to explore them.

But Thomas Jefferson understood the profound importance of this talk here in the quiet of the clergy study. It was to leave on him an influence that was to dominate all of his life, his thinking and his decisions while President of the United States. Even with the fragmentary information possessed by Dr. Walker in 1755, the shape of things to come in North America emerged out of Indian legend, campfire guesses, and the dreams and wish fulfillments of writers, monarchs and cartographers.

The continent was hung on a single huge hinge—the Mississippi. It was secured by the Great Lakes at the northern end and New Orleans at the southern. The St. Lawrence connected with rivers that led to the Lakes, and the Lakes gave easy reach to the Mississippi. The French owned all of that northern, western and southern territory, or claimed it, and were willing to fight for it. The English, occupied with fish and farms and ships, held only a little more than the coastal colonies, and now were being threatened there by a war with the French.

The French were in the Ohio Valley, and in 1753 Governor Dinwiddie had sent Colonel George Washington to get them out of it.

116

Washington had been forced to surrender to the French the next year at Fort Necessity, and was with General Braddock when that brave but stupid officer was killed in the recent defeat. The French and their Indian allies had proven themselves strong enemies; the war might go on for several more years, and wreck Dr. Walker's great plan of exploration.

Thomas Jefferson had heard the details of the Walker plan discussed so many times that he had them permanently memorized. It was on a vast scale, he realized, and some men who had been told about it were skeptical, called it impossible. But others—and only a few very important men had been informed—believed implicitly in its success, and in the need for the journey. Dr. Walker was ready to lead a party right across the continent, traverse the Mississippi, go up the fabulous Missouri into the unmapped and only vaguely known regions to the west, where a range of mountains, or at least high hills, lay, and past them, within marching distance, the Pacific Ocean.

There were various sources for the basis of surmise which supported Dr. Walker's conviction that the journey could be made. Most of

On the Susquehanna

them were French, and prominent among these was the book by the Baron Lahontan et Heslèche. The baron had a fine record of service as an officer and explorer. He had spent a considerable period of time in the Mississippi Valley, and entered the country west of it. Lahontan was to be trusted, then, quite implicitly, and other French officers who had been stationed in the Mississippi Valley.

An Englishman, Daniel Coxe, had also written an informative book. The title of it was *Carolana*. According to Coxe, the headwaters of the Missouri River were in a mountain range. He described it from accounts given to him by Indians. He wrote that on the west side of the range was a river which flowed down to "a large lake called Thayago, which pours its water through a large navigable river into a boundless sea."

The Missouri, Coxe stated, was navigable all the way to the source. He wrote that this "proceeds from a ridge of hills somewhat north of New Mexico, passable by horse, foot or wagon in less than half a day." It was from there, of course, a very simple proposition to get to the lake called Thayago, and the river which flowed from the lake downslope to the Pacific.

Dr. Walker believed what Coxe had written, and his conviction was shared by the Reverend Maury. The clergyman was exceptionally well educated, and generally able to discern fact from fiction. But the frontier dream entrapped him, too, and the covetous, empire-seizing ambitions that had driven all men of English origin since the middle of the sixteenth century. There was, of course, a subtle admixture of fact in Coxe's fancy, and also in that of the Baron Lahontan et Heslèche. They were so compulsive in their thinking that they lied without full awareness, fused in single concepts the elements of truth and untruth.

The Reverend Maury concluded from the evidence at hand that England was at last to achieve her possession of the continent. Then she would go on, and take hold of the rest of the known world. Euphoria claimed the sober-minded clergyman; he had been badly infected by his friend, Dr. Walker. His thinking was not wholly distorted, though, and he understood some of the phases of the North American power struggle with clarity.

118

He wrote home to an uncle in England a long very revealing and valuable letter. His central thesis was shrewdly reasoned. He wrote that whichever nation won the present war and was owner of the Ohio and the Great Lakes must become in the course of a few years "sole and absolute lord of North America." He envisioned the Hudson River as "the grand emporium of all East Indian commodities," and, if not the Hudson, the Potomac.

The letter was explicit, and technical. Reverend Maury wrote about canoe speeds and carrying capacities. He wrote with surprising foresight about the feasibility of canoe transport on the western rivers, particularly the affluents of the Mississippi. It would still be some years before the powerful Canadian fur companies would establish east-west traffic over a nearly 4,000-mile-long lake and river route with birchbark canoes that carried four tons of cargo apiece.

But he saw everything in relation to the accuracy of Coxe's report about the easy march from New Mexico, the range of hills which were in reality the Rocky Mountains, the completely imaginary Lake Thayago, and the equally non-existent river that connected it with the Pacific. The Reverend Maury had based his logic on a quicksand of falsehood. He was happy to report, believing Coxe, that there was no more need to seek for the Northwest Passage. The costly, dangerous attempts that had taken so many lives could be abandoned. For here was the route to China, as he described it in his letter to his uncle.

China-bound traffic and that on the return voyage to England would move along the Hudson or the Potomac. The English planters who lived beside those waterways would enjoy immense wealth. The river valleys would become "the general mart of the European World, at least for the rich and costly products of the East, and a mart at which chapmen might be furnished with all those commodities on much easier terms than the tedious and hazardous and expensive navigation to those countries can at present afford. What an exhaustless fund of wealth would be opened, superior to Potosi and all the other South American mines! What an extent of region!"

Then a sense of caution appeared in the letter, written June 10, 1756, and speaking of "a worthy friend and neighbor of mine." This was Dr. Walker. He was to lead a far-ranging expedition into the western 119 wilderness. The plans had been evolved for three years. They were held in the top-secret category. The bearer of the letter was advised by

Reverend Maury to heave it overside if his ship was closely pursued by a French privateer vessel.

Reverend Maury wrote: "Some persons were sent in search of that river Missouri, if that be the right name for it, in order to discover whether it had any such communication with the Pacific Ocean; they were to follow that river if they found it and make exact reports of the country they passed through, the distance they traveled, what sort of navigation those rivers and lakes afforded, &c., &c."

The outbreak of war had halted the expedition. Dr. Walker was not given the chance to lead it. But it had been very carefully organized, and the idea was not abandoned, therefore the need for secrecy. Thomas Jefferson was among those who cherished it. When he left the Reverend Maury's school and went to college at William and Mary, and afterwards, as he began his career as a lawyer, he retained the continental dream.

Virginia was actively engaged in the bitter and bloodily fought French-English war. Her troops served in it; her entire future depended upon the victory. All of the English colonies were under attack. French Canada encircled them. Battles had been fought along the Monongahela and the Ohio. But early in the war, up in the northeastern corner of English-held territory, the French had invaded Nova Scotia. They had erected forts at the head of the Bay of Fundy, and incited the Acadians to revolt.

Thomas Jefferson, while still a student in the quiet of Williamsburg, recognized the enormity of the struggle. This, he knew, was being fought for the control of North America. And only along the rivers could troops, their arms, equipment and supplies be moved. Some of them, although remote, not even marked on the maps, were of primary strategic importance. Their use might decide the war.

## 9

H E WALKED, VEERING, STUMBLING, SLOW TO GET
up from the snow-covered ground, so weak from hunger
and exhaustion that he moaned as he breathed. The remnants of his uniform were soaked with snow melt, his sweat, and blood from the scratches
where he had fallen among timber or rocks. Twigs, leaves, bits of bark
were in his shoulder-long hair; he wore no recognizable sign of rank. Still,
he moved like a soldier. When he tripped and fell, he kept his musket
from injury, and when he rose he swung back into place with mechanical
gestures his powder horn and cartridge box.

The powder horn bore his initials, beautifully inscribed in the
dark bone. This man was Major Robert Rogers, the commanding officer
of His Majesty's Rangers which late in October 1759 served King George
II. Now Rogers was kept going by the insistence of the river that swept
in wild rapids through a gorge close alongside him. He sought to reach

Major Robert Rogers

the bottom of the gorge, where the rapids subsided, and in calm water catch the raft his comrades would release from above at his signal.

He and his three comrades were some of the survivors of the force of more than 100 men Rogers had led against the Canadian settlement of St. Francis, and afterwards in the retreat from it. St. Francis was a large village near Montreal occupied by Indians of several tribes who at French orders had repeatedly, without mercy, raided the New England frontier.

Rogers had almost completely destroyed the place, which Lord Jeffrey Amherst, the British general in command, considered a key strongpoint of the French military system in eastern Canada. Rogers had been aware for days that a combined force of at least 600 French and Indians pursued what was left of his detachment. He had split it, and split it again, hoping that small groups would be able to escape in the mountain wilderness and reach safety at Fort Number Four, only a few miles away here on this river, the Connecticut.

Something had gone very wrong. A relief party with provisions was supposed to meet the detachment at the junction of the Wells River and the Connecticut. The men found nothing except a fire that still blazed and told them that within an hour, probably less, their own people had been at the rendezvous. Musket volleys and shouts that finally became hysterical brought no response, though. Most of the men were convulsed with stomach cramps; their only food was groundnuts and lily roots. They could not march, swim or paddle.

Rogers left them and with his three comrades built a raft of pine logs. The river was their single chance of salvation. It would lead them down to Fort Number Four, which was certainly occupied. His comrades understood the need to use the river, although the water was numbing cold, and the boulders, snags, rapids and whirlpools were a great danger.

Rogers knew all of this country. He had conducted his own party from St. Francis without losing a man. He led it along a series of waterways, taking advantage of the valleys in which they lay. His path went from the southern end of Lake Memphremagog along the Barton River to Crystal Lake. Then there was a short overland march to the Passumpsic;

123

down that valley, he and his men reached the junction of the Wells and the Connecticut.

But he tried the almost impossible in his attempt to navigate the Connecticut. The swift, high-rushing crest hurled the unwieldy raft over the White River Falls. It was already caught in the foamy suction of the rapids before the men tumbled off, muskets high above their heads, knapsacks and blanket rolls a wrenching weight.

The raft smashed apart in the rapids, went over the falls as separate logs. The men watched, and turned away, followed Rogers along the bank past the falls. Rogers started to build a new raft while his comrades hunted for game. He lacked an axe, and tools of any sort. He felled pine trees by setting fires at their bases, and burned the logs to the right length. Vines and withes gave him the lashing for the raft and an unreliable-looking hawser. He made paddles from sticks and pieces of bark.

His comrades came back with a couple of red squirrels and a partridge. The food restored a degree of strength to the men. They handled the new raft with fair skill when they headed downstream. But, through the snow, against the roar of the river over its stony bed, Rogers heard the sound of the falls. These were called the Wattoquitchey, and were about fifty yards in length. The raft would never survive them while carrying the men.

Rogers motioned to his comrades. He indicated that they paddle and push the raft in to the left bank. Then he told them that he would go down to the bottom of the falls and catch the raft after they had released it from up here, sent it fairly out into the stream at the full length of the hawser.

One of the men was a captain of Rangers named Ogden. He argued with Rogers, told the major that it was too much of a risk to take. A man should try to ride the raft through the falls, Ogden said. If Major Rogers tried to swim out to it alone down below and got a stomach cramp—

Rogers did not seem to listen. He was moving away, his broad and heavy body hunched with stomach pain, his ragged moccasins, the soles gone, dragging thin crooked trails across the freshly fallen snow on the bank. The men who stood beside the raft were silent, but they got the raft ready to be launched in the way that he had ordered.

Rogers pushed himself out onto a shelving bench of rock when he came to the bottom of the falls. He could very vaguely see his comrades upstream, and was aware that they saw him. They shouted, and he waved back. His motions were clumsy as he took off his accoutrements, then his clothing and his moccasins. He did not feel the cold at first; his clothing had been sodden. But the wind began to bother him, and the snow. He slipped into the water after he had waved again at the men above to start the raft downstream.

It danced, jumped, bobbed in the black furrows of water that were scrolled with ivory-colored foam. He measured, took a long breath. Then he dived and swam.

The raft beat him back. He grasped, and his hands slipped from the logs. He swam, and came abreast, stretched and held on, then began to drag himself aboard. That hurt. He was scraped from the navel to the knees.

Still, the pain did not affect him. He pulled loose a paddle lashed to one of the uprights, swerved the raft towards the bank. Now his men would be safe. He kept on telling it to himself, and it reduced the pain.

Within half an hour after Rogers arrived at Fort Number Four provisions were being taken upstream in canoes. The starving men who waited at the Wells River were brought to the fort, and later returned to the main body of the British Army. Rogers went back again into the wilderness, seeking men from the missing detachments. He lost on the St. Francis expedition, when the full count was made, three officers, forty-six sergeants and privates. It was for an elite corps a very large number; all of its men were volunteers, and carefully screened at the time of enlistment.

Rogers was a hero in New England. With the destruction of St. Francis and practically all of its male population, he had lifted a frightful weight of fear from the frontier people. Raids based on St. Francis had penetrated deeply, anywhere from the Penobscot River region in Maine through New Hampshire, and several groups of marauders had gone further south.

Rogers had been born on the frontier, in Methuen, a village set in the wilderness in the northeastern section of the Massachusetts Bay Colony. He was of Ulster Scot stock, his father, James Rogers, a man who had little success farming the stony, stump-littered acres taken on a squatter's claim. There were already Indian raids when Robert Rogers was born in November 1731, and he was taught how to handle a musket as soon as he could lift it and hold it steady. He had been a forest hunter first, roamed the rivers, lakes and mountains of the northeastern border region. Then he made professional use of his skill as an Indian-fighter, joined the British Army, and was assigned to organize the corps that soon became famous as Rogers Rangers.

Now he was implacable in his determination to bring before a court-martial the man he considered responsible for the failure of the Wells River rendezvous. This was a veteran Rangers officer, Lieutenant Samuel Stevens. He was found guilty in April 1760 of the charges presented by Rogers, and dismissed from service.

Rogers knew Stevens well. They had served together for years, shared many campfires. But for Rogers the necessity for discipline was paramount. The Rangers risked their lives under almost every possible circumstance; capture for them meant quite invariably the stake, torture that could last twenty-four hours and more. So, while he commanded them, each man's life was held most precious, and this, above all else, must remain unshaken. The men should maintain absolute trust in him, right to the end.

The proof of his theory of morale was proven when in November 1760 the town of Montreal was taken by British troops. The Rangers participated in the victory, and Rogers wrote, "Thus at length, at the end of the fifth campaign, Montreal and the whole country of Canada was given up, and became subject to the King of Great Britain; a conquest perhaps of the greatest importance that is to be met with in British annals."

General Amherst sent for Rogers immediately after the town was secured. He talked alone with the tall, massive-shouldered Ranger. There was an extraordinarily difficult mission to be carried out, he told Rogers, and Rogers and a special force were herewith assigned to it.

Part of the French capitulation was the surrender of all French military installations. This included the western posts at Detroit and Michilimackinac and on the various rivers reaching towards the Mississippi. But it was wholly possible that the local French commanders would be

A log-house.

unwilling to accept terms made in Montreal. No British force had ever attempted to go further west than Fort Pitt, at the junction of the Allegheny and the Monongahela.

The season was late. Snow and ice conditions would soon greatly hinder passage. The shores of the rivers, the lakes that must be used to get to the French posts were held by Indian tribes hostile to the British. The force that Amherst assigned to Rogers was small. Enemy action could block it, conceivably destroy it, or leave it in the winter wilderness with dwindling ammunition to succumb gradually to starvation.

Rogers received on September 12th his written orders from Amherst. He was given two Ranger companies, an engineer officer from the regular British Army, and a man who had formerly lived in Detroit who would serve as guide. The orders read for him to go up the St. Lawrence, keep close to the northern shore of Lake Ontario until opposite Fort Niagara. He was to cross over there, take his force into Lake Erie by way of the portage and the Niagara River. Then he was to go to Presque Isle, near the southern shore of Lake Erie, and leave the Rangers.

General Monckton was supposedly at Fort Pitt, and Rogers was ordered to find him, wherever he was.

He carried Amherst's orders for Monckton. These told Monckton to dispatch British regulars from Fort Pitt as a garrison force at Detroit. The Indian problem was given consideration by Sir William Johnson, who had been in conference with Amherst. It was the firm belief of Sir William, who had a Mohawk wife, owned an enormous estate on the Mohawk and ranked high in the Iroquois councils, that peace could be made with the western tribes. His Indian commissary, a man named George Croghan, was at present at Fort Pitt. Another order was entrusted to Rogers. It was from Sir William Johnson and directed Croghan to join the Rogers expedition and help pacify the Indians.

Rogers must have seriously doubted the value of that order. It added to the imponderables he would meet in the western wilderness. He mustered his force and at noon on September 13, 1760, the men, their arms, ammunition, gear and provisions distributed in fifteen boats, he started upstream from Montreal.

He recognized the extent of the ordeal ahead. He wrote in his journal that the force entered at once "a passage of seventy leagues with fearful rapids to mount, which wears out the best men." Rogers sent his men away from the Montreal wharves in whaleboats of Royal Navy design, and not in the much lighter and handier birchbark canoes which the French used.

He had been familiar since early boyhood with the graceful native craft. But he was a British officer, took orders from a British general. So his men rowed in the swirling, frothy water of the lower rapids. Then they hauled, heaved and strained themselves, some past the limits of their strength, to move twenty-seven-foot-long, clinker-built boats with six-foot beams and two-and-a-half-foot drafts. Rogers expected his men to be equally as tough as himself.

They negotiated the rapids and came on the evening of September 19th into calm water. Then Rogers was forced to halt for a day, although because of the lateness of the season each hour was precious. The boats needed repair, and ten men were disabled. Work was continuous on the boats. The disabled men were detached and told to make their way overland to the British post at Oswego.

But storm conditions held Rogers in camp. He paced nervously beside the river while he waited for better weather, his green uniform and round black cap with its black feathers spattered by spray. He decided at midnight of September 22nd that the voyage should be continued.

He was a real empire-builder. The fever to explore the unknown and to discover vast wealth coursed incessantly in him. No scratching on an arid mountainside for him, in his father's fashion. He was not going to end up as a backwoods farmer, his wife old before she was thirty, his own back permanently stooped from the axe, the harrow and the plow.

This was his last assignment as a Ranger officer. When he had finished it, he would return to civilian life. But he had made a fine name for himself as a soldier. Merchants would be eager to give him a partnership in their fur-trade ventures when he got to the western posts. He would start his fortune with them, use the money gathered as a trader to finance trips of exploration into the regions beyond the Great Lakes, and beyond the Mississippi.

The Rangers rowed all night when Rogers led the flotilla upstream. Starlight helped the oarsmen. They kept a smooth stroke. These were men who had learned their boat skill on Lake George and Lake Champlain in the long campaign fought against the French, where a single oar-blade splash or a thole-pin creak could give the enemy sufficient information to deliver a close-range musket volley.

When the starlight faded and the black, silver-streaked water was covered with mist, the sun cast a faint russet glow upon the river. It became lemon-yellow, then scarlet, and at last pure gold. The men pushed back their double-ribboned Glengarry caps as they began to sweat. They took off their shirts, and rowed bare to the waist. Many of the torsos bore scars from old combat wounds. The Rangers boasted, while off duty and engaged in tavern drinking with British Army regulars, that their unit had been awarded very few battle honors, or medals. A Ranger's wounds, the Rangers said, were his medals.

Rogers kept the flotilla moving until it entered Lake Ontario. Camp was pitched on the ruins of Fort Frontenac, built by the early French. The Rangers were curious about the place; almost the complete muster were frontiersmen, and they shared Rogers' elation over the victory which opened up this enormous territory. It meant new homesites for them and their families on richer, finer land than any to be found in New England, and maybe a couple of handfuls of shillings a year from the fur trade.

But storms held the expedition at Frontenac for several days. When good weather came, Rogers led the flotilla along Lake Ontario for two days and a night without a break. The good weather was only relative; there was fog, and rain. The shore of the lake he followed was uncharted. He used a hand compass, and at night he illuminated it with phosphorous contained in a bottle. A candle or a torch would be useless in the wind.

He brought the expedition across the lake to Fort Niagara. The boats leaked from the pounding they had taken. Some were in very bad shape. Rogers ordered them to move in single line formation, so boat could help boat. The seams in the craft commanded by Lieutenant Caesar McCormick suddenly spread, and water jetted high in the boat, swamped her. The men and their gear were saved, though, and they were landed safely with the others at Fort Niagara.

Rogers became profoundly impatient after his arrival at Niagara. The post was filled with English traders all eager to go west and start in business at Detroit and Michilimackinac. A partnership was arranged by Rogers with a pair of traders. Then he took a birchbark canoe, two officers and eight Rangers, and shoved off for Fort Pitt. He wanted to deliver Amherst's orders to Monckton, get along into the western country.

He had been warned by veteran French *voyageurs* at Niagara that the southern route along Lake Erie was extremely dangerous at this time of year. Storms were frequent, and the shore afforded very little shelter. Rogers disregarded the warnings; he and his party reached Fort Pitt on October 16th despite the bad weather. General Monckton was given his orders. George Croghan, the Indian commissary, sent Iroquois and Delaware emissaries to Detroit to treat with the tribes there, and a company of Royal Americans was dispatched as the Detroit garrison force.

Rogers, most of his duties executed, was more impatient than ever to reach Detroit. But when he left Fort Pitt he went to Presqu'Isle, on Lake Erie, where he was supposed to keep a rendezvous with his two companies of Rangers. They were in camp on the island after a very rough voyage from Niagara in the whaleboats. Rogers had foreseen that, and brought all of the available carpenters with him from Fort Pitt. The injured boats were repaired, and new ones, among them several sturdy bateaux, built.

Rogers pushed off on the morning of November 4th, headed for Detroit. He met Indians along the way up Lake Erie towards the Detroit River. They had all heard of the French defeat, and wanted to greet the victors. Rogers met Ottawas, then Hurons and Potawatomies. The usual fusillades of musket shots fired at the sky were exchanged, and he gave gifts and served the chiefs with rum.

He was extremely wary, though. He moved slowly into the curving river with its heavily wooded banks and islands that created narrow passages. Emissaries were busy carrying messages between him and the commandant of the French garrison, Captain Bellestre. But there were Indian villages on both sides of the river, and ambush was always possible.

Captain Bellestre chose to accept in full the terms of surrender. The ceremony was held on November 29th at noon in sharp, clear sunlight. Rogers formed the British troops on a grassy field outside the western gate of the stockade that surrounded the small French village. The Rangers were as smart as possible in their campaign-battered green uniforms. The Royal American detachment wore red coats, blue breeches and knee-length white gaiters. Around both units—shouting, dancing, gesticulating —surged hundreds of braves who belonged to the tribes of the region. They were painted in complex designs from the waistbands of their buck-skin kirtles to their scalp locks, and those were stiff with clay and daubed vermilion.

A French officer in a white-silk uniform marched out of the western gate. He saluted Rogers, and expressed Captain Bellestre's compliments. Rogers stood rigidly front and center, and returned the salute. The French officer said that Captain Bellestre was at Major Rogers' command. Rogers called an order and two officers and thirty-six men of the Royal Americans entered the stockade.

The French garrison force stood under arms there on the parade ground. The Royal Americans halted, facing them, and stood at attention. Captain Bellestre gave an order; halyards were jerked, and the fleur-de-lis flag of France came from the mast. A Royal American sergeant rapidly ran up the British colors, and as the breeze spread that, the troops outside the stockade cheered and the Indians made yelping cries.

Rogers felt tremendous elation. This was for him, he wrote in his journal, a moment that would change the history of the entire continent. The western territories in all their vastness now belonged to Great Britain. For a span of sixty years, the French had held on here, but people at home, at the court of Versailles, could not have realized the extent of the wealth that belonged to them overseas, or they would not so easily relinquish it.

Rogers inspected the bastions of the fort at Detroit, examined the plank-walled houses with their dormer windows and sloped roofs. The town inside the stockade was laid out along regular streets, and was very neat. But Rogers did not give it much attention. His thought was given to treaties that should be signed as soon as possible with the tribes, and a fast march further west to Michilimackinac and his own affairs.

George Croghan, the Indian agent, brought together the tribes, solemnly presented the chiefs to Rogers. They were given appropriate gifts, and again rum was used to establish friendship. One of the Ottawa war chiefs was a tall, deep-eyed man named Pontiac. He kept sober, refused all offers of rum, and Rogers, who drank on every possible occasion, remarked the fact, remembered it.

Rogers left for Michilimackinac directly after the conference with the tribes was finished. He disregarded the advice of the veteran *voyageurs* at Detroit; it was December 8th, with winter weather already severe. Ice floes drove him and his party of more than forty men back from Lake Huron. He almost lost them, and his own life, too. He wrote in his journal, "To our great mortification we were obliged to return to Detroit."

But he was content to stay at the post only long enough to acquire the deed to 20,000 acres of land on the southern shore of Lake Superior. He had been told by traders who dealt with the western tribes of the copper mines in the Superior region. This, he hoped, would give him the fortune he keenly needed.

He started east on the same day the deed was executed, signed by four Chippewa chiefs and decorated with a belt of black wampum. He was not prepared to spend the winter in garrison. He took a party of Rangers with him and went down the Detroit River to Lake Erie, marched over the lake ice, and on January 2nd camped on the southern shore of Sandusky Bay. Then he went southeasterly, through what is now northern and central Ohio.

Snow was deep, and the temperature below freezing, even at noon. But game was plentiful in these forests of black and white oaks, hickory, maple and locust. The Rangers killed fat-breasted turkeys, deer, elk, bears dislodged from their snow-bank repose and beaver holed up in ponds. The beaver were killed more for pleasure than provender; only the broad fat tail was edible.

The party passed Indian villages where inside the log stockades, safe against the wolves, herds of horses, cows and hogs were kept. Rogers recorded these facts in his journal. This was the 1761 western frontier in winter. When the detachment was near Fort Pitt, he turned over command to Lieutenant McCormick, a trusted officer. They were to take a northeasterly route overland to Albany, through Iroquois country. He kept on alone to Fort Pitt.

He crossed the solidly frozen Allegheny to the fort on January 23rd and was greeted with no great surprise. Indians had reported his presence in the forest. He stayed three days with the garrison, to get rested a bit and equipped with new moccasins and snowshoes.

When he left Fort Pitt, he was headed for Philadelphia. The country was unknown to him, and he marched alone, without a map. But he followed the rivers, then the mountain ridges, used his woodsman's sense, and on February 9th he came into Philadelphia. He had not thought of the march as exceptional; in his journal he called the route he took the "common road."

The people of Philadelphia, though, rang the church bells in his honor. Pennsylvania had suffered her share of Indian troubles, and Benjamin Franklin had treated with dangerously aroused tribes on her border. Rogers was given a hero's welcome. He left two days later for New York.

He entered British headquarters there on February 14th and asked the duty officer to take his name to General Amherst. The general did not keep him waiting long. Rogers had conducted an expedition in open boats through more than 800 miles of territory that was entirely strange to him. The maps and charts supplied for his use were incomplete. But he had carried out his orders in every respect, and with the loss of only one man.

Rogers was twenty-nine years old, and the toast of New York. He bought a new uniform, clubbed his hair, learned to drink Madeira instead of rum, and found that despite his big lumpy nose he was attractive to women. There was no future for him, though, except in the British Army. He was quick to accept the commission as captain of regulars offered him by Amherst.

The Cherokees had started war along the southeastern frontier. Amherst issued travel orders and Rogers boarded a transport in New York harbor. Rogers was on his way to South Carolina. But when he landed at Cape Fear and took command of a local infantry company, the Cherokees had already surrendered.

Rogers was abruptly confronted with the problem of retirement on half-pay, the settlement of a huge amount of debts he had variously accrued, and the fact that during his last leave he had become engaged to Miss Elizabeth Browne, of Portsmouth, New Hampshire. He sought work as Indian agent in South Carolina, for which he was highly qualified. When a local favorite got the assignment, Rogers went on to North Carolina. He found the governor of that province, a burly and brilliant Irishman, seventy-two-year-old Arthur Dobbs, much more receptive.

Dobbs had started out as an engineer, then become a professional civil servant. He had many close friends in the spheres of highest influence in London, and a single, almost deranging obsession. Dobbs had brought himself to the unshakable belief that a water passage led to the Pacific from Hudson Bay. He had spent more than eighteen years of his life trying to forge the belief into reality. The Hudson's Bay Company had been his chief target while he was a member of Parliament; he attacked it in a series of bills he sponsored, and demanded that its charter be withdrawn because it had failed to explore sufficiently the adjacent territory.

Rogers came to him not only as a kindred believer in the Northwest Passage, but a man who had been recently in the west, knew the terrain, had met the tribes of the Great Lakes region. From the Great Lakes to the Shining Mountains, then the straits of Anian and the South

Sea was no great journey in Arthur Dobbs' reckoning. He had, though, just before he met Rogers, tired of the struggle, and written a final pamphlet:

> The person who had promoted this Discovery, after it had been so long dormant, to which he applied his Thought and Time for eighteen years, in order to improve the Wealth, Trade and Navigation of Britain, hopes it won't be taken amiss of him, that after so many Years Trouble and Attendance at a Great Expence to his Private Fortune, and Loss to his Family, that he should hereafter retire and leave the Prosecution of the Discovery of the Passage and the Extension, of the British Trade to some more happy Adventurer.

Rogers appeared at just the right time for Dobbs. He was manifestly the "Adventurer" of Dobbs' description in the pamphlet. The two spent weeks together in 1761, Rogers as the guest of the governor. They sat almost side by side in the shade of the long, high gallery, the mansion quiet in the afternoon heat behind them. Maps, books, pamphlets were spread on chairs and a table. There was a decanter of Madeira, a bowl of Virginia very fine cut, a rack of long-stemmed Waterford clay pipes, and paper, ink, quills for any notes Rogers might wish to make. He made a number.

The stalwart old governor inspired him. He would find his fortune after all in the western territories, and along with it the Northwest Passage. He and Governor Dobbs parted great friends, and Rogers, still perilously in debt, went back to New York. Rogers lacked any sort of income for a successful marriage, and his fiancée's father, the Reverend Browne, expressed total gloom regarding it. But Betsey was very impatient, and the ceremony was performed in Portsmouth.

Rogers returned right afterwards to British headquarters at New York in an effort to sell his South Carolina commission and lighten some of his debt load. He sold it to an officer who preferred southern service, and handed the money to his creditors. Then he was given a commission as captain in a company of New York regulars and sent to Albany for active duty.

His luck had definitely changed, he wrote Betsey. He was preeminently a frontier officer, had established his reputation as an Indian

Sketch of Detroit in 1780.

fighter. Now, in 1763, all along the western frontier, the tribes had raised the tomahawk, furiously rebelled against the inept, harsh and often arrogantly stupid restraints of British rule.

War parties organized and shrewdly led by Pontiac, the Ottawa chief, had taken every British post in the Great Lakes region except Detroit, and that was under fierce siege. Over in western Pennsylvania, only Fort Pitt survived the Indian attackers, and was also surrounded and besieged. A relief column sent to Detroit was ambushed along the way, and the few survivors who got back to Fort Niagara were shattered men, unfit for further duty. Captain James Dalyell, an experienced officer and Amherst's aide, was ordered to take a relief force through to Detroit with Rogers as his second-in-command.

Dalyell was brave but without experience in guerrilla warfare. He made a foolish show of strength outside Detroit, and in the display he and many of his troops lost their lives. Rogers covered the retreat, brought the remnants of the force into the stockade. Then he held off the Indian attackers until with bad weather, on October 31st, even Pontiac gave up the attempt.

Rogers, as soon as peace was assured, went east to spend Christmas with Betsey. He left Detroit in extreme winter, the rivers and the lakes hard-frozen, deep in snow drifts, the forest almost impassable. But that did not deter Rogers; he was reunited with his wife at holiday time, and was once more a deservedly popular hero.

But General Thomas Gage had replaced Lord Amherst as the commander-in-chief of the British forces in North America. He disliked Rogers, considered him to be a bumptious, loud-mouthed colonial. His dislike of Rogers was cleverly inflamed by Sir William Johnson, who as an Irish peasant boy had come to the Mohawk Valley and with shrewd dealing, squaw-man tactics and sheer audacity won a knighthood and fabulous wealth. Johnson's motive for disliking Rogers was obvious; the big Ranger officer was the only other colonial who could treat with the Indians, and defeat them in battle, and whose fame among the tribes eclipsed his own.

Sir William Johnson was General Gage's close adviser. The general, who had enough intelligence to recognize he knew nothing about Indian affairs, listened intently to what Johnson said. He entrusted all of the negotiations for peace to Johnson, and the Irishman saw vast profit for himself forthcoming from the assignment. A salient part of the advice Johnson offered was not to give Rogers command of a frontier fort or a Ranger unit. Rogers, because of his still pressing debts, might put personal concern and possible profit from the fur trade ahead of allegiance to the king.

There was no further assignment to duty for Rogers. He was met by cold, inimical formality when he came to New York headquarters and presented himself as ready for service. Fat, wily Sir William was no longer in New York, but at Johnson Hall, his opulent estate on the Mohawk close to the frontier, where he was in touch with Pontiac and the other dissident chiefs. Rogers was not a particularly subtle man; still, he was aware that he must go to London to better his circumstances and surmount the barrier of hostility raised against him in America.

He sailed for England without even informing Betsey. His military record was well known in London, and he bore letters of introduction from Arthur Dobbs to a number of important people. He impressed them with his tremendous fund of knowledge about the wilderness, his physical presence, and his ability to drink wine, gin, rum and brandy all day and nearly all night. But he wrote two books during his stay, and a play about Pontiac. One of the books was his personal journal. The other he called *A Concise Account of North America*, and in it was a large amount of information about the American interior regions, and a very faulty geographical description of how the Northwest Passage could be reached.

He wrote with great feeling about the Indians. His attitude towards them was surprisingly objective in light of the fact that he was frontier-born and hundreds of his friends and military comrades had been killed in Indian combat. He emphasized that among the tribes "every man is naturally free and independent. No one or more on earth has any right to deprive him of his freedom and independency, and nothing can be a compensation for the loss of it."

Rogers had received little if any schooling. His education came from the perusal of whatever was handy in bivouacs, winter barracks or the tap-rooms of taverns. But his eloquence brought him the admiration, then the friendship, of some of the leading London savants and government officials. He filed after consultation with them a petition for support from the government. He outlined a three-year plan for the discovery of the Northwest Passage, asked Parliament to finance it.

He wanted to explore the interior of the "Wide-Spread Empire, which the Glorious Successes of the Late War added to His Majesty's Dominions." The plan detailed the manner in which he would go to the head of the Mississippi and from that to "the River called by the Indians Ouragon, which flows into a Bay that projects North-Easterly into the Country from the Pacific Ocean."

Parliament did not grant him the funds to make the exploration. But while he was still in London in the fall of 1765 he was appointed governor of Michilimackinac. He was given to understand privately by his high-placed friends that in the very near future he would be awarded the commission for the Northwest Passage exploration. It was all that a man of his sanguine nature needed. He took a packet ship out of London and on January 9, 1766, arrived in New York.

General Gage was furious when Rogers showed him the papers of appointment. Gage wrote secretly and at once to Sir William, telling him to take care of Rogers, divest the man by any means of his post as governor of Michilimackinac. This was completely in accord with Johnson's determination to get rid of Rogers forever in the northwestern territory.

But Rogers, sure of himself because of his powerful London backing, sent for Betsey, then traveled in style towards his new post. They went up the Hudson from New York by sloop, were rendered all due honors at Albany, then went along the Mohawk and Lake Ontario to Fort Oswego. Here, in one of the greatest Indian congresses yet assembled, Sir William dealt with Pontiac and the other tribal chiefs who in the recent campaign had proven redoubtable enemies.

Rogers talked at length with Pontiac. He told the proud and brilliant Ottawa chief that he had written a play about him that was being produced in London, the home of the Great White Father. Then

Fort Oswego in 1798.

he questioned Pontiac about Michilimackinac, and the river called Ouragon, and where that might lead.

Pontiac had much to say in favor of Rogers' appointment as governor at Michilimackinac. But he had no clear knowledge of any western river called Ouragon, and his conversation was mainly given to the British plan for control of the fur trade. The Board of Trade, with the advice of Gage and Johnson, had passed an order that in the future all fur business was to be transacted at British posts.

No free traders would be allowed to roam in the wilderness, live with the remote tribes and make their own deals. This, Pontiac said, could only bring great trouble. If the tribes failed to get the axes, the knives, the powder and muskets they needed from British traders, they would buy them from French and Spanish happy to make a summer visit to the villages.

Rogers saw the same weaknesses in the British plan, and agreed with Pontiac. He was, though, a British officer, and a newly appointed royal governor. Sir William Johnson watched all of his actions, Rogers realized, and was either present personally when there was a conversation with Pontiac, or sent one of his subordinates to listen to everything said.

Rogers decided to get on west to Michilimackinac. He felt uneasy in Johnson's presence; while he admired the man's ability to treat with Indians, and respected him for his power, he was troubled by a profound sense of distrust. He was not fully aware of the fact, only perceived it in a vague way—Sir William sought to destroy him.

The party which Rogers led took a sloop from Oswego to Niagara, rode in Army carts around the falls, then boarded the schooner *Charlotte*. She took them to Detroit, where they transferred to another schooner, and on August 10, 1766, through the brilliance of noon sunlight, Rogers and his wife saw Michilimackinac.

It was the most important post at the time in North America, and one of the most important military installations in the world. The nation that owned and held Michilimackinac was master of the heartland regions of North America, could dominate the St. Lawrence, the Mississippi, all of the intervening rivers and the Great Lakes.

Lake Huron shimmered blue. Stands of pine were green-black and magnificent on the shores of the peninsula. The sandy bluffs of

View of Michilimackinac.

Mackinac Island were bone-white off to starboard, and ahead were the Straits of Michilimackinac that led to Lake Michigan and the Mississippi. Out past Mackinac Island, to the northward, Huron stretched towards the Sault Sainte Marie, Lake Superior and the unknown.

But Michilimackinac was almost a travesty of a western post. Bark had peeled from the stockade logs and some of them were askew. Huge, barnlike structures lay among the sand dunes at the edge of the beach, and those, Rogers knew, were the traders' warehouses. They were shabby, and stunk of uncured furs. Beyond was a little white huddle of houses where gardens grew in miserable disorder, and then three straggling Indian settlements.

A nine-pound cannon fired a shot above the water gate in Rogers' honor. The gate swung open; troops who wore red coats emerged. Canoes and bateaux left the beach, jammed from bow to stern with traders who

141

shouted in ecstatic greeting at Rogers, fired volleys from muskets held like pistols. Rogers experienced vast elation. Here—shabby, dirty, dusty or not—was the place where he was going to make his fortune and his truly great fame.

Rogers spent the winter at Michilimackinac. He entered into deals with several of the traders and, wholly contrary to his orders from Gage, relaxed the ban on trade among the tribes. A number of the veteran merchants, men whose bases were in Montreal, left during the fall to hibernate with favorite squaws in distant villages and pick up a fine collection of furs for sale in the spring.

The fur trade was really incidental to Rogers, though. He dreamed incessantly of the Northwest Passage discovery. Two of his former Ranger officers, Captain Jonathan Carver, an accomplished cartographer, and Captain James Tute, had gone west in the preceding September with explicit orders to find the passage. Rogers paid them himself, eight shillings apiece a day, and expected in every mail forwarded from Montreal to receive favorable word from London. His influential friends there would finally get him the commission to finish the work, and pay for it.

He had described the Ourigon in his orders to Captain Tute. He called it "the great River Ourigon that falls into the Passific Ocean about the latitude Fifty." His knowledge, distorted by his weeks of conversation with Arthur Dobbs and reliance on almost worthless maps, now betrayed him. He wrote that the river "runs Westward for near three hundred Leagues, when it is at no great distance from each other joyn'd by one from the South, and a little up the Stream by one from the North; about these forkes you will find an Inhabited Cuntry and Great Riches."

Tute and Carver had gone west from Michilimackinac in birchbark canoes, supplied and equipped to pass the winter without return to the post. If the Northwest Passage search proved futile, Carver was to leave his winter quarters on the Upper Mississippi and with Tute explore the region that held the Ourigon. Then, of course, they were to head back to the fort with their momentous news.

It was an anxious and miserable winter for Rogers. His wife was unhappy, and he drank too much, talked too much about the deals he had made with traders. Then spring came, and the ice buckled, moaning and grinding, in the straits, and open water showed. The dirty parade-

142

ground snow gave way to tender grass, and birds sang in the forest, gulls squatted on the crests of the sand dunes.

Rogers sent out word for a gathering of all of the western tribes. The usual assembly in late spring was a great occasion for the Indians, and Peter Pond, a hard-bitten trader who had spent years in the Great Lakes region, left an account of the 1755 visit. The tribes massed at Green Bay, and in a single fleet of birchbark canoes headed for Michilimackinac.

They came out from Green Bay into Lake Michigan through Poverty Isle Passage. The warriors wore their best buckskins, wampum belts, necklaces, armlets and paint. Their canoes were freshly built, or recently put in commission. Those were big craft, thirty feet long, with pole masts for the use of a buckskin squaresail when the wind was astern. Gaudy tribal totems were on the high-curved bows. The flags or banners of various chiefs were flown from the mast trucks. The canoes rode low in the water; they were loaded from bow to stern thwart with bales of prime furs. There was barely room for the paddlers, and they worked with a shortened stroke.

They filed across the lake, each craft exactly in formation, towards Little Fox Island, then Big Fox, and Ile aux Galets. Looking astern when Big Fox was abeam, they could see the familiar image of Little Fox reflected perfectly in the sky. Sturgeon Bay was on the other side of Ile aux Galets, and from there the flagpole at Michilimackinac showed above the peninsula sand dunes. Peter Pond wrote of the scene, which was repeated almost exactly when Rogers witnessed it:

> The way ther was fair and pleasant we all proseaded together across Lake Mishiagan at the end of two days well appeard on the lake about five miles from Macenac and aprocht in order. We had flags on the masts of our canoes—eavery chief his flock. My canoes bearing the largest in that part of the cuntrey and haveing a large Youon (Union) flage I histed it and when within a mile and a half I took ye lead and the Indians followed close behind. The flag in the fort was histed—ye cannon of the garrison began to play smartly—the shores were lind with people of all sorts who seat up such a crey and hooping that seat the tribes in the fleat a going to that degrea that you could not hear a parson speak. At length we reacht shore and ye cannon seasd.

143

The convocation Rogers arranged in 1767 brought in first the nearby tribes, Potawatomies, Chippewas, Ottawas, Missiauguas. More than 1,000 of them came thronging ashore, and Rogers took care to meet them outside the stockade. He wore his little infantryman's hat, his silver-corded, dark green Rangers' tunic, and buckskin trousers and moccasins. He was gay, confident, quick to bestow gifts and offer toasts in undiluted rum.

There was no way for him to understand that this was the apogee of his life; after this, everything would be decline, denial, treachery, and slow, stupid tragedy. Other tribes were arriving on the beach alongside the water gate. He waded out to greet the more powerful chiefs. His voice boomed; his handslaps resounded on sweaty, muscular backs.

Whole oxen were being roasted in barbecue pits on the beach. New rum kegs were trundled out from the fort, tapped, and emptied. The red-stone calumet with its dangling three white eagle feathers was passed, smoke was ceremoniously blown. Here were the Fox chiefs from the upper Fox River, the Menominees from Green Bay, Sauks from the Wisconsin River, Winnebagos from country southwest of Green Bay, Mascoutens from near Racine, Nipissings from Lake Nipigong, Crees from Lake Winnipeg, and the early arrivals.

But there were also chiefs who came from much further away. There were Chippewas from the Kaministiquia River on Lake Superior, and more of the same tribe from Madeline Island, in Superior, and from Sault Sainte Marie, and Lake of the Woods, and the Rainy Lake region; and Dakotas, who were really a branch of the great Sioux nation and came from the upper Mississippi, their villages in the prairie immensity very few white men had even seen.

The chiefs left Michilimackinac calling Rogers their perpetual friend. He believed them. They had given him invaluable information about the northwestern territory, although none of them had been able to locate accurately the Ourigon. Promises had been made about future deliveries of furs, and this was reassurance he badly needed. His debts had increased again, and he was keeping Carver and Tute at their exploration work at his own expense.

144

Lookouts in the bastion of the fort reported on August 30th the appearance of a small canoe flotilla from the lee of Mackinac Island, to the northwest. It was Carver and Tute and their Indian companions. Rogers went to the beach and waited for them to land.

The pair of former Ranger officers used a considerable amount of language in their report to Rogers. The meaning of it was clear, though, from the answer given by Tute to Rogers' first question. The Northwest Passage did not exist. Nor the Oregon* River. Both were campfire dreams, or mapmakers' inventions.

Rogers stayed on at Michilimackinac. He was still governor, and he might yet recoup his fortune in the fur trade. But he had not accounted for General Gage and Sir William Johnson in his reckoning. Charges of treason were brought against him, and he was taken fettered from Michilimackinac to stand court-martial in Montreal.

He was acquitted, and yet he was a ruined man. General Gage was too powerful, kept him from reinstatement in the British Army. There was also the problem of Rogers' debts, and his very heavy drinking. His marriage broke up, and Rogers went to London.

He died there finally, alone, dishonored, on May 18, 1795, and his landlord claimed his effects for back rent and damage done the room. Rogers had cried out in the night when drunk and beaten against the walls. He was far from Michilimackinac, and an immeasurable distance from the Northwest Passage.

* Captain Tute's spelling, and the first time it was used.

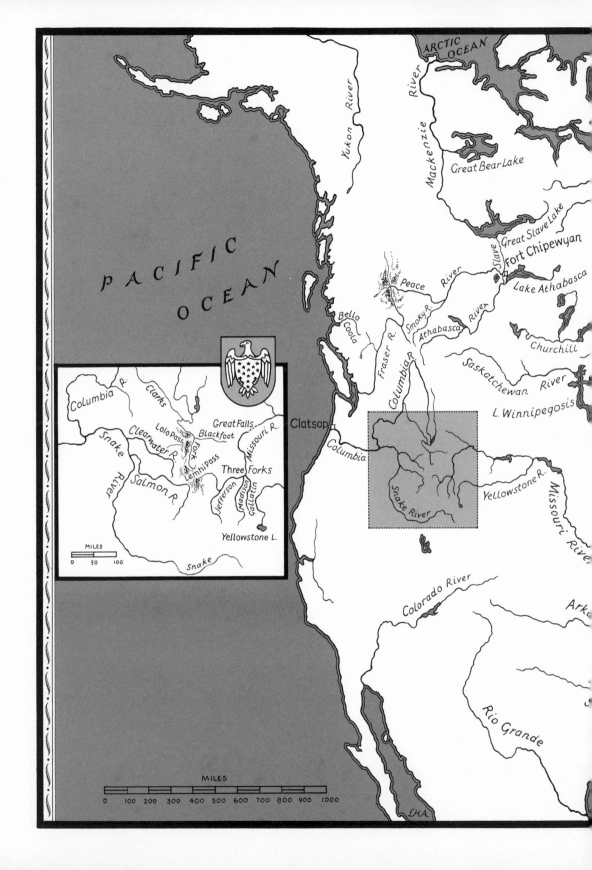

PACIFIC OCEAN

ARCTIC OCEAN

Yukon River

Mackenzie River

Great Bear Lake

Great Slave Lake

Slave River

Fort Chipewyan

Lake Athabasca

Peace River

Smoky R.

Athabasca River

Churchill

Bella Coola

Fraser R.

Columbia R.

Saskatchewan River

L. Winnipegosis

Clatsop

Columbia

Snake River

Yellowstone R.

Missouri River

Colorado River

Ark

Rio Grande

MILES

0   100  200  300  400  500  600  700  800  900  1000

### Inset map

Columbia R.

Clarks

Lolo Pass

Fork

Blackfoot

Great Falls

Missouri R.

Clearwater R.

Lemhi Pass

Three Forks

Snake River

Salmon R.

Jefferson

Madison

Gallatin

Yellowstone L.

Snake

MILES

0   50   100

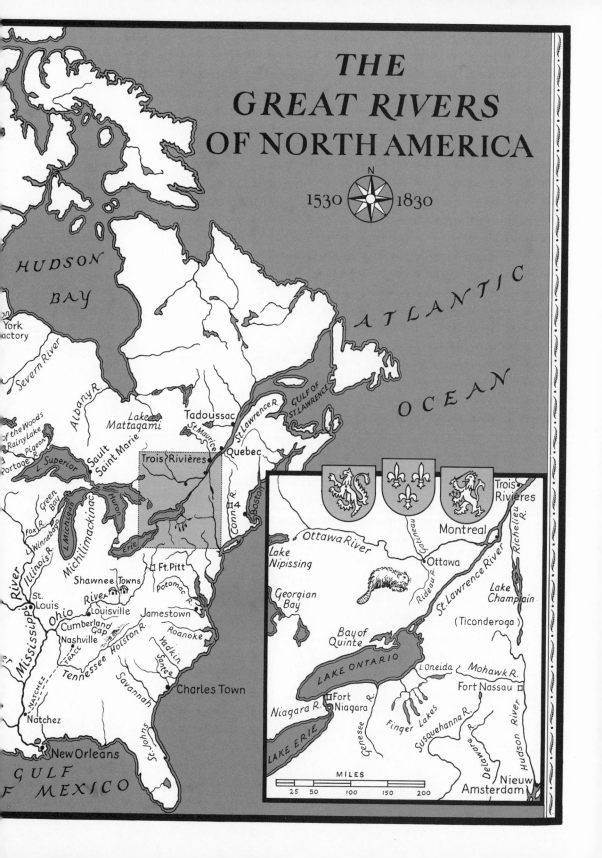

# THE GREAT RIVERS OF NORTH AMERICA

**N**

1530 ◈ 1830

HUDSON

BAY

ATLANTIC

OCEAN

York Factory

Severn River

of the Woods
Rainy Lake
Pigeon R.
Portage R.

Albany R.

Lake Mattagami

Tadoussac

St. Lawrence R.

GULF OF ST. LAWRENCE

St. Maurice

Quebec

L. Superior

Sault Saint Marie

Trois Rivières

Green Bay

Fox R.

L. Winnebago

Illinois R.

L. Michigan

Huron

Michilimackinac

Erie

Conn R.

Boston

Mississippi River

St. Louis

Ohio

Shawnee Towns

River

Louisville

Cumberland Gap

Nashville

TRACE

Tennessee

Holston R.

NATCHEZ

Natchez

Yadkin

Santee

Savannah

St. Johns

New Orleans

GULF OF MEXICO

□ Ft. Pitt

Potomac R.

Jamestown

Roanoke

Charles Town

Ottawa River

Lake Nipissing

Georgian Bay

Gatineau

Ottawa

Rideau R.

St. Lawrence River

Richelieu R.

Trois Rivières

Montreal

Lake Champlain

(Ticonderoga)

Bay of Quinte

LAKE ONTARIO

L. Oneida

Mohawk R.

Fort Nassau □

□ Fort Niagara

Niagara R.

Genesee R.

Finger Lakes

Susquehanna R.

Delaware R.

Hudson River

Nieuw Amsterdam

LAKE ERIE

MILES

25  50      100      150      200

## 10

MICHILIMACKINAC HAD DRAWN THE DREAMS OF another extraordinary man nearly a century before. He was René Robert Cavelier, Sieur de La Salle. He recognized much more clearly than Rogers how the St. Lawrence river system, the Great Lakes and the Mississippi could be linked and made to supply wealth probably just as great as that to be found in China.

When he first arrived in Canada in 1666, he believed in the China dream. He was twenty-three, a Norman born in Rouen, his father a wealthy merchant there. With his father's money, he bought a seigneury on Lake St. Louis, near Montreal. He called it Saint-Sulpice, and began to farm the land. But the *habitants* who were his neighbors heard him talk so much about China they gave his property the name of La Chine, and openly mocked him.

He gave up the idea of any kind of China venture, stopped tilling the soil. His basic ambition to explore inland North America was un-

René Robert Cavelier, Sieur de La Salle

changed, though, and to further it he went into the fur trade, built a stockaded post on his property. He made friends among the Indians, particularly some Senecas, familiar with the western region of the Iroquois territory. Winters when trade was slow were spent in study of buckskin maps made by Senecas, in long conversations about the Great Lakes and the Mississippi, and plans for exploration.

149

La Salle sold the La Chine seigneury three years after he bought it. He used the money to finance an expedition to the Ohio. His Seneca guide took him across the portages from river to river until they reached what the Iroquois called "The Beautiful Water." They floated down the Ohio to the site of present-day Louisville, happily bucked the current on the return journey. Then, as part of his overall plan, he built in 1679 a wooden-hulled sailing vessel on the Niagara River near Buffalo.

He named her *Le Griffon*, sailed her past Michilimackinac into Lake Michigan and went ashore at Green Bay. The Dutch pilot, a man trained on salt water, took command of the vessel, and La Salle began the exploration of Lake Michigan by canoe. His ambition was unrelenting; he built a fort and left a garrison to occupy it at St. Joseph; he and his canoe crew entered the St. Joseph River. They portaged to the Kankakee, and paddled down the Illinois to Starved Rock.

La Salle built a fort on the summit of the hill at Starved Rock. He wanted to protect the local Indians against roving war parties of Iroquois. When the stockade was finished, he took his men north to Fort Frontenac. They had made a 1,000-mile journey by canoe and portage in sixty-five days. La Salle went back during the depths of winter the next year and repeated almost the entire route. He was preparing for the descent from the Great Lakes to the Mississippi.

It was his intention to make the Mississippi voyage aboard a strongly built sailing vessel armed with cannon. Others, earlier French explorers had turned away from the river because of fear of Spanish attack; a couple of musket volleys would sink their fragile bark canoes. But lack of time and suitable material forced La Salle to leave the ship half-completed in the Illinois River.

He used birchbark canoes instead, and put those in service during December 1681 while the rivers were still thick with ice. His party made sledges, and hauled the canoes from the stream the Indians called the Checagou to the Illinois. He had with him twenty-two Frenchmen, eighteen Indian men, ten Indian women and three Indian children.

La Salle had given great care to the composition of the party. The Indians were chosen from eastern tribes, Micmacs, Abenakis, and even Wampanoags who were survivors of King Philip's War in New England. There was a war in progress between the Iroquois and the proud, defiant Illinois, and La Salle wished to avoid any possibility of involvement.

His lieutenant was a tall, tough professional soldier named Henri de Tonty. One of Tonty's hands had been lost in battle from a grenade explosion. The Indians called him "Iron Hand," and when an Illinois brave tried to kill him in a sudden treacherous knife attack Tonty had terribly clubbed the attacker with the hooklike device he wore. The Catholic Church was represented by Father Zenobius Membré, who held the duties of chaplain and historian for the party.

Ice kept the party ashore from February 6th to February 13th at the junction of the Illinois and the Mississippi. Then the dream was at last reality. The canoes were launched, the supplies, the personal gear, the weapons put aboard, and the women, who sat quickly, holding the children close. The paddlers followed, and the soldiers, who balanced their muskets, then La Salle himself. He took his place on the bow thwart of the first canoe. Father Membré and Tonty rode in separate craft; should there be an accident, they would have a chance at individual rescue. La Salle raised his right hand; it was the signal for the flotilla to shove off.

The tremendous river, furiously carrying its burden of gray, shattered ice floes, swung curve upon curve to the southward. Jolliet and Marquette had called it Mississippi, a corruption of several Indian names. La Salle was content with it. He had waited sixteen years to get here, and that for him was enough.

The Mississippi moved in such majesty that he and his people, who had seen many rivers, regarded it with awe. They sat almost completely silent in the canoes. When La Salle lifted his arm in a gesture, paddling stopped. The craft, their hulls mottled with resin-caulked patches, drifted in the brown thrust of current. The ice floes clunked against each other, groaned and mumbled. But most of the sounds came from shore.

Birds called among the tall trees. Animals that smelled or sensed man and wanted to get further away and hide hurried through the underbrush, twigs snapping, leaves rustling. Sometimes, though, a bison or an elk or a white-tailed deer was surprised while it drank, head bent to the water. Then there was the unforgettable scene when black bears, the males six-foot-high beasts, had been found as they swam the river.

More than fifty bears made the passage. They went from east to

151

west, leaving the safety of the shallows where finches chirped and hopped on twisted cottonwood roots. The big males swam in front, long snouts lifted, the five-toed paws clear from the surface to take short, powerful strokes. The females kept the cubs swimming, nudged them, growled and pushed. The column emerged glistening from the river, shook off the excess moisture in iridescent spray, went trotting into the forest.

There was, below the entrance to the river that was later to be called Missouri, the buffalo that floated, distended, stinking, and a feast for carrion crows. The beast, from the condition of the carcass, had been carried down-current several hundred miles. A broken spear stub projected from one flank. La Salle's men pulled that out; the tip was of flint, and made by a tribe that lived nowhere near the Mississippi.

La Salle talked at length with Henri de Tonty, his lieutenant, about it when camp was pitched ashore for the night. But the best they could do was conjecture the source and direction of the river that had brought the buffalo into the Mississippi. Relations between the Spanish traders and the members of the southwestern tribes had obviously broken down; there were no iron articles here in the Mississippi Valley, and as recently as 1673 a number had been reported.

La Salle was meticulous in his treatment of the tribes he met along the river. He, Tonty and Father Membré visited often in the dome-shaped council houses of the Osage, the Creeks, the Chickasaws and the Choctaws. The calumet was ceremoniously smoked, and afterwards, at each village, La Salle took possession of the region in the name of His Majesty, Louis XIV. Prayers were said by Father Membré, and the Bourbon coats-of-arms raised and secured.

The tribes that lived on the broad grassy mounds which reared like small islands from the flatlands near the river banks had been here for many centuries, La Salle knew. Their ancestors, fish-eaters and growers of corn, had increased the height of the mounds generation by generation, one structure built upon the ruins of another, all thickly layered with fish bones.

They were in the main a gentle people of some culture, these tribes of the Muskhogean nation. They sought peace. Their chiefs were willing to accept Louis XIV as ruler, although, possibly, they lacked a full understanding of who the Sun King was.

La Salle and his party proceeded without serious incident towards the Gulf. He was anxious to reach the mouth of the river, wrest the title to it and to the Gulf from the Spanish. There were squalls, though, and spring thunderstorms, floods, encounters with surly Indians who asked tribute from the French for further passage. Membré, a Recollect friar, kept an account of the voyage. He checked with La Salle, listed the major landmarks, the Ohio, the Missouri, the Chickasaw Bluffs, the hill at Natchez, the caves, the vast wide-sprawling bends, the islands.

The rest was too complex to record: the dusk thunder, pealing, smashing across the valley; wind that plucked cottonwoods and sycamores from the banks, flung them out into the river in parabolic flight; waves that came white-crested aboard the canoes, threatening to sink the craft where everybody bailed, even the sorely frightened children. Trees that had been uprooted somewhere above drifted past the flotilla, and in the greenish lightning shimmer the eyes of raccoons and opossums showed blank but bright among the branches and soaked, torn foliage. The animals rode the driftwood with despairing grace; around them in the water were the bodies of less fortunate beasts, knocked unconscious or badly hurt early in the storm.

The storm left the valley. The mist was solid from bank to bank until the sun lifted it. Then, under the sun blaze, the water was no longer brown, but blue. The sycamores, the cypresses, the cottonwoods and the willows were golden with the noonday light. Birds sang, dived, caught fish, chased insects, pecked at wild grapes. Their melody was so sweet that the *voyageurs* at the paddle began to sing. They answered the bold, ringing cadences of the thrushes with a tune about "Gentille Alouette," the skylark.

Big and sleek catfish broke the river surface all around the canoes in search of flies and worms. There were perch, too, and sunfish whose scales were green, gold and silver. The canoemen were ready. They cast for the fish with poles made of hickory or hazel, dumped the catches flopping into creels made from willow withes and small branches.

La Salle was strangely disappointed when the expedition entered the lower reaches of the river. There were nowhere in the valley Indians who carried firearms, or who had articles made of iron or steel. The danger of Spanish occupation of the territory at the mouth of the river

153

was much less than he had expected. He saw on the wall of a hut in one village a Spanish sword and three rusted guns, obviously unused for years. That was all. He gave the order for the flotilla to keep on quickly to the Gulf; chance of Spanish attack was very small.

Father Membré wrote about the arrival: "Advancing on, we discovered the open sea, so that on the ninth of April, with all possible solemnity, we performed the ceremony of planting the cross and raising the arms of France. After we had chanted the hymn of the church, 'Vexilla Regis' and the 'Te Deum,' the Sieur de La Salle, in the name of His Majesty, took possession of that river, of all rivers that enter it and of all the country watered by them."

La Salle named the territory Louisiana. It was a claim only equalled by those Columbus made in the name of Ferdinand and Isabella. The Spanish had failed to consolidate their position along the Gulf, join their Florida and Mexican colonies by a settlement at the mouth of the Mississippi.

Within the space of eighty years, France had penetrated westward to the Great Lakes and the headwaters of the enormous river, and now were in possession of the northern and southern entrances to the continent. They held an almost insuperable advantage over both England and Spain. Their control of the vital inland system of transportation extended all the way from the head of tidewater at Trois Rivières to Michilimackinac and Sault Sainte Marie, down the length of the Mississippi from the Falls of St. Anthony to the canebrake hummock where La Salle stood in the Gulf and raised the white-and-gold Bourbon flag.

La Salle had divided his party into three groups to explore the three main passes of the river that led through the low marshy land of the estuary to the Gulf. With the ceremony of possession completed, he brought the canoe flotilla into compact, single formation again and started the tremendous upstream journey back to Quebec.

He made it without serious loss or delay. La Salle was undoubtedly one of the finest river men in North American history. When he returned to Quebec, he had a large part of the continent's geography accurately located in his mind, although most of it was confined to the regions east of the Mississippi. He recognized the salient importance of the Great Lakes chain, and proposed to Jean Talon, the Intendant, the

Chicago in 1820 as seen from the lake, with the Chicago River and its branches in the background.

erection of defensive forts at regular intervals between the St. Lawrence and the Gulf.

He understood in addition the value of the enormous Laurentian Shield, which was marked on the east by Sault Sainte Marie, on the west by the westernmost end of Lake Superior, and on the south by the southerly end of Lake Michigan, where the Chicago River drained into it. La Salle wanted, first, a French trading post on Lake Ontario that would take the fur business away from the English and their allies, the Iroquois. Transportation costs could be sharply reduced, he pointed out to Talon, if sailing vessels were used to haul cargo on the Great Lakes instead of canoes.

His own vessel, *Le Griffon*, had been lost on Huron, but that did

155

not dismay him. He conceived of a fleet of cargo-carrying ships built, manned and sailed on the Lakes. They would handle the extremely profitable traffic in furs. There was within the triangle of the Laurentian Shield a constant flux of tribes who traded among themselves. The Ottawas were famous as middlemen, and sold the Crees and a number of the other western tribes old knives, cracked kettles and worn-out nets for the finest beaver pelts. Those were of French manufacture, and the Ottawas put a high mark-up price on them, sometimes triple what was asked at Montreal.

La Salle wanted to build other sailing vessels for Mississippi River service. He knew from his travel through the valley that the southern furs were not of the same quality as the Great Lakes yield. But they were still worth export, and with them could be shipped buffalo hides, buffalo wool, and deerskins. The major factor in his calculations was to keep the dominance of the Indian trade. With England checked east of the Alleghenies and the Spanish confined to the southwest, there would be time for exploration beyond the Mississippi, and into the Shining Mountains. Vestiges of the old South Seas dream and of passage to China persisted in La Salle's thinking.

He was not welcomed with any particular warmth when he returned to Quebec from the Mississippi expedition. His personal debts were sadly tangled, and large. He was regarded as a visionary whose radical ideas were almost laughable. La Salle went to France.

Louis XIV had considered La Salle's exploration useless. But, at Versailles, La Salle was persuasive. Louis decided that it would be worthwhile to hold onto Louisiana, if only to annoy the king of Spain. He gave La Salle a fleet of four ships, and in 1684 they sailed for the Gulf of Mexico with both men and women colonists aboard.

Navigation went wrong in the Gulf. There was no sure way for La Salle to determine where he had emerged from the Mississippi. He set out overland with a few men to find the river. It was a difficult journey, and it ended in mutiny. He was murdered, and his body left naked on a Texas prairie. Henri de Tonty, hearing months later of what had happened, tried to discover it, and the murderers. But he was threatened by Indian attack, could not complete the search.

A succession of Royal Governors and Intendants, who served as the king's personal representatives, fumbled with the future of France in North America after La Salle was killed. They were appointed, maintained and withdrawn for reasons that were often in conflict with her best interests. But in 1749 it was recognized that a French force must enter and occupy the Ohio Valley to stop English expansion.

The force was led by Celeron de Bienville, a celebrated officer, and contained Indians. No mercy was given the English settlers. The trading post at Pickawillany was destroyed in the summer of 1752, the garrison annihilated. The French built posts in the manner suggested long before by La Salle. Among the protective chain of installations were Fort Presqu'Isle, at the present-day site of Erie, Pennsylvania, Fort Le Boeuf at French Creek Portage, and Fort Venango, at the junction of French Creek with the Allegheny River.

George Washington, who at twenty-one was a frontier veteran and a colonel of militia, was sent to protest the French action and scout their posts. He took his orders from Lieutenant Governor Robert Dinwiddie of Virginia. Washington made a tour of Venango and Le Boeuf. He returned in January, 1754, and told Dinwiddie that the French intended to occupy the entire Ohio Valley. They would not be driven from it without war.

The war began in April, 1754, and lasted seven years. When it was finished, France had forever lost her cause in North America. She still held New Orleans, and tenuous title to the vast region known as Louisiana. But Quebec, Montreal, Trois Rivières, Detroit and Michilimackinac were gone, and with them the strategic forts at Ticonderoga and Crown Point that had dominated the approaches to Albany, the Hudson River, and New York.

The irony behind the origin of the name, La Chine, became for Frenchmen an almost unbearably bitter reminder of frustration.

THE ENGLISH KING HAD GIVEN HIM, AN IRISH PEAS-
ant's son, a baronetcy, and now he paid for it in full. He betrayed absolutely, with finality, his sworn friends and allies, the Indian
people who for decades had cherished his friendship. Sir William Johnson spoke to them with a passionate eloquence that was rare for him,
famous among the Iroquois as an orator.

He wore buckskins and his gold-brocaded crimson robe. He disregarded the Englishmen seated beside him. Now he was Warraghiyeh,
and proudly pronounced the Mohawk name as he began to speak. He
addressed the Indians. There were 3,400 of them. They stood row on
row, straight, silent and motionless, ranked together by tribes, their canoes hauled out behind them on the river bank.

This was the greatest of the Indian conferences. It was called
formally by the English the Boundary Line Congress, and was held here
in late October 1768 at Fort Stanwix, at the western end of the Mohawk

158

Sir William Johnson

Valley. The warriors had learned since the war six years earlier how to accept English gifts, although they still missed the French ease and grace of giving, and the imagination displayed in the variety of French gifts. Now all of the English medals were worn and the English muskets carried. But even among his own adopted Mohawk tribe there was an attitude of sullen dissatisfaction which Johnson immediately noticed.

He tried to eradicate it with the utmost of his eloquence. He entered into flights of speech that brought grunts of approval from the sachems, and he took fresh incentive from the fact. His voice boomed on through the golden, hazy afternoon while overhead, along the river, flights of Canadian ducks and geese flew whirring south, and in the fort the guard was changed with a bang of heels and musket butts, a staccato of orders.

Johnson used his extraordinary power to penetrate the Indian mentality. He played upon the warriors' pride; now they were the allies of the great English king overseas who had so humbled the French. He appealed to their avarice and profound desire for adornment; the big plank tables in the main hall of the fort were heaped high with trade goods which he had personally chosen and arranged. And a sutler, at a prearranged signal from Johnson, put the spigot in a rum cask, filled a pannikin.

The warriors took their glances from Johnson. They stared through the part-open stockade gate, fascinated, smelling the rum, locating the source. Then they looked beyond and, with the afternoon sunlight upon the fabrics, the brass buttons, the mirrors, the beads, the knives, saw the heaps of trade-goods. Johnson rapidly finished his peroration. He nodded to the white men and to the interpreters who would transact the details of the treaty. He had done his part.

The white men formed an unusual group. Among them were Governor Penn of Pennsylvania and Benjamin Franklin's son, who served as governor of New Jersey, and representatives of the Virginia colonial government, and the Reverend Eleazar Wheelock, who was here to acquire a land grant that would help him propagate the faith and also establish Dartmouth College for the direct benefit of his Indian students.

Sir William Johnson represented the New York interests. He was approached at discreet intervals by men who worked for the huge landowning companies, the Ohio Company, which as early as 1749 held 200,000 acres in an area bounded by the Ohio and the Great Kanawha Rivers and the Allegheny Mountains, the Susquehanna Company, under charter from Connecticut, and the Mississippi Company, headed by George Washington, who had bought military-bounty grants that amounted to 2.5 million acres at the junction of the Ohio and the Mississippi.

These men had no particular sensitivity regarding Indians, considered them to be proud, foolish if sometimes dangerous children. But the negotiations had entered a very difficult stage. Not enough rum was being drunk by the warriors to please Johnson. The land agents waited anxiously and kept to themselves as much as possible.

It was not until November 1st that the boundary line was drawn and approved. Then, in the language that the Indian signatories insisted upon for the treaty, they showed their contempt of the white men: "We have given him [the king] a great and valuable country, and we know that what we shall now get for it must be far short of its value."

The Iroquois sachems and the chiefs of the tribes allied with them had traded away, for 1,000 Spanish dollars, western Pennsylvania. The rest of the transaction included the disposal of West Virginia and Kentucky and millions of acres in the Ohio Valley. Their price totalled £10,000, and Sir William Johnson lacked the cash to make complete payment.

He was untroubled, though, and borrowed what he needed from his neighbors, the Mohawk sachems. They had just sold what he called "a little farm" and was in reality the enormous Kayderosseras grant. He knew that he could rely upon their affection for him. They had visited him often at his new and imposing estate, Johnson Hall. He maintained there a large council house, cabins, sheds, and tents for the use of his Indian friends.

It was a common saying in the Mohawk Valley that all Indian trails led to the home of Warraghiyeh, the tribes' one true friend. He sat with the visitors when they were finished eating the food he offered. Rum was shared, and tobacco. Tunes were played throughout the evening on the soft-tuned Indian flute, and they echoed dimly in the mist that rose from the river over the pastures and the brook.

161

A part of Fort Johnson.

But, Johnson knew, his pastures and his brook, even Johnson Hall itself, might not remain long as they were. This was a time of great change. The Mohawk Valley would never be the same after the Boundary Line agreement was put into effect. The barriers that the Iroquois had used for more than 200 years to block the river to settler movement westward were swept away, destroyed by the treaty.

There was not much that he could do to save the tribes, even if he so wished. The pressures were too strong. What lands the tribes still claimed would be taken from them whenever the white men wanted. But it was not the king or the king's officers who controlled North America. It was the land companies. Sir William Johnson, for very practical reasons, was on their side.

Land hunger had become a fever that burned with terrific, searing heat in the minds of the people in the English colonies. They saw themselves as the possessors of the entire continent, and each man saw himself as rich. The fever left a lasting trauma that affected the thinking of such men as Jefferson, Washington and Franklin. Land, more land—and there was always more to the still unexplored westward—was the answer to the colonies' problems.

The fever infected the American mind for a long time. Many values were distorted; the source of the disease lay very deep, yet discernible, in the psyche of the colonists. They or their direct forebears had been in the main extremely poor when they arrived from the British Isles and Europe. Their history was common because of a single, very powerful factor. They had come to the New World as the dispossessed, the homeless, lacking even a husbandman's tools and a housewife's chattels, forced to work as hired people, field-hands, indentured servants.

Land would bring freedom, and equality. It was there, along those wilderness rivers. The sun led to it through the river valleys. The Indians talked endlessly of it, sang about it, took wealth from it. Men who lived in the New England colonies and in Pennsylvania and Maryland and Virginia told their wives that they had waited long enough. They must go west, and go now.

The British government had decreed in 1763 a Proclamation Line that followed the crests of the Allegheny Mountains. Land west of that was supposed to belong to the tribes, and to be used only by the fur traders. But men known as "long hunters" because of their protracted journeys in the wilderness had been through the territory and guided parties of settlers across the mountains.

Benjamin Cutbird, one of the first long hunters, had gone over the mountains in 1766 and along the Tennessee-Kentucky border to the Mississippi, and south on the river by Indian dugout canoe to New Orleans, where he sold his haul of furs. Daniel Boone, who came from the upper Yadkin River, was early in the trans-Appalachian country in the winter of 1767–68, and explored the region along the present border of Kentucky and West Virginia.

When Sir William Johnson was through with his great friends, the Iroquois, at the Fort Stanwix treaty conference in 1768, the tribes had sold to the Indiana Company, in which he held a large interest, 1,800,000 acres. This tract stretched southeast of the Ohio River from an extension of the Mason-Dixon, at the southern boundary line of Pennsylvania, to the Little Kanawha River.

The Revolution stopped the surge of movement westward. But with the end of the war it tremendously increased, many of the men settlers holding veterans' grants to wilderness land. The frontier* was being constantly thrust further inland. It was opened by the fur traders and long hunters, who in the years after the Revolution were quickly followed by the settlers.

There were five main entrances to the west within the English colonies themselves. The Mohawk River led by way of Lake Ontario to the Ohio Valley. The Susequehanna and the Monongahela route served the people of Pennsylvania and Maryland who wanted to cross the Alleghenies. The Monongahela was used again in connection with the Potomac; there was also the Roanoke-Kanawha route; and from the valley of Virginia the Tennessee and Cumberland Rivers could be reached.

People from New England, New York and New Jersey chose the Mohawk River route. There were some hardy Maine and New Hampshire men who took their families through Canada, along the Richelieu and the St. Lawrence, headed for the Great Lakes. But most of the migration was centered southward. The broad-beamed and slow Hudson River sloops, heavily overloaded, brought hundreds of settlers to the mouth of the Mohawk, nine miles beyond Albany. A tangle of shipping occupied all of the wharf space at Albany, and the skippers preferred to anchor above, make the transfer there.

Some of the people were Dutch-speaking, tenant runaways from Rensselaerswyck and the other great patroon estates on the Hudson. The men were tough, desperate, ready to kill any deputy sheriff or bailiff who might try to question them too closely ashore. The sloop crew were Negro, the sailors proud of the fact that in the river tradition they spoke Dutch. They stood on the landing near the Rensselaerswyck runaways, watchful and ready to help.

164     There were others who went ashore from the sloops with the

---

* Usually an area containing no more than six people to a square mile.

*Plan* OF AN *AMERICAN* NEW CLEARED *FARM.*

determination to keep on going west no matter what happened. These were the Palatine Germans who had worked for the Livingstones down-river at the family manor. A long series of broken promises had been given them in exchange for years of labor making naval stores.

The Livingstone cupidity had also contributed another large group to the migrants. These were wild-looking men, women and children whose clothing was scorched and grimed, and who carried with them the sharp, unmistakable tang of charcoal. They were the forge workers and charcoal burners who for generations had kept in operation the Livingstone iron trade and got very little for it. Now they had left the rough, granite-block forges, the charcoal pits, the huge ox-drawn wains, and the miserable huts they had occupied in the Taconic Mountains on the east bank of the Hudson. They were Welsh, Irish, Scots, and some of them had intermarried with the Wappinger tribe. Freedom had become again for them a very precious word.

165

There were more prosperous people who joined the exodus along the Mohawk. They were from Connecticut and Massachusetts. The urge to move west was so compulsive that almost entire townships were deserted. The journey was usually begun in the spring, just as soon as the roads were dry enough to take the weight of the emigrant wagons.

The New Englanders went west in relative comfort, and this was remarked and not forgotten by the former indentured folk they met beyond Albany. The main route to Albany was passable, and crossed through northern Connecticut from Hartford, used the town roads between Goshen, Cornwall and Canaan. It traversed the Housatonic near Salisbury by ferry, and then followed the Great Road that ran from Boston to Albany.

Soil erosion, repeated crops of rocks forced up each spring in the fields by frost, and winters that lasted for eight months were the major incentives for the New Englanders. But they left behind them stout barns, houses that were already walled with clapboards or shingles instead of logs, and fields which for decades had been clear of stumps.

The women rode in the big, well sprung wagons that were drawn either by a span of oxen or double teams of horses. The women brought with them their house furniture, and in the wagon loads were Hitchcock chairs, cherrywood lowboys and highboys, spool bedsteads, tall columned clocks, bone china, silverware, mirrors and books.

The men walked and handled the teams. They wore cowhide boots and broad-brimmed hats. Many carried muskets; the roads were not entirely safe from outlaw attacks, even in Connecticut. The boys of sufficient age herded the stock, the milk cows, an occasional bull, a heifer, and the spare horses. Their sisters took over when the wagons got in trouble. That was frequent.

There were deep pot-holes, and swampy stretches where the wagons submerged to the wheel hubs and the teams strained sweating, white-frothed with lather. The boys waded into the mud and led the frantic animals by hand, talking to them, gentling them, while the men heaved at saplings to lift the axles, keep the rig moving ahead. Then the women and the little children got down to lighten the load, and the women took the boys' places with the horses.

The women knew the horses with great familiarity. They had been present when the mares had foaled, and these animals were born. During periods of sickness and bitter winter, they had fed the colts venison broth, covered them with blankets and fresh dry hay. Now they lifted their skirts and petticoats high, and, softly speaking to the horses by name, strode ahead in the mud.

Most of the wagons got through to Albany. But there were dismal wrecks, each worth several hundred dollars when built, in the worst of the swamp reaches and at the bottoms of the mountain slopes. Brakes had failed on the mountains, or snubbing ropes snapped, or harness breeching broke. Anyhow, the wagons were lost, and the best that could be done was dismantle them, take what was fit to carry back to the farms that just a few days before had been abandoned.

Water transportation of any kind was better than this, the men told themselves. They talked to their wives at night in the roadside camps about the Mohawk. The smooth, easy-flowing Mohawk, then the Great Lakes. Men remembered the rest of their lives the hopelessly mired wagons in the swamp patches, and the veering, crashing descent down Goshen or Sharon Mountain. When they reached Albany, they were ready to sell their wives' silverware or their best pairs of boots for space aboard a westbound boat.

Most any kind of craft that would float was being put in use at Albany. Families or groups of settlers who came from the same township went up the Mohawk in square-bowed batteaux made out of unfinished planks and green timber. They helped the boatmen pole, haul and row, and at night, when camp was made on the bank, they were too tired to eat, stretched out, and, despite the mosquitoes, deeply slept.

But as they progressed west and they became accustomed to the river work, their fatigue lessened. They took much more interest in the valley. They stared with intense curiosity at what were called the Iroquois "castles"—the stockaded towns where the carved, curious statues were raised over the gateways beside the poles that had once been decorated by scalps. The Iroquois squaws, dumpy, dressed in cheap trade cotton dresses, were a disappointment; they did not even look up from the corn rows as the boats passed. The warriors did not seem fierce at all, and either spent their time picking ticks from their short-haired mongrel dogs or at the fish weir nets in the river.

The river names excited memory, and some of the pioneer men had served here, at Oriskany, at Fort Schuyler, now about to be called Utica, and Canandaigua, and Fort Stanwix. There were flatboats with roofed, strongly built cargo shelters that moved among the batteaux. Some of them were almost 100 feet long, twice the size of the batteaux, and with a broader beam, more draft, a sharper bow. The crews were mixed, Dutchmen and Negroes from the Hudson, and Mohawks and a few Senecas. They were very professional about their work, shouted for clearance along the fairway at the middle of the stream, their captain, usually a Dutchman, sounding a warning on his big tin horn at the bends.

The old fur-trading posts along the river had been made into taverns that were known as "ordinaries." The term was much too fancy, the New England people said. The ordinaries exhibited a sign in front, and a whale-oil lantern after dark; inside, they were crowded, noisy and filthy, their prices invariably high.

They served as the hangouts for the flatboat crews, and the New England men kept their families separate in the main room, sat with their muskets beside them. Ale, beer, wine and rum flip were drunk nearly all night long by the flatboat crews. Ugly fights took place in the taproom and the stable yard. Bodies were sometimes found at dawn, floating in the river.

The poorer folks who could not afford the ordinaries camped in the forest on the way west. The men earned passage for themselves and their families as workaways aboard flatboats or batteaux. They also repaired and put into commission old skiffs and Indian dugout canoes, built rafts from timber they felled and trimmed on the river bank. Their food was the fish they caught, the game they trapped or shot, and corn and pumpkins taken in barter from the Iroquois squaws for small manufactured articles or for work the men had done to fix musket locks, straighten awls and reshape fish hooks.

Every man who was the head of a family collected his essential pioneer gear during the first weeks of the voyage. He could not exist in the wilderness without an auger, a frow, bar lead and bullet moulds, an axe, a tomahawk. He needed also blacksmith's "traps"—files, hammers, U-irons, a buck saw and a hand saw. His wife treasured her big kettle, her little kettle, and her yellow yarn blankets. His children, especially the boys, increased their forest and river skills.

The boys learned how to make snares and traps, and to fire the long-barreled, clumsy muskets. When their fathers allowed them the use of precious powder, they stood braced against the recoil shock and knocked squirrels out of trees at a distance of 200 yards. On the river, they paddled, rowed, tended towrope and anchor cable, made landings after dark, ran rapids and recognized shoals, shallows and snags.

They and their parents spoke of the Great Lakes as "the English Seas." The Mississippi was for them "the New Orleans River." Those names were wrong, they knew; they were often corrected when they came in contact with the educated New England people. But that did not bother them. Most of the New England people were from Connecticut, and going to the Western Reserve on Lake Erie. A land company owned it, a man named Moses Cleaveland had laid it out, and to live there cost so much an acre.

The former Rensselaerswyck and Livingstone manor workers decided they would keep on, past the Western Reserve, into the Ohio Valley country. It must be real wilderness there, and the two rivers, the Monongahela and the Allegheny, flowed into it, formed the Ohio. Some of the valley land should still be free.

But at Fort Pitt, jammed with soldiers, traders, peddlers, trappers and land speculators, they found more New England people. An immense tract of the prime Ohio Valley land had been acquired from the government by a Congregational preacher. He was also a promoter and lobbyist, and a Yale graduate. His name was Manasseh Cutler. He had signed on October 27, 1787, a contract with the Treasury Board for the Ohio Company of Associates, which he represented. The company bought a million and a half acres of land at the junction of the Muskingum and Ohio Rivers. It paid eight cents an acre.

The New Englanders congregated at Fort Pitt were in charge of General Rufus Putnam, who had served in the Continental Army in the Revolution. It had been the general's task to bring the settlers who had invested in the Ohio Company of Associates safe to their new homes.

169

The last part of the journey from Fort Pitt was made down the Ohio aboard flatboats. There were sixty people in the group that General

Putnam personally led. He celebrated the fact that they were New Englanders by naming one of their flatboats *Mayflower*.

They arrived April 7, 1788, at the town site chosen by the company. The men immediately began to clear the land and build a village. But their Puritan fervor lagged, and although most of them came from families long known for piety in Connecticut, Massachusetts, New Hampshire and Rhode Island, they named the town Marietta. They wished to express a romantic liking for the frivolous and ill-fated French queen, Marie Antoinette.

The Reverend Manasseh Cutler showed further impatience with the constraints of New England thinking when he came west. He drove out in a sulky. This rather fragile two-wheeled vehicle, with a seat for only one person and designed for harness racing on a graded, smooth track, made quite an impression along the reverend's route.

Military wagoners, tavern hostlers and village blacksmiths, ferrymen and boatmen spread his fame. Waves of astonished rumor preceded him to Marietta. He came ashore from the flatboat that had carried him from Fort Pitt, his horse and the sulky battered but in working condition. He urged the horse nimbly over the gangway to the landing. Then he jumped down from the sulky and accepted the greetings of General Putnam and the settlers. It had been a nice ride, he said, with, of course, a few bumps.

But, further south, the proud and powerful Cherokee nation fiercely blocked pioneer expansion towards the Ohio. They defended their ancient homeland, the beautiful, mountain-surrounded Valley of the Tennessee. Their name for the river was Tanase, or Tenese, and Chota, the sacred capital village, was near the west bank of the Little Tennessee.

Both the English and the French who tried to penetrate the valley in the eighteenth century called the Tennessee "the River of Cherokees." It doubled mysteriously on itself, they found, before it traversed the Great Smoky Mountains and joined the Ohio. Some of the ridges through which it cut were 6,000 feet high, and the tallest in the eastern part of the continent. The deep, tortuously winding gorges were flanked with spruce and balsam. They were magnificent in their stark grandeur. But the spring freshets roared out of them with terrific, destructive velocity and caused widespread floods across the flatlands beyond.

The Cherokees lived in "town houses" very similar to those built by the mound-dweller tribes of the Mississippi Valley. The Cherokees, though, put up theirs in a rectangular rather than round shape. They drove heavy posts into the ground and covered the entire structure, walls and roof with clay over a framework of canes.

Fires were kept going in clay basins in the centers of the single large rooms of the houses. There was a high seat, fashioned from clay, for the chief or the priests in the council house. Around it were seats for the tribal assembly, and those were covered with mats and split canes.

All of the houses were periodically pulled down, burned and levelled. Then new ones were built on the same sites, and gradually the village mounds were larger, higher. This was again in the tradition of the Mississippi tribes. But the Cherokees linked their heritage with the east. They, like the rest of the eastern tribes, called the Delawares "Grandfather" and showed them ceremonial deference.

The Chickasaws were allied with the Cherokees, and claimed the land between the Tennessee and the Mississippi. But they never occupied within historically recorded time villages on the Tennessee. The enormous Tennessee Valley, more than 40,000 square miles in size, was owned and defended by the Cherokees, who kept the white men from full possession of it for sixty-two years after the Revolution.

The Tennessee Valley was in reality the inner bastion of the Indian race throughout all of the country east of the Mississippi. The successive movements of white migration were stubbornly repelled by the Cherokees. Their resistance forced the settlers from the natural southwest course towards the Mississippi. They fought against penetration that came from the valley of Virginia in a southerly drift of land-hungry wanderers, some of whom had started in Maryland and Pennsylvania.

The Cherokees held their main villages on the river. Their canoes were dugout craft made of pine or poplar, and usually between thirty to forty feet in length. But they also put in the water other dugouts that were sixty feet long and manned by twenty paddlers. All of the strategic points on both banks were guarded, defended. A mobile force of warriors followed a shrewdly conceived defense plan for the whole valley.

But Daniel Boone was in the valley from North Carolina in 1760 and left a legend on a beech tree. He carved with typical frontier vanity:

171

"D. Boone cilled a Bar." This was in the Watauga Creek region of the valley, and it was soon invested by other white men. Four settlements were along the Watauga by 1770, and from them in a northwesterly direction the Wilderness Road led towards the Cumberland Gap.

The Cherokees, defeated in a series of bitterly fought actions, signed in 1777 a treaty of submission. But then they retreated deeper into the wilderness, and built new villages where the Tennessee twisted across the Cumberland Mountain ridges. Their principal chiefs, Dragging Canoe, Ostenaco and Willenawah, were ready for revenge, pillage and continued war.

Despite the known hostility of the Cherokees and the extraordinarily severe conditions of the 1779–80 winter, Colonel John Donelson decided to move west on the river. The colonel was from Virginia, had served in the Revolution, and held a reputation as an intrepid commander. He led a party of more than 200 people that included a number of women and children.

His contingent was the water-borne division of a carefully developed migration west of considerable size. The objective was French Lick, on the Cumberland. Colonel Donelson proposed to navigate in flatboats and pirogues the entire length of the Tennessee, then make the still more difficult passage up-current along the Ohio and the Cumberland to the settlers' future home. An advance party of veteran woodsmen led by James Robertson had set out overland for French Lick the preceding fall, across the Cumberland plateau and through Kentucky. They were to build cabins and prepare for the arrival of the Donelson party.

But Colonel Donelson was greatly daring. The rebellious, revenge-eager Cherokees had received supplies of arms and ammunition from British agents in Florida. Renegade whites, Tories who had lost everything in the Revolution, served under the Cherokee chief, Dragging Canoe, along with Creek volunteers and runaway Negro slaves. Dragging Canoe had by the end of 1778 a fighting force of 1,000 men.

Donelson kept on with the construction of his flotilla, confident that he could defeat any Indian attacks. The craft he called his flagship, a roughly built flatboat, was launched in a snow storm. He gave her the name of *Adventure* and put her in the Holston River, a tributary of the Tennessee, near Fort Patrick Henry. Then he finished assembling the rest of the craft. He loaded aboard the men, women, children and their household goods, and shoved off three days before Christmas. They had ahead of them a 1,000-mile voyage.

He wrote an account of it: *Journal of a Voyage, intended by God's permission, the good boat Adventure, from Fort Patrick Henry, on the Holston River, to the French Salt Springs on the Cumberland River, kept by John Donelson.*

The craft in which he sailed had been built at Boatyard, now Kingsport, Tennessee. She was a large flatboat of the type known as a broadhorn. Her flat-bottomed hull was heavy, made of thick, trimmed logs, and Donelson described her decks as being "well-bulwarked against gunfire." The cabin was solidly roofed, and contained bunks with spruce-bough mattresses and a stone fireplace. Her crew, protected by the bulwarks, moved her with poles. The steersman was also sheltered from gunfire by a bulwark aft, and navigated with a long sweep.

But none of the other craft was as thoroughly protected. The people who rode in the open pirogues were exposed to the weather and

Sketch of a flatbottom boat.

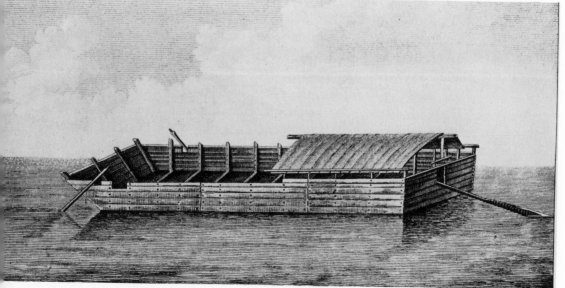

intensely suffered. Snow gales swept down through the valley. Boats were capsized, or driven aground. Their crews when rescued were in bad condition. Frostbite was common; there were several cases of gangrene.

The flotilla made little progress. Colonel Donelson was for the first time seriously worried. He had counted on the severe winter to check Indian attack. But it was now March. The snow was gone. Blustering rain squalls made navigation difficult, forced the steersmen to keep in close to the banks. Men on lookout peered hour after hour through the rain to find the landmarks the pilots sought. They searched for signs of Indians, too, among the dull green expanses of the cane bottoms, the somber clusters of cedars on the lower slopes, the tall stands of pines and leafless hardwoods above, along the ridges.

Men saw game move in the gray sedge grass, and across the open savannahs. But no Cherokees showed themselves. This, the great valley of eastern Tennessee, seemed empty of human life except for the file of boats that slowly traversed the whirlpools and eddies and the stubbornly swerving current. The cloud-flanked hills, the huge and dark mountains that pierced the upper clouds made the scene oppressive. The people in the boats spoke only in response to orders or when the loneliness could no longer be endured.

Colonel Donelson was aware that he should not turn back, and must complete the voyage. He and the people in his charge had entered a region of Cherokee ambush. Their single chance of escape was to remain on the river and try to navigate it. The greatest danger for them would come when they reached what were called the Five Lower Towns. These lay along a stretch of the river called The Narrows.

One of the Cherokee towns commanded the entrance to the difficult passage known as "The Suck." Another town, Nickajack, was just below The Narrows, and two more were further downstream. Donelson had been badly informed about their reoccupation by the Cherokees. Still, to send his people overland would mean that they would either die of hunger in the wilderness or be caught and massacred by the Cherokees within hours of their landing. He had another motive for continuing. A corn crop had been planted by the advance party at French Lick, and was an essential item in next winter's rations for the settlers.

Families on their way downstream.

The weather became fair, and with good visibility Indians appeared on the river banks. They were Cherokee warriors, who shouted to the settlers that they wanted to board the boats, prove themselves friends. Donelson had more than thirty people aboard *Adventure*, and the other craft were all heavily loaded. There was no space or time for friendly overtures, and Donelson suspected treachery.

Ahead, mountains descended sharply to the water. A massive promontory jutted forth, the slopes very steep. Donelson recognized Lookout Mountain. He made a signal to the rest of the flotilla to steer a course along the center of the river.

A Cherokee warrior fired from the underbrush and the musket ball skipped in white spurts across the bronze-colored surface, missed a boat at the head of the column. Then there was a fusillade. The other marksmen were better. Boats were hit. A man named Payne was killed when the flotilla breasted Moccasin Bend.

But the current was fast. The flotilla kept going, the steersmen crouched at the sweeps, their shipmates busily answering the Cherokee fire. The last boat in the column belonged to Thomas Stuart. She held that position because there were twenty-eight people aboard, and smallpox had broken out among them. Donelson had ordered them to keep well astern due to the possibility of infection.

The Cherokees concentrated their fire on the Stuart boat. Her steersman was knocked down by a bullet. She began to drift in towards the bank. Men aboard the other boats sent volleys into the Cherokees on the bank. That was too late. Warriors were in canoes. They paddled out and boarded. They carried tomahawks and scalping knives, and some of them were killed as they went aboard. But the people they fought were weak, sick.

A few shots, muffled and fired at very close range, came from the flatboat cabin. Then the Cherokee whoops were dominant. A shout punctuated them, and screams. The boat veered towards the bank and bodies were slung splashing over the side. Colonel Donelson looked around and watched the other boats.

They were heading with the torrential current into the whirl-pools of The Suck. It rushed through a high-walled gorge, and, above, careless of the targets they offered against the afternoon sunlight, Indians stood along the summits and fired rapidly repeated volleys.

Those formed a cross-fire which the flotilla could not evade. Boat followed boat into it and through it. Powder smoke in a grayish-blue cloud rose above the red-black bodies of the warriors in their war paint, and over the river where men hauled at sweeps and poles and took re-loaded muskets from their women and children.

Boulders close to midstream were a menace in the gorge. The boats rounded them with the current dragging and the musket volleys a ragged whine overhead, bullets finding the bulwarks with a flat sound, the sound softer, slower when a body was hit. The steersman was wounded aboard the boat owned by Abel Gower. Other men had already been struck, and none of them could immediately take his place.

The boat was hurled broadside by the current, began to swing towards the boulders. A young girl, Nancy Gower, took the steering sweep. She brought the boat back, clear from danger. But her mother, staring out from the cabin, noticed blood that broadly stained Nancy's skirt. Nancy had been wounded in the thigh, and said nothing about it. When a man relieved her at the sweep, she went into the cabin and had her mother treat the wound and bandage it.

Donelson kept the flotilla in column as much as possible when he heard the warning roar of Muscle Shoals. He realized once more that he was committed, must take his people through it. Indians kept pace along the banks or sent word downstream. Any attempt to land here would end in massacre.

He shouted orders for the various boats to change their trim for the Muscle Shoals passage. Cargo was carefully shifted so that they would ride more easily in the violence of the rapids. The water was very high, he saw, so that they could navigate safely among the rocks. He wrote a clear description of the scene:

> When we approached them they had a dreadful appearance to those who had never seen them before. The water being high made a terrible roaring, which could be heard at some distance among the driftwood heaped frightfully upon the points of the islands, the current running in every possible direction. Here we did not know how soon we should be dashed to pieces, and all our troubles ended at once.
>
> Our boats frequently dragged on the bottom, and appeared constantly in danger of striking: they warped as much as in a rough sea. But, by the hand of Providence, we are now preserved from this danger also. I know not the length of this wonderful shoals: it had been represented to me to be twenty-five or thirty miles; if so, we must have descended very rapidly, as indeed we did, for we passed in about three hours. Came to, and encamped on the northern shore, not far below the shoals, for the night.

177

The weary, bloody, shocked survivors were not aware of it, but they had no more serious danger ahead of them. The Cherokees did not pursue them any further than the Shoals, and on the lower river the flotilla was able to make better time. High water helped them, and they floated 250 miles within a week to the junction of the Tennessee and the Ohio.

They found fair weather, with the Ohio ashine in sunlight, the soft green of new foliage beyond the canebrakes and gauntly twisted white sycamores along the banks. They moored the boats and went ashore, camped at the site of present-day Paducah. The men already understood the huge amount of hard labor that now confronted them.

The Ohio was in fast, rapid flow, swollen by spring freshets. The boats were not built for upstream work, lacked cleated walkways for the pole handlers and cordelle gear for the hawsers used along the banks to haul the craft against the current. The crews were in bad shape from hunger and fatigue, and the last of the party's provisions were almost expended. Donelson was also unable to tell them the distance yet to go to their destination. Donelson wrote:

> The scene is rendered still more melancholy, as several boats will not attempt to ascend the rapid current. Some intend to descend the Mississippi to Natchez; others are bound for Illinois—among the rest my son-in-law and daughter. We now part, perhaps, to meet no more, for I am determined to pursue my course, happen what will.

Colonel Donelson had become an excellent river man. It took the party more than a month to pole, push, shove and haul up the Ohio to the Cumberland, then up the Cumberland to French Lick. But he brought all the boats that remained under his command safely there. They rigged crude squaresails when the wind was in the right quarter and blew from astern. Hunters detached by Donelson and entrusted with precious powder went ashore and killed game. The party lived on buffalo meat, wild swan, ground nuts and wild asparagus.

Lookouts aboard the lead boat reported at the end of March that they saw white men on the bank. This was a party of surveyors in charge of Richard Henderson, a land speculator who had started the French Lick settlement. His party was assigned to run the line between Virginia and North Carolina.

178

The settlers kept on, now joyous, up the Cumberland. They landed below the bluffs where the settlement was located, climbed rapidly to the cabins that were ready for them. It was April 24, 1780, and they had been on the rivers for four months, navigated a course more than 1,000 miles long since Christmas.

They had lost thirty-three people, through Indian attack or capture, or drowning, or exposure. Nine of them carried scars from Indian bullet wounds. This was a common experience on the frontier, though; the survivors went at once about their work at the new settlement.

French Lick flourished. It attracted other settlers from eastern Tennessee. They were among the people who founded Nashville. Their enterprise opened the Cumberland Valley. One of Colonel Donelson's daughters, Rachel, who was fifteen at the time of the voyage from the Holston, later married Andrew Jackson, the seventh President of the United States.

But the most significant result of the western expansion towards the Mississippi lacked drama of any kind. A Kentucky pioneer farmer left his homestead around 1785 and went to Pennsylvania and loaded a flatboat with flour. Then he floated down the Monongahela to the Ohio, and from that river into the Mississippi. He bartered his flour for furs in New Orleans. A ship took him and the furs to Havana, where he sold them for sugar. The sugar cargo was sold by him in Philadelphia, and when he was paid he walked home.

There was an empire within an empire between the coastal states, the "old colonies" and the Mississippi. The French, because of wanton disregard at court and political and religious differences, had lost it. The British, for different reasons, but also due to stupidity at high governmental levels, had lost it, too, would never, in spite of continued plans of redemption, get it back. It belonged to the new nation that had hardly begun to reckon the extent of her incredible wealth.

## 12

THERE WERE OTHER NEW INLAND EMPIRES. THE boundaries were very flexible, almost constantly changing with the pressures of war, peace, and the immensely expanded demands of the fur trade. One had its capital at the trading post started on the Mississippi in 1764 by Pierre Laclede Liguest. He was a Frenchman who had come upriver from New Orleans, and he soon held the Indian trade of the Missouri and of the Ohio. This did not please the British much, but Liguest was smart, ambitious, stubborn. A settlement grew around his post and became the city of St. Louis.

The British did better in the Great Lakes region. Michilimackinac was the capital of an empire whose rulers dictated terms to Montreal and to Albany, and whose power stretched to Lake Superior and the vitally important post that had been built at Grand Portage. It was difficult, though, in the years right after the Revolution, to decide precisely who was in command at Michilimackinac. Many of the men who gathered there were violently independent, chose to live in the wilderness so that they might evade any authority. They came only to Michilimackinac to sell their furs, replenish their supplies of trade goods, and get roaring, gouging, stabbing drunk for a night or two.

They were nearly all renegades who if they had stayed along the seaboard would have been hanged for various crimes. General Gage left a brief but vigorous description of them: "Many of these have inhabited the Indian country for 12 to 30 years, differing little from the Natives except in Colour, and being more addicted to vice."

His term for them was "vagabonds," and it was justified. They were English, or French, or a mixture of both with most of the Great Lakes tribes. Their clothing was Indian, and their speech polyglot. They were squawmen, and often swapped or deserted their squaws. Their crimes, some of which they were perhaps falsely accused, were shooting government hunters within sight of the post, and hijacking each other for furs, trade goods, or drunken dislike. A number of the Frenchmen did not even enter the post; they dealt through traders who were in better repute and had been granted licenses.

The capital of the third inland empire was Grand Portage, at the northeastern corner of Lake Superior. The Pigeon River gave the place its name. The river rushed in rocky, unnavigable falls for nine miles before it tumbled into the lake. All canoe cargo was unloaded at the cedar-log wharves below Fort Grand Portage, then packed around the falls. The headwaters of the Pigeon River led to what was the richest fur-bearing region in the world—the High Country.

Frenchmen hung on stubbornly at Grand Portage. They called themselves proudly *Les Seigneurs des Lacs et des Forêts.* They were independent operators, and malcontents who disliked or feared civilization, and profoundly distrusted each other. Nobody was allowed to stand behind them when they sat at the long plank table in the huge, barnlike main hall at Fort Grand Portage. Heavy-bladed scalping knives were carried in beaded scabbards at their hips; pistols were in their belts. They drank the finest imported liquors, but they seldom permitted themselves a night of unrestrained carousal. Each of them owned a fortune in furs, and a killer took all, could easily disappear in the High Country wilderness.

Grand Portage—trading post
on the northern shore of
Lake Superior.

An exceptionally courageous French explorer and fur trader, Pierre
Gaultier de Varennes, Sieur de la Vérendrye, was the first white man in
the High Country after Groseillers and Radisson. He entered it sixty
years later, in the 1720s, and realized from the quality of the furs brought
him by the local tribes the immense amount of wealth to be gathered
there. So that it might be kept not only for himself but for his king, he
built a series of stockaded posts to protect the route. He built Fort Charles,
near Lake of the Woods, as a base for the Grand Portage area, and Fort
Maurepas on Lake Winnebago.

With great diplomatic skill and patience, he established a treaty
of peace between the Crees and the Sioux. Then he began barter with
both tribes. He built Fort Rouge at the mouth of the Red River in 1737,
Fort La Reine at Portage La Prairie in 1738, and also Fort Dauphin. But

he became enmeshed in the same kind of credit difficulties that later ruined Major Robert Rogers and many other fur traders.

The Montreal merchants who supplied him with trade goods demanded payment. When Sieur de la Vérendrye was unable to make it, and his two sons failed in an attempt to find either the Shining Mountains or any trace of the Northwest Passage, the king withdrew his fur monopoly rights. This was in 1744, and for almost fifty years afterwards the High Country was left unexplored, the maze of rivers and lakes unused by white men, the log, sod-roofed forts in ruins, even their locations forgotten.

The Hudson's Bay Company, which since 1670 had traded on the northern rim of the continent, decided finally in 1765 to explore the High Country. A trio of smart traders, William Pink, Joseph Smith and Isaac

Batt, went into the region from Hudson Bay. Their purpose was to get the tribes to bring furs down to York Factory on the Nelson River. But the tribes were reluctant, and the trade did not prosper.

Then, in 1768, a tough Scot named James Finlay made an epic canoe voyage from Montreal. He went on alone past Michilimackinac, portaged around the Sault Sainte Marie, paddled the length of Lake Superior, hauled his canoe and his gear over the nine-mile Pigeon River carry at Grand Portage. Then he got back in the canoe again and kept going to Assiniboin country in Saskatchewan. He gathered a fine load of furs in the High Country, returned to Montreal before the rivers and lakes froze, and was well paid for his effort.

The Hudson's Bay Company heard of his entrance into the region, and referred to him contemptuously as a "Montreal pedlar," a term they used for the hardy French, English and Scots traders who followed the route he had taken. Thomas Corry was among the first of this lot, and a famous French *coureur de bois* known simply as Blondeau; a pair of equally famous wilderness veterans, Peter Pangman and Peter Pond; and Charles Paterson, William Holmes, and Alexander Henry, who had as his partners Benjamin and Joseph Frobisher.

Another group, composed almost entirely of Scots, came into the High Country next, and formed a loose kind of partnership. Among them were Simon McTavish, Alexander Mackenzie, Donald Cameron, Henry Bostwick, George McBeath, Charles Grant, John Ross and Ezekiel Solomon. Ezekiel Solomon said that he had joined the Scots to learn the finer points of fur trading. The group, in alliance with the earlier arrivals, took a tremendous amount of business away from the Hudson's Bay Company.

It was no longer possible for the company directors to describe the High Country traders as a temporary menace to trade, and badly financed men who were independent upon an impossible 1,800-mile canoe route from Grand Portage to Montreal. The company sent Matthew Cocking, the second-in-command at York Factory, inland in 1772 to investigate the activities of the "pedlars." Cocking risked his life on the way across-country to the Saskatchewan, then as he made contact with the Montreal men. He found that the Blackfeet, the most numerous local tribe, delivered in barter forty-five canoe-loads of prime furs. These the Montreal men

The trapper returns.

happily shipped east, via Grand Portage. The long, devious and difficult route worked, and worked very well.

The Northwest Company was formed, in direct opposition to the Hudson's Bay Company. It shipped out during the 1793 season 196,-000 beaver skins, 2,100 bear skins, 1,500 fox, 400 kit fox, 16,000 muskrat, 32,000 marten, 1,800 mink, 6,000 lynx, 6,000 wolverine, 1,600 fisher, 100 raccoon, 1,200 dressed deer, 700 elk, and 550 buffalo skins. The company operated almost completely in Canadian territory that bordered the United States along the Great Lakes. It supplied work for several thousand people, among them clerks, trading-post assistants and factors, seamen, furriers, auctioneers and retail and wholesale hat manufacturers overseas. The gross profit was in the hundreds of thousands of pounds, the net profit very considerable, and rapidly making the partners wealthy.

The system of transportation was very delicately balanced, though. The entire operation depended upon the good will, health and strength of the *voyageurs* who manned the canoes. They were the last and the best of the French Canadian river men. There was 150 years of tradition behind them; they were bandy-legged and enormously broad-shouldered and long-armed. It was their great-grandfathers who had ridden the rapids, hauled the portage loads and sailed through the storms with Champlain, Jolliet, Marquette, La Salle. The fact dominated their lives.

185

There were between Montreal and Lake of the Woods, by the Ottawa River route more than ninety portages. Those were from a few yards to nine miles long, and over them the *voyageurs* moved in single file. Each man carried at least two packs for an average distance of 600 to 800 yards. His breath back, he continued. When time pressed and the season was late, men went along the portage trails with four of the ninety-pound *pièces*, the tumplines yanking at their foreheads, the combined weight bending them almost double, spines and legs throbbing, aching with strain, feet numb in the sweat-soaked and slippery moccasins that were worn through at the end of a day.

The season was cruelly short for them, and during it they moved the cargoes both east and west. It began when ice left the rivers, along in April or May, and was finished no later than November. Heavy dugout craft called ice canoes were sometimes used in the fall months when ice had already begun to form. But they were difficult to navigate, and progress with them was slow. The *voyageurs* preferred to take their chances in the tender-hulled birchbark canoes. Crosses made of branches lashed together with withes were put up on the banks of rivers where men lost their lives, but many who drowned in the lakes or while paddling in darkness could not be so remembered.

The canoes that left Montreal in the spring bound west were the largest of their kind ever built. They were approximately thirty-five feet long and took four tons of cargo. The load, in addition to the crew of eight or ten men, was sixty-five ninety-pound packs of trade goods, 600 pounds of biscuit, 200 pounds of pork, three bushels of dried peas, two oilcloths to cover the cargo, a sail, an axe, a towline, a kettle, and a bailing sponge. The sponge, an imported item, was necessary because the fragility of the hull did not allow the use of a more rigid utensil.

The bowman and the steersman in these crews received higher pay than those who worked amidships and were called "middlemen." They knew more, and they performed with extreme skill in the rapids and when squalls abruptly threatened destruction during the Great Lakes traverses. Their annual pay was 150 *livres*,* which they, along with the rest of the crew, usually asked to have paid them in trade goods. The company

186

* About $600 in present day buying power.

was willing, and sold them goods which had almost as high a mark-up as that demanded of the Indians.

The *voyageurs* were vaguely aware that they were being exploited. Even their squaws, Sac and Fox women for the most part, explained it to them. But they were uncaring. Life, the life that counted, were the rivers—the surge of the craft beneath them as it danced, whipped, lunged between the darkly glistening rocks of a rapids—and the lakes at dawn in mist, the birds just awakening, and the fires on the beaches at night, the songs, the stories, the jokes, taunts, boasts and laughter, the word that no man could express but each man kept in his heart—the *camaraderie*.

The canoes maintained an average paddling speed of six miles an hour. The wind right, and from astern, the small squaresail was rigged amidships, or, lacking that, one of the cargo oilcloths. Then the speed might increase to nine miles an hour. But when there was bad weather on the lakes, the canoe brigades were held shorebound. They waited sometimes for as long as a week for Huron or Superior to clear. It was after such a delay that men carried four *pièces* at once at a portage, and steersmen kept the craft moving in the rivers at night, and navigated by starlight.

There were two kinds of canoe crews, and intense jealousy separated them. The crews that took the spring fleet as far as Grand Portage, then made the return trip from there to Montreal were known as *mangeurs du lard*, literally, lard-eaters. Space in the canoes was too limited for anything except concentrated foods, and there was little time to fish, hunt, or even gather berries. The crews lived on leached corn and buffalo tallow, and when they got to Grand Portage they varied that diet with a bit of wild rice.

Each of the lard-eaters was issued a blanket, a shirt and pants by their employer. The rest of their gear they supplied themselves, but it was almost standard. They favored red-wool stocking caps, wide woolen waist sashes, usually also red, beaded Indian garters worn just below their knees, and the finest sort of quill-decorated moccasins. The garters, the moccasins and their fancy tobacco pouches of various carefully treated animal skins were made by their squaws. Each man had a knife, worn in his belt at the hip, and treasured it just about as much as his clay pipe. Red had been chosen as the cap and sash color for quite practical reasons; a

187

man could be seen by his companions and rescued while he fought for his life in fast or rough water.

The lard-eaters met at Grand Portage the second kind of canoe crews. These were known as the *hivernants*, the winterers who spent the bleak and terrible, cold-locked months in the High Country. The winterers were paid more than the lard-eaters, and received more personal equipment from their employers, stroud-cloth coats, fur-lined moccasins and mittens, thick shirts. They claimed to be tougher than the lard-eaters, and were quite willing to prove it with their fists, feet or knives.

The lard-eaters hauled west in the bulky *canots du maître* bolts of coarse cloth, milled blankets and cotton sheeting, thread, fishline and twine, hardware, arms and ammunition, cutlery, iron-mongery, brass and copper kettles, silk and cotton handkerchiefs, hats, shoes, stockings, calicoes, blue beads, and penny prints made in England for the amusement of children but bought by the tribes as talismans against evil. The journey was broken by a week's lay-over at both Michilimackinac and Sault Sainte Marie, and the same would be true Montreal-bound.

The winterers were confined inside the walls of the trading posts, and generally in a single common room, for at least seven months. Their diet was unchanging unless varied by starvation. It was frozen whitefish or muskellunge, eaten saltless. There was always rum, though, and plenty

*Canot du maître*

of tobacco. Some of the post managers were learning, too, how to maintain a winter's supply of pemmican made in the Indian style.

Peter Pond, Connecticut-born, had found in the High Country that the Indian staple was much more satisfactory and that a man did not lose his appetite for it. He introduced it among the garrisons of the posts. The men welcomed it, came to like the compound of thinly sliced buffalo meat, marrow, choke cherries and mint leaves. Pond was a veteran with many years in the wilderness. He had served under Sir William Johnson and taken part in the capture of Montreal. But, he admitted, if he was forced to look into the eyes of any more frozen whitefish, he would go berserk.

Pond held an ugly record in the High Country. His words about going berserk were not taken lightly by the men who knew him. He was accused, although never directly, of having killed a competitor in the fur trade, and was believed responsible for the death of another. But he was extraordinarily well informed about the region, had explored almost all of it, and his time during the winter months was occupied with map-making, geographical research, discussion and speculation. He was convinced that the Northwest Passage existed, and that eventually he would be able to discover it.

The other men of lesser mental scope in the post garrisons were not allowed the release from monotony that Pond enjoyed. Most of the winterers were entirely illiterate. They came from the meanest of circumstances in the Province of Quebec, or had been born to Indian mothers somewhere along the canoe route west. Their employment here was because of their exceptional physical strength and their ability to transport, by the complex of High Country rivers, lakes and portages, fur cargo down to Fort Grand Portage and trade goods back.

The week or so they spent at Grand Portage when the Montreal canoe fleet arrived was the only opportunity they had for enjoyment. All winter long, and ever since last summer, they had been thinking about this. Now they were *en regal*. They drank, ate, danced, sang, drank, fought, sang and argued, drank some more, and sprawled out on the open prairie with squaws too drunk to protest. It was a *regal*, even though they awoke with hangovers that left them speechless, spent their year's

189

wages in a couple of nights, and picked up syphilis which had been recently imported from Montreal.

Back at the posts on Rainy Lake and Lake of the Woods, the Saskatchewan and the Athabasca, the memory of a *regal* faded, became confused with that of the year before. They all seemed the same, and none of them filled the awful chasm of loneliness that kept on widening. The High Country men lacked the reassurance of the knowledge that their debauches at Grand Portage greatly resembled their Viking ancestors' bouts of wassail. They knew only that the cold, the dark, the wind beyond the walls were about to burst in and overpower them.

The winterers sang. They sat shoulder to shoulder before the immense stone hearth of the chimney where wood was tossed until the fire leapt crimson-crested, rustling and roaring with the force of its heat. The songs were old ones, often repeated:

> *J'ai cueilli la belle rose*
> *J'ai cueilli la belle rose,*
> *Qui pendait au rosier blanc.*
> *La belle rose*
> *Qui pendait au rosier blanc,*
> *La belle rose du rosier blanc.*

There were no roses in the High Country, and these men had not seen one in years. The song was sung out of sheer nostalgia. They had another song which, quite self-consciously, they had developed, using an old Norman folk tune. It concerned them personally, and their work, so it was popular:

> *Tu es mon compagnon de voyage!*
> *Je veux mourir dans mon canot.*
> *Le laboreur aime sa charrue, le chasseur son fusil, son chien;*
> *Le musicien aime sa musique; moi, mon canot est tout mon bien.*

But songs about canoes bored them, here in this womanless High Country. They returned to their youth—distance, the passage of years diminishing if not erasing the poverty and the misery of the rigidly regulated life in the Province of Quebec. Montreal appeared in a nostalgia-

190

brightened series of images. The summer dusk touched the river with crimson, and the Angelus was sweetly played. People sat on the broad wooden settles which flanked the front doors of their homes and quietly talked.

Children played with each other and dogs and kittens in the cobbled street. A peasant girl passed, her coif and kerchief gleaming white in the sunset light, her bundle of purchases balanced on her shoulder. She had a long walk home into the country before her, most of it in darkness. Her strides were steady and determined in her square-toed, cowhide shoes.

The song about her sent her on her way:

> Lev' ton pied léger, bergère,
> Lev' ton pied légèrement!

But after a time the singing around the fireplace stopped. The men were silent. Wind screamed in the chimney. The window coverings, made of greased deerhide parchment, bent and almost buckled inward with the blasts. There was no light except the fire, although it was near noon. A snow gale held out of due north, off the Arctic Ocean, would blow for days to come. A man who stepped outside the door, no matter how he was dressed, and no matter what he did, would die within ten minutes.

The winterers were inculcated with a fantastically confused mass of distorted Christianity and Indian folklore. What they had learned from the priests in their youth was intertwined with a belief in the *loup-garou*, the hideous werewolf of French Canadian mythology, and the *windigo*, the faceless and cannibalistic spirit which the Indians greatly feared. That screaming in the chimney might well be the *windigo*, angry and about to come down.

Some of the winterers had bought at the post trade counter the colored pictures made for children in England. They slipped them out from their pockets and looked at them, to ward off evil. Their ignorance and the degree of their superstitition were not uncommon, though. Samuel de Champlain had accepted as fact stories about a monster. La Vérendrye, an educated man, recorded with care the folklore fables told him by the High Country tribes, gave credence to many of them.

191

He had marched as far west as the foothills of the Rocky Mountains, met with the "Horse Indians," who were Blackfeet and offered wolf skins in barter. The Blackfeet had dealt since with the Assiniboins, who were canoe people and came to the High Country posts, brought fascinating accounts of the western regions as well as furs. The stories originally told by the Blackfeet were increased in stature at the various posts on the way east, and were really astounding when they reached Montreal. A considerable number, though, received serious consideration from otherwise responsible merchants, officials and military officers.

These men were asked to believe that:

Beyond the sunset lived Indians of the size of giants. There were deadly serpents, which, forming big hoops by taking their tails in their mouths, could roll downhill, seize their victims, and crush them to death. There was a pure salt mountain located 1,000 miles upstream from the mouth of the Missouri River. This was 180 miles long and forty-five miles wide. No trees grew on the mountain, and not a blade of grass. Streams of pure salt rushed forth from caves in its flanks. No trees would grow on a wide prairie near the mountain, either, but the grass there was remarkably abundant. It was pasture land for millions of enormous animals. Another area held castles adorned with turrets and towers, the walls of bright red stone. They were built and occupied by the giant Indians.

Peter Pond was an outstanding skeptic, and failed to respond to this array of misinformation. He went alone into the High Country and spent the winter of 1776–77 on the northern branch of the Saskatchewan River. He brought his supplies with him, because in that treeless muskeg waste there was little game to be found. When the fall gales descended, he was warm and secure within a stockade shelter, "forted up" against the weather or any wandering Indians.

He was just as wary about Hudson's Bay Company agents after spring opened the river to traffic. His presence here was unwelcome to the company. High Country furs were the finest in the world, and the company wanted absolute possession. It had sent in a party to build a post on the same fork of the Saskatchewan. They called it Hudson's Bay House, and might at any time dispatch an expert musket shot to visit him.

But the Hudson's Bay people were not as murderously inclined as Pond had imagined. He ventured deep into the wilderness the next season, and traded to the northward, near Lake Athabasca. His trade with the local tribes was brisk, and his yield of furs excellent. Hatred of the Hudson's Bay Company because of their monopolistic practices moved him to tell other independent traders about the wealth in the region.

The newly arrived men were so successful that in 1778 the Hudson's Bay Company entered formal complaint with the Board of Trade in London:

> The greatly increased number of Canadian Traders that now over-spread all this country and have absolutely blocked up every Passage to their Honors' Inland Settlement, as most of these to York fort.

The Board of Trade used direct means. It shut down all shipping on the Great Lakes. The independent traders in the High Country were cut off from their single source of goods at Montreal. They retreated to Michilimackinac. Some of them passed the rest of the Revolutionary War years there in drunkenness, gambling and squaw-swapping. The rest went into the Ohio region, or down the Mississippi, partway up the Missouri.

When the war ended, they went back to the High Country. The British government accepted a Board of Trade estimate that 800 men entered into trade with the northern tribes. But at Michilimackinac, which served as a transfer point for all of the independents' cargo movement, the figure was said to be badly underestimated. Several thousand men, experienced traders, *coureurs de bois*, discharged soldiers, frontier rejects, and deserters from both the Continental and British Armies had headed north from Grand Portage to make their fortunes.

Peter Pond was among the first. He returned to Lake Athabasca, where he had traded and built a post. His knowledge of western America from Prairie du Chien to the northern reaches of the High Country was quite detailed, if in some respects inaccurate. He maintained the conviction that there was only "a narrow strip" of country between Lake Athabasca and the Pacific Ocean.

One of his former partners, Alexander Henry, shared the conviction and firmly upheld it. He was, like Pond, of American birth, came from New Jersey. He had served under Amherst in the French-Indian war, afterward worked as a trader at Albany. With a canoe-load of

193

Albany goods, he moved on to Michilimackinac, where he met Pond and they formed their partnership. He and Pond were together in the pre-Revolutionary years when Indians who bore Spanish knives ascended the Mississippi and came to trade at Prairie du Chien.

Alexander Henry took it on himself in 1781 to write a letter to Sir Joseph Banks, the president of the Royal Society. The language in which it was phrased must have surprised Sir Joseph, and the idea it expressed was bold. Henry proposed that the Royal Society should finance exploration of the High Country. He named various trustworthy guides who were capable of taking the expedition from Lake Athabasca to the Pacific Coast, and Pond's name was at the top of the list. But he did not receive a reply, and at the end of the Revolution he went back to the High Country for trade purposes alone.

Alexander Mackenzie was the man who finally punctured the huge, gaudy and mysterious bubble created by the wishful thinking about the Straits of Anian, the Northwest Passage and the Shining Mountains. He came to the High Country in 1785, when he was twenty-two, and after six years of trading-company service. Five of them had been spent in the Montreal counting-room of a famous Canadian firm, Gregory and McLeod. He was a big and gawky, blond-headed boy of sixteen when he joined the firm as a junior clerk. His energy was so great that the other clerks called him "Perpetual Motion."

He incessantly pestered Gregory, the senior partner, to be assigned to one of the firm's posts in the High Country. But Gregory was cautious, wanted to temper Mackenzie's impetuosity. When Mackenzie was released from clerk's-stool bondage, Gregory sent him first to Detroit, to handle there a separate trading enterprise with complete responsibility for it. Mackenzie was very successful, and a year later he was assigned to the High Country.

He took over the management of a trading post in the Churchill River district. This was near Lake Athabasca, and gave a splendid yield of furs. Mackenzie had become an important man, and was made a partner in the Northwest Company. He recognized almost at once the tremendous rivalry exerted by the Hudson's Bay Company. The much older and more powerful organization was out to destroy the company he represented.

The Hudson's Bay Company was able to maintain its monopoly

over the sea approaches to the **High Country**. Years ago, Groseillers and Radisson had proven to the satisfaction of the board of governors that the major rivers of the region were north-flowing, emptied into the Arctic Ocean. Three or four vessels of less than 200-ton displacement handled the entire cargo operation, outward-bound and homeward-bound, for the company.

It had built four key posts, all at the mouths of rivers flowing into Hudson Bay. They were Prince of Wales Fort, York Factory, Severn House and Albany House. The company had an inflexible policy of enormously high prices, consistently cheated its Indian customers, and at trading time fuddled their wits with cheap alcohol, also sold for a large figure. The factors in charge of the posts took only beaver pelts in barter, and secured a 2,000 per cent profit.

Mackenzie compared the prices that he could offer in competition with the Hudson's Bay Company, and calculated the net profit. His firm would realize nothing like 2,000 per cent. The transportation costs between Montreal and the High Country built up a very substantial overhead.

He received in barter for a common musket ten prime beaver pelts. A pound of gunpowder brought two pelts. Four pounds of shot were worth a single pelt, and a pound of glass beads, two pelts. A cloth coat was sold for six pelts, and a petticoat for five. Spencer's black twisted tobacco, a particular favorite with both warriors and squaws, sold at a foot length for a pelt. A bottle of rum, traded at Northwest Company standard price, was worth two pelts.

The profit, when first toted on the company books in the Churchill River post, looked very impressive. But the Northwest Company had twenty-three partners, and employed 2,000 people, factors, clerks, canoemen, trappers. With the expansion of the trade route further into the High Country, it was impossible to make the transfer of pelts and trade goods in the same season. Men could not paddle and portage canoes that fast.

Mackenzie was aware that the company was threatened by serious economic strain. He reported to his partners:

195

The tract of transport [from Montreal] occupies an extent of from three to 4,000 miles, through upwards of 60 large lakes and numerous rivers. Those waters are intercepted by more than 200 rapids, along which the articles of merchandise are chiefly carried on men's backs, and over 130 carrying places, from twenty-five paces to 13 miles in length, where the canoes and cargoes proceed by the same toilsome and perilous operations.

The partners, content with their share of the company profit, were unwilling to give thorough consideration to Mackenzie's report. Still, he knew that all along the trade route, from the St. Lawrence River basin to Lake Superior, the Indian tribes were uneasy, resentful of the loss of their lands to the white men, and preparing themselves for eventual, widespread war. The sea-otter trade on the Northwest Coast was another threat to the future of the company. More than a dozen British vessels were engaged in it, and furs were being shipped to very active markets in Canton and London. If the company was to survive, it must find some means of access to the Pacific. The Northwest Passage dream was to be proven soon, or completely abandoned.

Mackenzie held the strong respect of his partners despite their lack of interest in his report. He was assigned next to the Lake Athabasca region, and made a senior partner. The territory for which he was responsible was larger than France and could be made to yield incalculable wealth in furs. He had started out as a barely educated junior clerk nine years earlier; now he was one of the major figures in Canada.

He realized that in the present phase of his career he needed the help of a man he could absolutely trust. He sent home to Stornaway, in the Outer Hebrides, for his young cousin. He and Roderick Mackenzie had grown up together on the Isle of Lewis, run the red deer through the gorse, caught salmon in the burns, sailed offshore in small craft when northeasters slammed down from Cape Wrath upon the Minch. He and his cousin were Rory and Alex to each other, closely bound by family ties and the intense loyalty of the Highland clan relationship.

When Rory Mackenzie arrived, the cousins built an elaborate structure on the shore of Lake Athabasca. They chose the site where Peter Pond's old trading post had stood, and the Connecticut man was with them while the work was done. The Mackenzies put up a formidable fort protected by blockhouses at each corner and surrounded by a high stockade. Their name for it was Fort Chipewayan, and it was soon famous.

Rory Mackenzie had brought a large collection of books from Montreal, some his own choice and the others ordered by his cousin. Alexander Mackenzie told the other Athabasca traders about them, offered use of the books. But the men preferred rum and solitude, and the library was mainly of a technical character. It was chosen to give all possible knowledge about the Northwest Passage, and narratives of various voyages of discovery by Drake, Gilbert and Dampier were included.

Peter Pond passed the winter of 1778–79 with the Mackenzies at Fort Chipewayan. The veteran trader had in his possession a copy of Captain James Cook's voyages, and he had spent months making a map of the High Country. He was greatly excited by what he believed to be his discovery of the Northwest Passage route. Striding back and forth in the flare of firelight in the main hall of the fort, tapping his map for emphasis, and glaring from time to time at the pair of Scots, motionless in their chairs, he said that he was ready to send it to Empress Catherine of Russia.

She should have the information he had gathered, Pond said. The Russians were at least making some sort of effort to explore the Bering Sea region and find the Northwest Passage. While nothing was done by the English—or the Scots.

Pond stood still and gazed at Alexander Mackenzie. The tough, scarred, squint-eyed Connecticut Yankee was suddenly a very dramatic figure, and in his voice were unconcealed sadness, and jealousy. He was too old, he said. He was fifty. There were behind him too many years of war, marching, paddling, hauling and carousing. He could not lead a party out to the Pacific Coast and bring it back safe. But Alexander Mackenzie could.

Mackenzie accepted the challenge. He doubted the validity of Pond's sense of distance. The Yankee lacked knowledge of latitude and longitude, and any kind of astronomy. But Mackenzie recognized that a search for the Northwest Passage must be made without further delay and, if that failed, an overland route to the Pacific discovered. The sea-otter trade on the coast and the activities of the Hudson's Bay Company very gravely threatened the Northwest Company. It must expand to survive, and the only way it could go was west.

Mackenzie spent most of the winter in preparation for the voyage. He left Chipewayan right after dawn on June 2, 1789, and with a flotilla of three canoes manned by Indian hunters started north. Rory Mackenzie was in command at the fort, ordered musket volleys to be fired as a good-luck salute by the garrison.

Mosquitoes in brown thick swarms met the flotilla on Great Slave Lake, and the canoes butted between chunks of floe ice. Caribou shot by the party's hunters gave fresh meat, and berries were gathered along the banks of the river that led north from the vast lake.

The river was north-flowing, and the canoe work easy. But on the morning of July 2nd, staring across the tundra waste on his left hand, Mackenzie saw among cloud the serried ridges of a mountain range whose crests were snow-covered. They reached unbrokenly all along the western horizon. These were the Rocky Mountains, and Mackenzie knew that the Northwest Passage belonged only in dream. The possibility that a river ran from here into what Peter Pond called "Cook's Inlet" was also illusion.

Mackenzie kept on, though. He took an observation that established his position at 69.7 degrees north, 200 miles above the Arctic Circle. The party went past the mouth of the Great Bear River. Then, on July 12th the three canoes, still in single file, river style, entered the Arctic Ocean and began to buck the onshore rollers.

The party spent three days in the open ocean. Mackenzie felt a tremendous exhilaration. He chased whales, explored the coastal islands, made estimates of the tides. Still, he was saddened by the memory of Peter Pond's often repeated prophecy that men would go to "Unalaska, and so to Kamskatka, and thence to England through Russia." The canoe crews had become unhappy, too. They explained that they thought birchbark craft were not right for hunting whale, and that the Eskimos on the coast and the Indians who lived along the river were both known as cannibals.

Mackenzie gave the order to head back upriver for Fort Chipewayan. He named the river Disappointment. But he was determined to continue with his exploration, find a westward route to the coast. He had learned enough on this voyage to make him believe that it was feasible if the mountain range was approached further south.

He got back to Fort Chipewayan 102 days after his departure. His cousin and Peter Pond conducted most of the affairs of the post during the next few months. He was busy transcribing the notes from his journal and making a new map. Then, at the end of the summer, when the annual meeting of the Northwest Company was held at Fort Grand Portage, he reported to the assembled partners.

He was eloquent, and spoke at length. The partners were told that he had discovered and explored the second-largest river, after the Mississippi, in North America. He had gone in ordinary birchbark canoe through 3,000 miles of wilderness, traversed country occupied by cannibalistic tribes, entered the Arctic Ocean, and returned without serious incident or injury.

The partners sat in rows on benches in the Great Hall of Fort Grand Portage. Their thoughts were occupied by profit percentages. A keg of gunpowder that cost two dollars in London was sold for $140 here, and possibly the mark-up could be increased. With the termination of this meeting, the hall would be turned into a space for trade with the tribes. Mackenzie's report made sense perhaps, but what he said did not press, and was something to be considered later.

Mackenzie restrained his anger. The treatment given him by his partners only heightened his resolve to go back to Scotland. He was not through with the Northwest Company. But he was going to take a course in practical navigation. When he had mastered the subject, he would head west and find that overland route.

The attempt was made the next year, in the fall of 1792, right after Mackenzie had returned to Fort Chipewayan. Time was of extreme importance because of the mounting competition, and he was determined to go as far west as possible before winter stopped him. He left the post in charge of Rory Mackenzie and Peter Pond, took his party up the Peace River from Lake Athabasca. They were all veteran High Country men and formed the crew for a single canoe.

But a week out of Chipewayan, still in early October, they found ice at dawn in the river. Mackenzie kept driving them upstream for three weeks more. The calculations he had performed at home in Scotland while he was planning this voyage had shown him that Chipewayan was no more than 900 miles from the Pacific Coast. He had no accurate idea, though, of the distance overland, following the meanderings of rivers, lakes and portages.

He chose to pass the winter where the Smoky River joined the Peace. It was already so cold that axe blades shattered when swung against wood. The party lived precariously in tents and lean-tos until the stockade was built and the cabins roofed, fully chinked and equipped with chimneys.

The winter passed without incident, and a new canoe was built during the first clement days of spring. It was a typical High Country craft, made from a single piece of birchbark stretched over a white-cedar frame. The bow was raised and curved in traditional style, and Mackenzie reckoned the craft would serve the expedition for at least 1,000 miles of hard going. He wrote in his journal that two men could carry her three or four miles over good terrain without a halt.

He started the party west again on May 9, 1793, the river running with wild force. The canoe carried almost 3,000 pounds of cargo, including the crew of nine men and Mackenzie's mongrel dog. There was very little freeboard, and she began to leak badly. The crew, all French Canadian *voyageurs* except the second-in-command, a young Highland Scot named Alexander Mackay, asked to beach the canoe.

Mackenzie gave the order, and the *voyageurs* tightened and re-caulked the seams. Then the voyage continued steadily, through grassy prairie land where elk and buffalo grazed by the thousands. The party emerged from that into tremendous forest, and to the westward the peaks of the Rockies were visible.

The men were forced to haul the canoe, wading chest-deep, or using block and tackle from the bank. They had climbed so high that ice formed in the kettle at night, and to breathe was painful. The portage work demanded their last reserves of strength. Mackay, witty and gay, and a favorite among them, became short-spoken with fatigue, and Mackenzie's orders were obeyed in silence.

But then, in a deep valley, they came to the headwaters of the Peace River. It ended in a pond surrounded by meadow. Ducks, swans and geese were on the pond, and the supper ration was increased. The men regained their spirit. This, Mackenzie told them, was the Great Divide. They were the first white men to reach it.

The party kept on west the next day along a nameless river. There were many portages, many more than the Indian guides had indicated. The canoe was swept out of control in a rapids, and a very precious piece of cargo, the keg that held the musket balls, was lost. But nothing would turn Mackenzie back now that they had crossed the divide.

A frame was built from saplings to protect the canoe, and it was cross-lashed, and dragged. But it was so badly battered that after a few days' march further west it was abandoned. A new one was built, and that also was left behind, placed high on a platform to keep it safe from bears.

The party had entered tangled, almost impenetrable forest, and rain was continuous. The single ration was pemmican, and there was not much of that. Mackenzie wrote in his journal, "In short, our situation was such as to afford us just cause for alarm."

The rain stopped, though, and the Indians they met were friendly. The Indians said it was only a short march—three days—to the river that led to the sea. Mackenzie started the men forward once more, their progress very slow, their feet swollen by the unaccustomed marching.

Then, below them, across the sweep of forest, they saw the river. This was the Bella Coola. It curved through a wide green plain towards the sea. An Indian village was on the nearest bank, and smoke rose in straight pillars from the broad stone chimneys of the houses.

The party reached the village after dark. The men were lame, barely able to walk. Mackenzie halted them outside it, went on by himself. Dogs barked and sniffed at him. Squaws stared up from fires where they roasted salmon on greenwood spits. Then he was in front of a house that was raised high above the ground on posts. A notched log served as a ladder.

Mackenzie still carried his pack, slung from his shoulders. A sword that he had brought from Scotland was at his left hip. He had a pistol in his belt. But he went into the house with his hands at his sides, away from the weapons.

The house was reserved for the village warriors, and there was just this single, long, and smoke-filled room. A number of fires burned, set among stones on the floor. The warriors gathered at the fires looked up at Mackenzie. He was holding out his hand to each of them in turn.

His blond hair lay thick, matted with bugs and shreds of bark, on his shoulders. He was gaunt, and his cheekbones were prominent. His moccasins flapped around his ankles, the soles torn loose. But the warriors returned his greeting. The chief of the tribe made Mackenzie understand that his name was Soocomlick, and that the Scot should sit down and eat.

Mackenzie later called that place Friendly Village. The party restored its strength there, and, in a pair of big, high-bowed dugout canoes offered by Soocomlick, kept going downriver to the sea. They left the village on July 18th, and four days later Mackenzie took out his theodolite, his chronometer and journal. He made his observation with extreme care, then marked on the shore side of the boulder he had used as a base:

ALEXANDER MACKENZIE, FROM CAN-
ADA, BY LAND, THE TWENTY-SECOND
OF JULY, ONE THOUSAND SEVEN
HUNDRED AND NINETY-THREE

Mackenzie and his party got back in good shape to Chipewayan. He left it for Montreal, London and Edinburgh. He was an international celebrity, famous as the man who had found the "Western Sea," and King George III knighted him. One of the most beautiful women in Scotland, an heiress, married him, and he was wealthy in his own right.

But he broke from his partners in the Northwest Company. Their thinking remained static and narrow, and he joined the opposition. The company later failed, and Peter Pond, jobless, an old man, got out of the High Country. He was still suspected of having murdered two competitors in the early days. He went home to Connecticut and died very poor, almost forgotten. Right until the end, though, he claimed that his wealthy friend, Mackenzie, had not discovered the real overland route to the Pacific.

That must wait for another, even luckier man.

202

## 13

I<small>T WAS A GENTLE RIVER NAMED THE</small> P<small>ERKIOMEN.</small>
The name was Indian, he knew, and the name of the nearby
river, the Schuylkill, was Dutch. The largest in the region, which was
wide-flowing and went to the sea, was named for Lord de la Warr. The
early English had done well here in Pennsylvania, and the local grist-mill
had once belonged to William Penn.

History did not mean much to John James Audubon, though. He
knew about the river names, and the fact that his father's estate was
called Mill Grove because of the grist-mill, and with that his curiosity
stopped. He had seen fine and great rivers in France, particularly the
Loire at Nantes, where he had been raised and first became interested in
birds.

The valley of the Perkiomen in spring had more species than the
Loire. Audubon pursued them from dawn until after darkness. This was
1803, and he was almost eighteen, still in many respects he was boyish. He

was alone at Mill Grove except for the caretaker couple, a staid pair of Quakers. So he spent as much time as possible away from the property, was delighted by the river.

The Perkiomen broke pale and clear over limestone ledges. It surged about the roots of the giant elms and formed pools, and fish came there from downstream to spawn. Ospreys, known locally as fish hawks, followed them. The hawks waited high up, drifting very slowly with the wind, for the wind and sun conditions to be right. Then they dived, the fish in silhouette against the dark river bottom.

Audubon secured fish-hawk specimens. He measured and sketched them, but without much success. He was more fortunate with a family of phoebes he discovered. The beautiful little birds lived in a limestone cavern under the steep river bank. He reached it by sliding down the bank and hanging onto the trunks of trees. His motions afterwards were gradual, and subdued; he did not wish to alarm the birds.

The parent phoebes worked at building the nest, delicately adding bits of lichen, moss and grass. Audubon moved close and inspected it. There were six white, red-speckled eggs. He deftly picked up the fledglings, kept them on the palm of his hand for several minutes with no complaint from the parents.

Still, his sketches of various specimens were unsatisfactory. He made hundreds and threw them all away in disappointment. Then he shot a kingfisher, and experimented with it. He passed wires through the body, fixed the body to a board, and found the method which he used during his entire career.

Audubon took time off from his ornithological studies to go to local parties. He was broad-shouldered and handsome, tanned by the summer sun, and wore excellent clothes he had brought from France. His French accent, his ability to perform the intricate dances with grace, and the fact that his father, Captain Jean Audubon, was the absentee owner of the valuable Mill Grove property, were enough to make him attractive. He was very popular among the valley belles, but he soon chose a favorite.

She was Lucy Bakewell, the sixteen-year-old daughter of a neighbor. Her father was William Bakewell, a wealthy English emigrant who

John J. Audubon

had bought Fatland Ford. It was a huge white mansion with tall columns, set near Mill Grove on a ridge. Lucy's brothers went skating that winter on the river with Audubon, and sometimes she and other girls accompanied the boys.

Audubon towed Lucy on a small sledge. Her cheeks were bright with the cold, and her dark brown hair blew loose in the wind as Audubon skated fast. He bent hard to the sledge rope, his curl-toed skates leaving long, regular marks on the smooth ice, hearing the creak of the sledge runners, the rhythmic stroke of his skates, and the cries, the squeals of false alarm from the girls in the rest of the group.

Audubon and Lucy kept to themselves. He took her to see the cavern where the phoebes had lived. When Lucy visited Mill Grove with her parents, he proudly showed them his bird paintings. It was quite obvious to the Bakewells that their daughter was deeply in love, and they approved of the match with one major reservation. John James Audubon had no way of making a living, and no skill or knowledge beyond that in ornithology.

William Bakewell advised the young man to go home to France and talk with Captain Audubon about the advisability of marriage. Then he corresponded with the captain. The senior Audubon was a hard-headed man who had started to sea when he was twelve, retired to a life of comfort at his home outside Nantes. When John James arrived, he listened to him at length. He was willing to help finance the marriage to Lucy, he told his son, and wrote to that effect to William Bakewell.

John James returned elated to Pennsylvania. He brought along with him a young French friend, Ferdinand Rozier, who was supposed to become his partner in a trading firm on the frontier. But Lucy's father was not satisfied with the arrangement. He put Audubon to work in his counting-house in New York until he absolutely despaired of Audubon's ability to perform the work of a common clerk.

Audubon took what money he could get from his father and went west with Rozier. They bought general merchandise and planned to open a store in Louisville, which was almost completely a French settlement. It was still a small town when they reached it in the autumn of 1807, coming down by keelboat along the Ohio. There was a ready market for the merchandise, and they sold it quite easily in Louisville and the surrounding countryside.

Audubon had proven that he could support Lucy and himself. He went east, and on June 12, 1808, they were married. Audubon was impatient to get back to the frontier, and he and Lucy left Fatland Ford the morning after the ceremony.

They moved by public carriage along the rutted, stump-littered, often deeply mired roads that thousands of settlers used. The big, iron-shod wheels banged against rocks. Horses neighed and whinnied as whips were applied. Most of the rigs were the gaily painted and graceful Conestoga wagons. The boatlike bodies had red sideboards. The running gear was blue, and the protective covers, arched high on wooden bows above the bodies, were of tightly drawn white canvas. Whole families rode in the Conestogas—mothers nursing babies, older daughters taking care of younger, boys with the stock or helping their fathers with the teams.

John James Audubon, who was much more artist than anything else, was intensely excited by the vigor, the turmoil and the always changing composition of the spectacle. He marked in his memory the trip from Lancaster that led to the Susquehanna. The cupola of the courthouse at Harrisburg gleamed rotund and white. The Juniata, where the cumbersome carriage splashed through the ford with the floorboards awash, was a dark blue, the color of slate. Then, after the team had been halted several times for a breather on the upward slope, the road swung down over the great ridge.

This, John James told his bride, was the Blue Ridge. There, below, was the first of the real western country. Stands of hickory, hackberry and sugarberry grew at the roadside. Ravens coursed slowly on long slants in the valley breeze. The streams that spilled gleaming down the mountainside became rivers on the valley floor, widened as they reached towards the west.

The Monongahela was the next river, and after it the Allegheny. There was so much smoke and noise and confusion in Pittsburgh that Audubon told Lucy he was willing to leave it right away. The combined odor came from breweries, glassworks, forges, furnaces, stables and boatyards. Bituminous coal gave a tang to stale manure and wet lumber. Boat-

207

men in red-flannel shirts, wide-brimmed black hats and butternut pants stuffed into cowhide boots gave enthusiastic support to the tavern trade near the wharves. Audubon knew the type. He went into a tavern and made a deal for transportation for Lucy and himself to Louisville.

It was aboard a flatboat. They boarded with their luggage, then waited for the crew. The Monongahela, here in the flat bottom land at Pittsburgh, furnished the town with a floating population of several thousand people. Scores of boats, all of them occupied, were tied up alongside each other. Men fished. Women washed clothes. Boys swam, ducked their sisters, pushed old skiffs with poles, collected driftwood for the cooking done in sand-boxes out on deck.

Audubon was fascinated. He brought forth his sketchbook and drew the scene. He was, with only partial knowledge of it, a profoundly devoted river man. He was already explaining to Lucy the various kinds of boats and the purposes they served.

The barges were as big as Atlantic Coast schooners, with a length that often reached a hundred feet and a twenty-foot beam. They were really big floating boxes, with a shedlike structure over most of the length where the cargo was carried. This kind of craft needed twenty-five hands to work her upstream against the current. Three, four months were taken to make the return journey from New Orleans to the upper Ohio. Their cargo load was around fifty tons, and they hauled bales of furs, powder, lead, flour, pork, ironwork, textiles, and Monongahela whiskey. Headed back upriver, they brought coffee, sugar and merchandise of French manufacture for the markets at Saint Geneviève and St. Louis, the Ohio and its branches.

The keelboat was a faster craft. Her design was long, slender and elegant. She was built of local timber, usually at Pittsburgh, for a price of between two and three thousand dollars. Her hull was smoothly planked, and her general length was sixty feet, with cargo space for fifteen to thirty tons. The keel ran the full length of the boat, and she had a fifteen-to-eighteen-foot beam and three- or four-foot depth of hold. Her ordinary draft was from twenty to thirty inches.

208 The keelboat was the great cargo-carrier on all of the inland rivers. She was designed to navigate easily in shallow water during the summer season. Keelboats were used far up the Missouri, and in many

The Jolly Flatboatmen in Port, by George C. Bingham

of the Mississippi and Ohio tributaries. She had a big deckhouse, called a cargo box, that took two-thirds of her length and offered shelter to the crew in bad weather.

A keelboat needed a much larger crew than the other river craft. Forty men were an average complement for an upriver trip with cargo aboard. She was equipped with every propulsion device except steam. The cordelle, a manila-hemp hawser nearly 1,000 feet long, was used most of the time to move her.

One end of the cordelle was secured to the top of the thirty-foot mast, located at the center of the boat. The cordelle was then led down to the fore deck and attached to a bridle at the bow. The bridle kept the boat from swinging too far out from shore while she was in motion. The cordelle was passed through a large iron ring in the bow of the boat after being connected to the bridle. Then it was taken ashore and handled by most of the men of the crew.

They hauled the boat against the current by brute strength. The bridle was also supposed to keep the bow off the bank, but often failed to do that. The boat yawed inshore, and although the cordelle led from high on the mast and had great length, it fouled on tree limbs and among bushes. There was no regular towpath because of the changing conditions of the river bank. Men called bushwhackers went ahead with axes and cutlasses and cleared the way. Outer clothing was discarded during the summer months. Men worked in breechclouts, smeared with mud as protection from flies, gnats, mosquitoes.

When the bank was too rough for the crew to work in concerted effort, the shore end of the cordelle was secured to a tall and strong tree. All of the men except the bushwhackers boarded the boat and heaved in the hawser with the crude capstan at the bow, or hauled the boat ahead, hand over hand. The bushwhackers shifted the cordelle as the boat came abeam, and took it to another tree, or the crew waded ashore and hauled from there. This maneuver was called warping. It very quickly exhausted weak men, and they either left the crew or asked for work as cooks, without pay.

The captain, a man called *patron* in French Canadian style, steered the boat at all times. He stood aft on a pedestal high enough to let him see forward over the cargo box and handle the long stern sweep. The sweep blade was fixed to a stout pole that was set in a crotch at the stern of the boat, with the inboard end resting on the cargo-box roof. The *patron* needed a considerable amount of strength to move the sweep, and he leaned on it hard.

The *patron* gave few orders while the cordelle work was being performed. A major part of the responsibility for the movement of the boat was taken by the bow man, called in French a *bosseman*—a boatswain's mate. He was as physically powerful as the *patron*, and just about as river-wise.

210

The *bosseman* watched the river for snags, sandbars, cross-currents and driftwood that might do the craft harm. He also helped steer the boat by keeping her off the bank with a sharp-ended pole. The cordelle groaned and creaked and vibrated with strain right beside his head, and he had the duty of telling the crew to slack off before the mast snapped, or the hawser, which in all probability would behead him.

There were many stretches along the river where neither form of cordelle work moved a boat. Sandbars and shallows kept her too far offshore, or the bank mud was too deep for the men to negotiate to reach the bank. When the wind was fair, and this was true once or twice a week on average, the sail was set. It contained about 100 square feet of canvas, and was set on a stubby spar rigged across the mast. Men who had been in New Orleans and picked up salt-water ship talk called it a squaresail rig.

When there was no wind, long oars were used, three or four to each side of the boat. But they were often unable to move the boat because of mud and sandbars. The *patron* gave the order to get out the poles.

Warping a keelboat.

Poling was the hardest form of river work. It was slow, monotonous, and literally back-breaking. The poles were manufactured from ashwood in large quantities in St. Louis. One end was fashioned into a broad knob to fit in the hollow of a man's shoulder, and on the other was a wooden socket or shoe that was thrust against the river bottom.

A cleated walkway called a *passavant* was built on each side of the cargo box and reached the full length. No less than ten men lined up on the walkways, facing aft, and waiting for the order from the *patron*. When he called *"À bas les perches!"* they set the poles on the river bottom near the boat, the poles inclined aft. They pushed in unison, forcing the boat ahead and gradually walking aft. They bent nearly double over the poles, and reached down and caught the cleats, pulled themselves along while the upper ends of the poles rammed into shoulder bones and muscles.

The *patron* called, *"Levez les perches!"* as the first man came to the final cleat. The poles were raised; stumbling, gasping, the men turned and went forward, once more began to thrust against the bottom. The *patron* took advantage of the brief period of time while the poles were out of the water and momentum carried the boat forward. He steered her shrewdly into the least of the current, kept her as much as possible from the stubborn clasp of the mud.

Lucy Audubon, new to the western rivers, watched the effort of an upbound keelboat crew with a sense of shock. The mud-slathered men pulled themselves along the walkways almost on their knees. Their hair fell lank, filthy, to their shoulders, framed their haggard faces and fatigue-dulled eyes. Muscles knotted upon shoulders, backs, arms and legs, made the nearly naked bodies ugly. No men, she knew, had ever worked harder than this, not the slaves in the Phoenician and Roman galleys, nor the Barbary Coast captives. Yet these men fiercely maintained the boast that they were wholly free, lived as they wished.

Audubon had taken passage for Lucy and himself aboard a flatboat. The popular name was a Kentucky broadhorn, and in reality the craft was a huge raft securely lashed with chains. Several structures built of logs and planks were along the deck and were comfortably furnished. The Audubons had their own, with a broad bunk filled with spruce boughs, a table, chairs, and a fireplace. Downbound, the crew were

*"A bas les perches!"*

given little work, rowed occasionally to clear an island or get around a bend, the rest of the time lounged on deck, fished, whittled, wrestled, played cards and slept in the spring sun.

Life for them, Lucy had surmised, was a good deal like that spent by gypsies. The crew were river nomads. But her husband had told her that in New Orleans the raft would be sold, broken up for sale as lumber. The men, all of whom were from the upper rivers, would either go home overland, taking three months or four to the march, or join keelboat crews.

The sounds of that last keelboat crew's passage were still in her ears. There was the gasping, the groaning, as breath was inhaled. Then the *patron* called, his voice like the punctuation of an uncoiled whip: *"À bas les perches! Levez les perches! À bas—"*

Audubon told her that the crews were originally of French Canadian *voyageur* stock. The men who came after them were Creoles, of

Raftsmen Playing Cards,
by George C. Bingham

French and Spanish blood, born and raised in the Mississippi Valley. With the early 1800s, they were being supplanted by men who were from Kentucky, Ohio, Illinois and Arkansas. That lot were English-speaking, and just as tough as the Creole or French Canadian breed. They gave river men a bad reputation from New Orleans to Pittsburgh, and beyond.

They quite invariably sought trouble when they had tied up their boats for the night and went ashore in a river town. The champion fighter in each crew wore a red feather in his hat band as a challenge. He and his companions were armed with bowie knives and a jug or two of Monongahela. They refreshed themselves further in the town taverns, which they called doggeries. When drinking and boasting bored them, they started a fight.

The fights were either "fair" or "rough and tumble." Champions preferred the rough-and-tumble variety. They stopped only when one of the contestants was maimed or disfigured for life. Eyes were gouged, ears torn off, noses ripped, and jaw contours changed by the heels of hobnailed boots.

Audubon cited for Lucy the famous cry of challenge made by a river man as he sprang ashore, "Whoo-oop! I'm the old original iron-jawed, brass-mounted, copper-bellied corpsemaker from the wilds of Arkansas! Lay low and hold your breath, for I'm about to turn myself loose!"

Audubon and several of the senior members of the crew told her about Mike Fink, the river men's great hero. Mike Fink was supposed to have been slow-spoken, patient, but enormously strong, and an Indian fighter in his youth, and a crack shot. His estimate of himself was "half-man, half-alligator, and chock full of fight." During the years he served as a keelboat man, he fought his way in and out of every tavern along the Mississippi. His woman, also of prodigious strength and very beautiful, was called Pittsburgh Blue.

For Pittsburgh Blue first, and then for anybody who had the equanimity to stand and watch, Fink shot a cup of whiskey off the head of a trusting companion. Fink's aim became erratic finally, and he killed his companion. He left the keelboat trade and went far up the Missouri, worked as a fur-trapper. But the best friend of the man he had killed finally found him, and shot him.

The end of the story about Fink was true, Audubon explained to Lucy. There were many told about the man, though, which were completely imaginary, and recently, here on the Ohio, a visiting clergyman from the east had been badly fooled. An old-time river man told the visitor that he had known Mike Fink well. The clergyman was curious; he asked the keelboater if he remembered any peculiar incidents of Fink's life.

The keelboater said he could recall one. There was the occasion when Mike Fink had eaten a buffalo robe. The clergyman showed a little surprise. "With the hair on?"

"Certainly, with the hair on," the keelboater said. "Y'see, Mike drank so much whiskey he ruined the lining of his stomach. Doctor told him he needed a new coat for it to get himself in shape again. Mike figgered that when he had a new coat for his stomach, he'd get one that wouldn't mind the whiskey. A buffalo robe with the hair on it was the exact thing. So he took a good long breath, and he swallowed it. He could drink all the whiskey he wanted after that, and never even belch."    215

According to the man who had given him the story, Audubon said, the clergyman who heard it from the old-timer accepted it as fact.

The Audubons had long hours to pass in conversation. The broad-horn moved slowly down the Ohio, the speed three or four miles an hour. It was a 600-mile trip to Louisville, and the young couple recognized that they would pass weeks aboard, were relaxed, took keen delight from the beauty of the river valley in early summer.

Sunlight made the water shimmer, and sent glints of reflection from the sheer blue of the surface over the yellow-green willow fronds on the banks. The smell of the honey locusts and the lindens pervaded the valley. The tall lindens were in bloom. Bees moved in bright flight across the river from tree to tree. Their hum was met by the cackle of chickens, the lowing of cattle aboard the flatboats which formed part of the traffic around the craft that carried the Audubons.

There was an almost unbroken procession of various kinds of boats, everything from a ten-foot skiff to a stately barge that resembled a barn and took up just as much room in the fairway. Dugout canoes appeared from creeks. Craft called "covered sleds" or "ferry flats" drew abeam and went ahead, propelled by men who pulled industriously at long oars. Some of those, the *patron* in command of the broadhorn said, hauled as much as twelve tons of cargo, but were not built for it. They had no more freeboard than a frying pan, and would sink in the first heavy squall.

But the Audubons had become accustomed to the exaggerated statements made by river men. Their tranquility was unaffected, and they sat by themselves a great deal during the daylight hours, just gazing out over the Ohio. The warm, scented wind touched Lucy's sunburned face, and moved Audubon's long locks on his shoulders. The river wound through lush, green bottom land that rose gently to hills that lay under cloud shadow. The steep flanks of islands were marked by masses of driftwood, and the steersman shouted an order, lifted his long horn.

The two men stationed at the bow set themselves and pulled their oars in unison. The bow swung, and neatly, despite the length, the breadth, was brought into the current that would take the craft clear of the island. The low, repeated notes sounded by the steersman on the broad-mouthed tin horn warned other *patrons* of his action.

216

The raft entered the smooth inshore current below the island. The Audubons sat back. But Audubon explained to Lucy in detail the maneuver which had just been performed. He pointed out to her among the driftwood tangle of the next island the wreckage of several boats, the ribs and planks skeletal.

An island like that, he said, was called a towhead by river men. The usual pile-up happened when a *patron* tried to keep going at night, or in a squall. Those over there, the green-slimed tree branches that jerked into sight, then disappeared, only to jerk rapidly above the surface again, were called sawyers. They stayed out of sight for minutes at a time, and a steersman might easily think his boat moved through clear water. A sawyer could punch a hole through the hull of a keelboat, tear apart a broadhorn's lashings. Still, the other common kind of snag, which stayed stationary beneath the surface and was called a planter, was just as dangerous.

Audubon was intensely interested in the lore of the rivers. He found on the Ohio the sources of the knowledge he needed in his chosen field of ornithology. The broadhorn drifted past groves of sycamore and hornbeam, and canebrakes and meadows where he saw scarlet-marked grosbeaks, then thrushes whose melodies rang pulsant over the water. When it was almost dusk, the *patron* took the boat into shore, and Audubon heard and saw owls, and quick-wheeling bats.

There was still the threat of pirates on the river, and the people who rode the boats gathered together at night whenever possible. Several boats tied up at the same point on the bank, and camps were made. The Audubons slept covered by buffalo robes in rude tents, the firelight high and the sentry's tread steady.

Audubon was out of the tent by dawn, and in the forest. He was the hunter for his party. With the grace he had learned along the Perkiomen, he moved through the mist that clung close to the ground on the deer runs. His targets were the proudly strutting but extremely smart wild turkeys, and partridge and pigeon. He used his excellently made French rifle, too, when a raccoon reared up at a creek bank. The raccoon had been busy scooping turtle eggs from the sandy creek bottom, was replete, and a bit careless.

The shots warned the forest. Moving back towards the boat, 217 Audubon saw no other game except a wildcat high up in a black oak. The beast's eyes were tight-squinted, gleamed like those of a rattlesnake, and the ears lay flat to the skull, the hair at the base of the neck was raised in rage. Audubon moved faster; he had no curiosity about wildcats. He stopped only long enough on the river bank to shoot a brace of wood ducks, then he rejoined the boat and Lucy.

The crew added to the rations during the day. They sat on deck and fished, poles slanted over the side, and seemingly asleep beside them. But they were quick to act when a big catfish struck at the bait. White perch offered more of a fight. The brilliantly colored sunfish claimed Audubon's attention as they were swung flopping aboard. Their scales shone in a coruscation of silver, green and gold. The fishermen considered the sunfish to be the best catch. They carefully baited the bent-nail hooks on their hickory or hazel poles after they had brought one aboard, boasted about immediately catching another.

Lucy was impressed by the childish qualities of the boat men. She compared what she saw exhibited here aboard the broadhorn with what was exposed in the river towns when the Monongahela jugs were emptied, and the taverns invaded. She had seen screaming, knife-wielding men stagger through the light of pine-knot torches at a tavern door, their intestines held up into the torn flesh. They were champions, wore the red feather, went back to renew the fight, kill, or be killed.

Audubon, an immensely strong man, had sometimes been forced to intercede when one of the raft crew was getting his brains kicked out on the wharf planks. The crew respected him, listened to him, but there were strangers whose pride and reckless anger were kindled to homicidal fury by the fact alone that he was so strong. They wanted to contest against him, show their prowess, with a knife, a piece of cordwood, or their boot heels.

Audubon smiled when Lucy expressed her fear. He could take care of himself, he told her. The river men were *beaux garçons*, his friends. He understood, though, the reasons for her trepidation. He and Lucy often discussed the complex, difficult character of the river men, and later in his career, when he had spent years among them, he wrote of their problems with great sensitivity. He shared part of their urges and needs, and felt a close, common bond.

The river men belonged to the frontier in the same fashion as Davy Crockett or Daniel Boone. They disliked if they did not violently hate organized society. Beyond the mountains to the east were cities with paved streets and thousands of inhabitants, factories, and foundries, mills, schools, churches. While they were scornful of the fragments of the Indian tribes still to be found along the rivers, and of the Negroes who were about to take their work away from them, they were inferior in nearly all respects to the real frontiersmen.

Some of them, for big pay incentives and free whiskey, ventured in keelboats up the Missouri from St. Louis as far as the Yellowstone. Most of their number stayed in the Mississippi Valley. They were like catfish, a fur brigade veteran said. Take a river man away from Mississippi mud, and he died, then stunk.

The river men were completely dependent upon the civilization they despised. Their work inevitably linked them to it. The main route they followed, upriver, downriver, was Pittsburgh to New Orleans, with St. Louis as a stop-over, and all three were rapidly growing cities. So the boasts, the fights, the insensate brutality and the compulsive drinking had their source in fear.

The river men were profoundly afraid. Their single possession was their strength. When that was gone, they were finished. A hernia wrenched by the labor on the *passavant,* a hand broken in a doggery fight, syphilis picked up from a New Orleans whore or at Natchez-under-the-hill, those were sufficient. Then a man stayed ashore, and slowly starved. For a time, he could make out, fishing on the town levees, helping load a bit of cargo, and begging. But there were always more men, quicker, smarter, and ruthless, who took away what could be made that way. The answer afterwards was simple. It was the river on a dark night, with nobody around to try to help a drowning man.

The crew of the broadhorn the Audubons rode seemed gay, almost without worry of any sort. The weather was idyllic. Sunlit days spread into star-paled nights. The names of the rivers in the narrow valleys that were passed became steadily less familiar to Lucy. Among them were the Kenawha, the Muskingum and the Hockhocking. The towns that were left astern were Marietta, Gallipolis and Cincinnati. The moon shone full, and the *patron* decided to keep under way after darkness.

Audubon was intoxicated by the beauty of the night. He got out

219

his flute, and with Lucy beside him sat on a bench on the roof of the main cabin. All of the boatmen except the pair at the oars and the steersman at the stern sweep were instantly attracted by the sweet, shrill sound of the flute. They came up onto the cabin roof and began to dance.

It was jigging, heel and toe and away we go, in their heavy-soled boots. They clapped hands as they danced, and took partners, and Lucy rose and was a partner, around and around. Audubon stopped to get his breath. The boatmen sang while they waited for him. This was their most famous chantey:

> Some row up but we row down
>     All the way to Shawneetown—
> Pull away! Pull away!
>     Pull away to Shawneetown!

The voices, rough and yet true, carried over the water through the moon shafts, returned in echo from the dark shore, and the crew sang the second verse:

> Hard upon the beech oar!
>     She moves too slow,
> All the way to Shawneetown
>     A long time ago.

The dancing continued until almost dawn, and without alcohol. Audubon was reminded of a fact that he pondered much more when he was able to reflect fully upon his river years. The highest approbation that a river man received was to be called a "hoss," which meant he was extraordinarily strong, and brave. But Mike Fink was supposed to have said about a river man's chances of survival:

"I've seen trout swallow a perch, and a cat would come along and swallow the trout, and perhaps, on the Mississippi, the alligators use up the cat, and so on to the end of the row."

220 The faint, constant rumor of the falls of the Ohio told the Audubons that the boat was approaching Louisville. The voyage was almost finished. They collected their belongings and stood on the main-

cabin roof and watched the bluish-gray loom of the Silver Hills emerge from the chimney smoke that formed a brown thick cloud over Louisville. The *patron* shoved hard on the steering sweep; the broadhorn swerved from the river into Beargrass Creek. The wide mouth of the creek gave mooring space for many boats. This was the transshipment point for the lower river. Cargo was portaged three or four miles around the falls to Shippingport and reloaded there for the Mississippi run.

Lucy Audubon looked around her in fascination. Nothing that her husband had told her or that she had seen was preparation for this. Louisville was part of the frontier. Hunters in buckskin carrying rifles, tomahawks and skinning knives slouched past among blanketed Indians who Audubon said were Osages, Creeks, Chickasaws. There were traders who wore expensive beaver hats and many-pleated shirts, the butts of a pair of pistols in their trouser waistbands. Back-country farmers whose boots were clotted with red mire drove skinny, fly-pesked horses, rifles in one hand, whips in the other, their wives and daughters crouched on the wagon seats, homespun shortgowns close about their knees. The farmer folks stared furtively, almost defiantly at the crowded street. They, like the hunters, were alien here, belonged to the wilderness.

The Audubons went to stay at the very popular tavern called Indian Queen. The open courtyard in front of the log-walled building was filled with guests who sought to get to the water pump. Wagoners and pack-train men fed their animals at the stable door, forked hay from the loft, measured oats, tended harness galls.

There was a corn-husk mattress on the bed in the room the Audubons were told to occupy, and the sheets were calico. The usual procedure for Indian Queen guests, Audubon told Lucy, was for four, six, sometimes eight people to share the same bed. But Audubon's bulky shoulders, his firm glance of denial, and a few words were enough to allow the couple to keep the bed to themselves. Her husband, Lucy realized, was what river men spoke of as a "hoss," and would continue to take care of her without much trouble.

Despite its frontier aspects, the Audubons found Louisville contained a sophisticated and cultured group of people. French *émigrés*, 221 driven from their homes a few years before by the Terror and threat of the guillotine, had settled in the town or in nearby Shippingport. They tried to the best of their ability to restore the qualities of the life they had known in France. It was a recent experience for many of the local citizens to look in wonder at the window glass used by General George Rogers Clark in his home at Mulberry Hill. Now, the French families had established an elegance that included formal calls, evenings of dancing and music. Fine clothing was worn. The homes were furnished with pieces that did not come from France, but were almost as handsome.

Lucy, who had grown up among such objects at Fatland Ford, remarked a Chippendale chest-on-chest made in Philadelphia, and a Chippendale mahogany block-front chest of drawers. One of the homes held a Queen Anne carved walnut stool which bore the label of William Savery, the famous Philadelphia furniture maker. Most of these people had lived in Philadelphia before they made the move west, and brought their finest pieces with them.

Lucy met Berthouds, Tarascons, Cerfs and Fouchés. She danced the minuet with the grave attention given it by the French, and learned to accept flowery, involved compliments. She and Audubon were a very popular couple. Her fresh, bright-cheeked good looks attracted both the local Frenchmen and the Virginia planters who had settled in the region and started to raise tobacco. Audubon was just as attractive among the women. He was five feet ten, his dark hair thick about his wide and powerful shoulders. His brow was high, and his nose long and regular, his eyes deep-set, clear. He wore his clothing easily, and a number of the French women were reminded that he had studied in the *atelier* of the great painter, Jean Jacques David, in Paris. His clothing, his manners, and the skill with which he stepped the minuet showed a Parisian flair.

But Audubon was much more successful on the dance floor than in business. He and his partner Rozier had a hard time disposing of their stock of general merchandise at a profit. When Audubon made selling trips into the countryside, he spent a good part of his time in watching birds, or in sketching them. He was delighted when the stock the store sold had to be renewed, and he made a trip back east to purchase it.

Lucy stayed at the home of General Clark, or with the family of Major George Croghan. Both men were wealthy by frontier standards, and Croghan had served as Sir William Johnson's agent among the western tribes. Lucy was a welcome guest, and greatly admired by the children of both households, became their unofficial governess. Audubon did not hurry on his journeys east.

He wandered often from the main road through the broad and gently sloping valley in Kentucky. Elk had roamed this valley forty years before, he knew, and buffalo had grazed the blue grass on the hills. They were all gone now, although in some of the cabins where he passed the night he saw big spoons which had been carved from buffalo horn. The people who were his hosts got the spoons down for him, let him handle the patiently chipped edges. The old oath, "By the great horn spoon," came from these, and another common frontier saying, "Break it or make a spoon."

Audubon wandered over roads that had been Indian trails and, before that, buffalo paths. He found buffalo horns near salt licks, almost hidden in the long grass beside the ledges. He met Daniel Boone during a trip east, saw the old man several times afterwards.

Boone was still erect and strong in 1810, his eyes sharp, his hearing excellent. He wore a homespun hunting shirt, went bare-legged and wore moccasins. He was impressed by Audubon's wilderness knowledge and took Audubon hunting. His stories about early Kentucky and the upper reaches of the Missouri kept Audubon awake late into the night. Here was an authentic frontier character, Audubon knew, and his time with Boone was not wasted.

But the store at Louisville failed to prosper. Audubon and Rozier agreed to transfer the firm's business to Henderson, a small village 125 miles below Louisville on the Ohio. The store in Louisville was shut, and Rozier went ahead to Henderson. It was warm October weather, with little wind on the river. Audubon decided to take his family in a skiff.

The Audubon's first child, Victor, was a very small boy. But Lucy, with her tremendous trust in Audubon, was willing to make the passage. Audubon hired two Negro oarsmen to handle the skiff, and the family shoved off with their personal belongings aboard. Lucy sat with Victor in her arms, and Audubon with his rifle on his knees. He was ready for any birds that might serve him as specimens.

Haze lay upon the river in the October sunlight. The leaves of the maples, oaks and ironwoods had turned, were many-colored, bright. Wild grapevines stretched a skein of red and purple down the banks to

223

the water's edge. Mulberry sprays formed long curves that were purple and gold. The canebrakes were tinder dry, so bleached by the summer sun that the smallest bird was visible in flight across them. Deer stood on the ridges, nervous and watchful, antlers canted, their sharp hooves crashing the underbrush as they rushed away in fright.

The Ohio was almost motionless, burnished with sun through the thin haze, the ripples created by the oar blades radiantly spreading. A few skiffs passed, and a flatboat, then another. Their crews were quiet in the drowse of the day. They only nodded in greeting to the Audubons and the oarsmen.

Audubon motioned for the oarsmen to bring him in closer to the bank. He stood erect, surely balanced in the flat-bottomed skiff. His targets were the wild turkeys that paraded just a bit carelessly through the canebrakes. He shot several of them, and grouse, and blue-winged teal. The oarsmen waded ashore and gathered the game.

A campfire was made on the bank at dusk. The smaller birds were plucked, cleaned, hung on spits and cooked for supper. But the moon was high, and full, and there was no wind. Audubon gave the order to continue the voyage.

Lucy and the little boy dozed during the night. Audubon sat keenly awake, studying the river. He whispered to the husky oarsmen at dawn, stood and drew aim. It was just light enough for him to see a great horned owl that perched on a sandbar.

The shot killed the bird. It was a splendid specimen that he wanted very much. He put down his rifle, slid off his shoes and trousers, dived, and swam at once to the sandbar to get the owl.

But the sandbar was quicksand. He wallowed deeper, deeper, until the oarsmen shouted to him not to move any more. They rowed the boat close alongside. Lucy sat helpless, holding the child. The oarsmen collected driftwood that the current had piled on the bar, and with that and the oars they made a very temporary bridge. Then one man and after him the other crawled out onto it until, their hands coupled, Audubon could be reached.

224    They pulled mightily, and Audubon was lifted, and saved. He lost the owl. He was to remember the incident in great clarity, though, and the behavior of the Negroes. They were men who worked for a dollar

Fur Traders Descending the Missouri, by George C. Bingham

a day and their food to row the skiff 250 miles. He hardly knew their names, had hired them on the levee at Louisville from among a large group. Still, without hesitation, calmly and certainly, they had risked their lives to save his. Here were real river men.

Audubon had been born in Les Cayes, in the sugar-wealthy colony of Saint Domingue on the West Indian island of Hispaniola. His father had owned an extensive plantation there. He grew up among Negroes, was familiar with their strength, their ability, remembered from his years as a very young boy the boatyard workers, and the lightermen who

225

loaded the ships, the fishermen who came in from the Caribbean with tarpon, marlin and shark.

His father, who as the master of merchant ships had cruised the Guinea Coast, told him stories of the lanky, absolutely fearless Kroo tribesmen. They ran the huge offshore rollers in log canoes, paddled twenty miles out to sea to meet a ship. The Congo tribes moved vast quantities of cargo each year down that magnificent river, used dugout craft that set sails made of reeds.

Negroes had as much river heritage as any white men. Now, on the Ohio and particularly the Mississippi, they were beginning to perform the largest share of the labor. They worked as deckhands aboard the paddle-wheel steamers that had just started service on the Mississippi. More than that, though, they loaded and unloaded the vessels, and the principal cargo they handled was cotton, which their people had picked, baled and carted to the landings. Without the Negroes, it was very probable, Audubon realized, that in a few years there would be only a small amount of river traffic.

The Audubons in their skiff landed safely at the frontier village of Henderson. The pair of oarsmen were paid off and thanked by Audubon and headed out into the Ohio for the upstream haul back to Louisville. With a local boy helping to carry their belongings, the Audubons walked up the red-clay bank into the wide streets, ambitiously designed but flanked by a few log cabins.

Henderson was home for the Audubons for several years. Lucy shared her husband's interest, and they explored together the salt licks near the village where buffalo and elk had literally licked away the hillsides, caused cave-ins. There were many signs of the ancient Indian tribes of the region, known vaguely as the Mound People. Mussel shells were found by the thousands, and stone tools, banner stones that had been finished and polished with great care, bore thunderbird designs. Audubon brought forth from the maze of artifacts stone pipes decorated with the images of birds, and the heads of snakes, foxes, owls, the hooves of deer.

These discoveries and his ornithological study occupied Audubon when he was not at the store or in the back country on a peddling trip. He enjoyed the trips; he usually returned from them with new specimens for his bird collection. He took pleasure, too, in meeting along the back-country roads the strange assortment of people who were on their way to the Red Banks Trail.

The trail ran south from Henderson to Nashville, where it joined the famous and heavily travelled Natchez Trace. It cut northward to Vincennes, and there was a second branch which followed the Kentucky side of the river to a point opposite Shawneetown. That was a lawless little settlement which most travellers avoided. The population was American and French, and the remnants of various Indian tribes. The white men were border renegades, and among them were Harpes and Mason, well known as murderous river pirates.

The pair of young Frenchmen at Henderson considered a journey over the Natchez Trace as their business became progressively worse and they were faced with bankruptcy. They were convinced that although it was mid-winter they should take the rest of their stock and attempt to sell the goods in the French settlements on the Mississippi. But passage aboard a keelboat was better than a traverse of the Natchez Trace. Arrangements were made for Lucy and the boy, Victor, to stay with the family of a local doctor while Audubon was away. Then he and Rozier took a keelboat that left Henderson in a snow gale.

The crew were French Canadians, and the *patron* a veteran. He stayed clear of Shawneetown, but passed close to Cave-in-Rock, the notorious river-pirate hangout. Audubon stared keen-eyed up at the somber cave entrance, set high in a massive bank, a tall stand of pines above it on the ridge. But the weather was extremely cold, and there was no sign of pirates, or of any other craft on the river.

The *patron* steered the boat into Cache Creek the third night out of Henderson. It was an almost completely hidden little river which had been used not long before by Colonel Plug. He had been in the forefront of the river-pirate trade until killed, and his haunt was now deserted. The keelboat crew tied up to trees on the bank and took shelter in the small cabin, hip to thigh with the passengers under a pile of buffalo robes.

Audubon was amazed when he went out on deck at dawn to find a large group of Shawnees on the bank. They stood in total silence and regarded the craft. But after Audubon politely greeted them the chief explained that there were more than fifty families of the tribe encamped in the forest here. They were gathering a rich harvest of nuts and acorns, which in turn brought black bears, opossums and raccoons within easy musket range of the tipis.

The chief invited Audubon to go hunting, and he eagerly accepted. The Indians divided into two groups of fifty each. One of those flushed the white trumpeter swans that had perched in the forest near the river. The other group shot the magnificent birds as they rose in flight. The swans flew tightly massed among the trees, and the Indians with Audubon's help shot down more than fifty. The feathers from the birds, Audubon knew, would be sold and later decorate ladies' hats in Europe.

The Shawnees broke camp the next dawn. They loaded their dugouts and shoved off, the squaws at the paddles. The chief had told Audubon that their destination was the Arkansas River, and the keelboat *patron* watched the disappearing flotilla with some impatience. He informed his crew that if Shawnees could navigate, then he could, too. But he sent a volunteer to walk five miles across-country and report on the ice conditions at the juncture of the Ohio and the Mississippi.

The man came back to say that there was little ice in the main river. But the *patron* acted with caution. He ordered the crew to smooth the blades, the looms and handles of the sweeps to reduce friction when they were in use. New cordelles were plaited out of long strips of leather; the course, once the craft was in the Mississippi, would be upstream, with the full force of the current heading her.

Thick, loosely floating ice was found at the mouth of the Ohio when the *patron* brought the boat there with the last of that river's momentum. Here was the Mississippi, the stream the Indians called Old Big Deep Strong River. With the bitter north wind in his face and ice clunking against the boat hull, Audubon braced himself and stared out over the tremendous expanse.

The Mississippi pounded on a tangent to meet the Ohio. It flowed dull brown, mud-colored, along the westerly bank and the Illinois side, while here, on the easterly, the Ohio ran clear. They were two almost separate, discernible streams in the same river bed. But Audubon did not have much time to contemplate them. The *patron* was determined to head upstream despite the hazards of the ice, the wind, the current.

Audubon, with his exceptional strength, was of great assistance. It pleased him to perform the work. The primitive part of his nature was

228

aroused by the challenge which the elements offered. His father had been one of a family of twenty children, and had gone to sea at the age of twelve. John James Audubon remembered that when he slid the bight of the cordelle around his shoulders and started to haul.

He was forced to drag forward while bent nearly double. The wind struck the breath from his mouth, and was so cold that in a few minutes his eyebrows were frozen. Prongs of the wind pressed against his eye sockets and caused excruciating pain. He wore moccasins, the toes stuffed with moss, and they skidded in the mixture of bank snow and shattered ice. When he or the other men who hauled the cordelle fell, ice fragments cut through their trousers and their mittens. They did not curse, or talk; breath was too precious.

Seven miles of progress was made upstream the first day. The next day, it was less. The ice was now almost solid from bank to bank. The *patron* hoped to get abeam of Cape Girardeau, on the opposite shore, then swing across to Sainte Geneviève. But there was a broad reach abeam of Tywapitty Bottom where some islands gave shelter from the wind. The *patron* ordered camp built on the leeward side of an island. He sensed that a blizzard was about to descend upon the river.

The men chopped trees throughout the day, and into the night with the light of torches. They slid the logs into the water and made a cage to protect the boat, moored close in alongside the bank. Then, without stopping, they felled more trees for firewood. Audubon partly cleared the camp space, left a few tall oaks for shelter. A windbreak was built in the shape of a circular snow-block wall that surrounded the campfire.

Rozier took care of handling the cargo put ashore from the boat. It was carefully stacked inside the windbreak—dry goods in boxes, powder in kegs, and barrels of whiskey—then covered with a tarpaulin. The fire was enormous—four or five ash trees, only a few inches in diameter but sixty feet long, with their branches, leaves and underbrush heaped over them, and a top layer of oak logs.

Wolves approached the camp. They came to the perimeter of the windbreak and scrambled up to peer at the men. But the fire's heat drove them back. The men wrapped themselves in buffalo robes, cut holes in the river ice and fished. Audubon, with his rifle in the crook of his arm, stood and watched the wolves.

229

Crawling, bellies flat to the ice, the wolves stalked the swans. The birds were plump, and there was not much else around to satisfy the wolves' hunger. The swans remained on the ice until the gray, evil-eyed beasts were about 100 yards from them. Then the startling clangor of their call rang through the wind, and they took off, upriver. The wolves sprinted and sprang, but the swans were much faster in flight.

The swans played a game with the wolves. They came back, partway downriver, and landed again, invited attack. They drummed upon the ice with their wings, and the sound increased to reverberations like thunder. The wolves' pointed ears quivered; their fangs showed, and they growled. The swans took off in low, daring flight and sailed right over the wolves, within inches of the upward thrust of the muzzles. Then they sailed high up, in an expression of triumph and disdain for the wolves, landed, and began to make the same thunderous sounds. The wolves left and did not look back.

A party of Osages was encamped on the river bank near the island. The warriors and some of the squaws crossed the ice to visit at night when the keelboatmen's fire reared a huge scarlet dome in the darkness. Audubon expressed his interest in birds, and with sign language the warriors told him about the local species. The squaws fashioned baskets out of bark which they presented to the white men. It was a pleasant and charming scene, with the various seated figures in the foreground, the firelight incandescent on the snow, and in the background the forest, and the river.

Audubon took out his pad and crayons from his pack. He drew quick sketches—laughing Indians, the boatmen, the *patron*, and Rozier, deep in buffalo robes. Then, from memory, he drew opossums he had seen here around the camp, and rabbits skipping nimbly over a snow drift, squirrels bulge-cheeked with mouths full of acorns.

But the evening dragged, and Audubon could tell by the tension in the *patron's* face that the wind sounds and the ceaseless rumbling of the river ice meant the boat might soon be in great danger. Audubon put away the sketch pad, and wrote for a while in his journal, then pulled forth his flute. It was the same instrument he had played during the moonlit night on the Ohio.

He played familiar French tunes now, and almost instantly the boatmen responded. They sang to his accompaniment the oldest and best

230

known of the Northwest songs, "La Guillannée." It told of mistletoe, and New Year's Eve celebration. It was very gay, and even the *patron* began to sing and thump his thigh. Audubon played dancing tunes.

The boatmen got up and danced as partners. This convulsed the Osages. They had never seen white men dance before, and they had never seen white men take the role of women. Warriors and squaws laughed and rolled over, looked up and laughed some more. The chief, between tunes, asked Audubon a question which Audubon realized was sincere: The men who danced, were they crazy?

All of the merriment was expended before dawn, and the Osages went back to their tipis in the forest. The keelboat party faced the fact that provisions were growing very short, and any day, with fair weather, the ice jams upriver might break. The boat must be further protected before she was crushed by the rush of floes.

The log cage around the boat was reinforced. The Osages helped, and brought loads of canes from shore. The canes were lashed in fender fashion against the logs, and secured with more logs. Then, at midnight, the *patron* aroused the camp:

"The ice breaks! Get down to the boat! *Allez!*"

Far up the Ohio, ice had begun to loosen, and the river was in flood towards the Mississippi. The pressure upon the ice, solid from bank to bank in the main river, was fantastically violent. There were, first, distant salvoes as the floes struck each other and disintegrated. The Ohio was high over its banks. The spate surged into the Mississippi.

The Mississippi ice field heaved, rose, subsided, buckled, and released in immense cascades of splinters from whose bases widening fissures ran. Loose ice piled against the keelboat cage. The logs and the cane fenders were macerated. The men threw more logs into place, sprang back as the ice mounted, ground smashing where seconds ago they had stood.

The Osages helped. Logs were passed from hand to hand, thrust between the crevices the ice left. The men were exhausted. There was no more they could do. The Mississippi was rising; current coursed rapidly beneath the ice. But the boat had begun to ride easily within the cage as the ice was hurled abruptly into gigantic furrows and parapets and ridges, all headed downstream.

There was a single and vast detonation. The *patron* spoke in a quiet voice. The Mississippi, he said, had pushed her way past the Ohio ice. The big river was free.

It took four hours for the Mississippi to clear herself of the worst of the floes. When the *patron* took the keelboat out into the current, he almost lost her. She was severely battered by loose ice and all sorts of flotsam torn away upriver. But she reached Sainte Geneviève after long and anxious hours at the cordelle, the sweeps and the poles.

Sainte Geneviève was the oldest white settlement west of the Mississippi. It had been founded by *voyageurs,* and it was still very French. The people welcomed Audubon and Rozier, and bought all of the merchandise. Rozier fell quickly in love with a local girl, chose to stay in the settlement. Trade should remain good, he told Audubon. This place was almost as big as St. Louis, further upriver. Both settlements were rendezvous points for *voyageurs* and fur traders northward-bound, travelers on their way to New Orleans, trappers who had outfitted for the upper Missouri River country, and Indians, and missionaries.

But Audubon was not willing to confine his future to Sainte Geneviève. It did not appeal to him as a home for Lucy and his children. He parted amiably enough from Rozier and went back to Henderson. Then he took the first of several voyages down the Mississippi to New Orleans.

His knowledge of the river gradually formed, and he learned an immense amount about the birds that lived along it, began his famous series of drawings and paintings of them. But, during his Mississippi years, he became very familiar also with the people of the valley. Poverty took him aboard keelboats as a workaway and professional hunter. His skill, his increasing reputation as an artist, and Lucy's social sense and charm allowed him entrance into the great plantation houses of the New Orleans region. He lived really in two worlds, and moved at ease in both.

He made one trip to New Orleans as part of the complement that worked a pair of flatboats. The craft carried bulk salt from Shawneetown, where it was collected in great quantity, and miscellaneous cargo for sale along the river. There were ten men in the combined crews, and it was Audubon's job to supply them with game. He went out into the forest or the flatlands and hunted all day, returned to the boats just at dusk.

The owners of the boats transacted business at each village. When the mooring hawsers were secured, the boats were converted into stores. Plank counters were set up on deck and arrayed with merchandise. The village people came aboard slowly, diffident and distrustful. They had been cheated often, and been sold shoddy, faulty articles. But jugs of whiskey were prominently displayed, and chewing tobacco, and segars, ribbons, calicos, even petticoats and entire dresses. Trade was brisk, and usually ended only at dusk.

Audubon kept away from the boats as much as possible during the day. The owners' successful trading was a poignant reminder to him of his fiasco as a storekeeper and the fact that he would be separated for months from his beloved Lucy and his two sons. He spent most of his time aboard in the company of Captain Samuel Cumings, a renowned and veteran river pilot.

Captain Cumings was engaged in making the first reliable chart of the Ohio and Mississippi rivers for the use of navigators. It was later published with the title *The Western Pilot*, and gave detailed, accurate information regarding every village on the two main waterways and their tributaries, and included the precise courses to be followed to avoid the dangers of snags, rocks, shoals and towheads, cited the various channel depths.

New Orleans—a terminal for flatbottom boats and deepwater ships.

Audubon understood the importance of Captain Cumings' work. He helped take soundings and current readings, check bearings and bank contours. There had been many guide books about the Mississippi published and widely sold. Most of them were collections of highly confusing if not very dubious information. Zadok Cramer had published in 1811 his *Navigator*, and felt moved to tell his readers:

> The Pelican is said to have a melancholy countenance, and is very torpid. It is asserted that they seemed to be fond of musick.

Sometimes, because of the briskness of the trading or river conditions, the two boats moved no more than fifteen miles downstream during a day's run. But Audubon saw the red, yellow and black striations of the Chickasaw Bluffs fall astern in the river mist. He went ashore to hunt in flatlands overgrown by sawgrass, canebrakes and thickly tangled willows. The country was dry in this autumn season, but floods had often invaded here. The river had left deposits of mud and detritus miles inland, and he came to have enormous respect for its power.

Swift currents roiled the mud-brown surface that took a bronze sheen with intense sunlight. Captain Cumings pointed out hundreds of uncharted snags, sawyers and islands that bore flatboat wreckage. A sweep, gray with weather, showed above the strewn planks of a cargo box, and very probably, where the current swerved tight-gathered around rocks, men had drowned.

The party to which Audubon was attached had careful steersmen, though. They negotiated the White River cutoff, where cordelles were made from grapevines, and came back without incident into the Mississippi. Then they passed the Yazoo, and tied up at Natchez.

Audubon explored Natchez-under-the-hill with the same curiosity as any man who had spent weeks in hard labor on the river. It deserved the reputation given it, he found. Flatboats in serried rows had been hauled ashore through the bank mud and secured to the walls of low, slab-roof houses. There was a constant parade of whores, pimps, gamblers, thieves and drunken or part-sober river men along the narrow, twisting streets where hogs investigated garbage and skinny dogs fought.

The houses and the beached flatboats were used by the whores or were doggeries that sold only rotgut whiskey. Fights were common,

234

Fort Natchez

and almost constant. Three or four were conducted simultaneously while the blowsy, sagging-breasted whores yelled encouragement to their clients from the doorways of doggeries, or shouted that they had not yet been paid.

Teams of horses hauled through the street mire wooden sledges that carried water barrels filled from the river. The water was drunk by people who lived in Natchez-on-the-hill. It was put into the barrels at the bank right here, and could not be considered completely pure. But the teamsters seemed unconcerned. They sent the sledges adroitly around the drunks that lay unconscious, and only struck with their whips when a man still upright tried to embrace a horse.

Audubon climbed the hill to the upper town. He had seen too much of blood, smashed faces and dirty whores. It meant little to him that this miserable place had been the headquarters for the robbers who had recently infested the Natchez Trace. The Trace ran through Nashville, and became the Red Banks Trail which he had known well when he lived at Henderson. The stories of the "land pirates" were all old, and stale.

Horsemen galloped the hill past him. He stopped, his artist's attention caught by the ruins of the old Spanish fort in a gully. Then he came to the top of the wide and flat bluff. Chinaberry trees gave shade. The houses were substantial, and some built in the Spanish manner. The shops were neat, spacious. Planters put their wives down in front of them from carriages handled by coachmen. There were two churches, the spires high above the trees. Natchez-on-the-hill had an existence of its own, Audubon realized, and he belonged to the other, at the bottom of the bluff.

He was more than thirty-five years old, and so poor he could not support his wife and children. These prosperous planters would call him a failure. He had better get back down the hill with the rest of the riffraff whose only reason for existence was the river.

The Mississippi took him past Bayou Sara and Baton Rouge. Then the river widened. He saw that both banks were almost barren. Flood had swept them clear of houses, barns, fences, flocks and cattle. Captain Cumings told him that the local people spoke of the region as "the coast." It held a somber and forbidding aspect; darkness claimed the bayous, swamps and coves, and Spanish moss swayed from cottonwoods in thick screens above the water.

Audubon stood on deck for hours, nervously alert. There was a final broad bend and as the ungainly boat rounded it he saw the mast tracery, and the furled sails, and the flags. This was New Orleans. Those were ocean-going ships, and they were moored alongside the city levee.

He went ashore up a broad flight of steps cut in the levee, carrying his rifle and wearing ragged buckskins. But he was given no more than a quick glance. All sorts of people were accepted here. This was Congo Square.

Palmetto leaves were spread on the ground and used to display merchandise, fruit, vegetables and fish. Boxes painted in bright colors supported a clutter of dry-goods items. Many of the merchants were women, full-blooded Negroes or mulattoes, with silk turbans and huge, solid-gold loop earrings. There were Mexican men who also wore earrings, and

New England peddlers in butternut or shiny blue serge. The New Englanders' chief stock was tinware, bolts of cotton goods, and loudly ticking Connecticut clocks.

Choctaws with tattoo designs on their cheeks sold game in wicker baskets. They, along with the rest of the crowd, spoke in Creole patois. It was, Audubon found, easy for him to understand; most of it was French in which Spanish and African words had been mixed.

He went to talk with men he knew, *voyageurs* he had met in Sainte Geneviève. They sold kegs of bear and buffalo grease, and spread before them also for sale were game and practically every kind of bird to be found in the bayou country. Audubon saw red-winged blackbirds, bluebirds, bobos, ivory-billed woodpeckers and purple finches in large heaps.

Those sharply reminded him of his lifelong ambition to paint in accurate, complete detail all of the species of American birds. He said goodbye to his *voyageur* acquaintances and became practical. He was, after all, the son of a man of wealth and prominence in France. There were connections he could establish in this very French city that should help him, and eventually reunite him with Lucy.

Audubon left Congo Square. He walked past Cathedral St. Louis into the narrow streets where lamps were hung on ropes between the houses and the houses were blue, yellow, pale pink. He asked questions of coachmen who drove expensive cabriolets, and they directed him to the house he sought. He used his father's name there, and was made welcome.

Audubon, through his New Orleans connections, got a job as a tutor with the Pirrie family. They owned Feliciana plantation, at St. Francisville. That was an old Spanish-built village near Bayou Sara, upriver from New Orleans. Audubon believed that he was extremely lucky. He was being paid $60 a month to instruct the Pirrie children, but it was agreed that he would be free for half of each day. Those hours would be devoted to his bird-collection work and his painting.

Great beech trees, and tall yellow poplars, gum trees, and palmettos whose trunks were clotted with Spanish moss surrounded the plantation. Muscadine grapes grew wild; magnolias spilled a tumble of immense, fragrant flowers; holly flanked the paths near the house. Birds came in swift and brilliant flight to catch the insects that gathered there. Audubon took the birds he needed for specimens, painted them in life-size proportion.

There was wilderness to the west of the plantation, on the Red River, and the Sabine, in what the Pirrie family called "the Texas." Warriors who belonged to the Houma and Tunica tribes of the Choctaw nation and had been peaceful for years worked intermittently as field-hands. But they greatly preferred being in the wild country to the west, took Audubon with them at his suggestion. They taught him how to use a blow-gun to get his specimens, and delicately killed a number of the species he lacked.

It gave him satisfaction to pay the Indian hunters for their work, and month by month he put aside money for his family's passage down-river from Henderson. There was enough finally, and he sent for Lucy and the two boys, Victor and John.

He was radiant with joy when they arrived. But Lucy took care to get a job as governess with a plantation family in St. Francisville. She loved with all her heart the burly, sun-brown man she had married. John James Audubon was forever restless, though. It would not be long before he was off again, following some river.

## 14

---

Thomas Jefferson had never forgotten the conversations in Dr. Maury's study years ago in the Virginia of his boyhood. Throughout all of his activities and interests, the resolve to bring about exploration west of the Mississippi remained inflexible, often dominant in his thinking. He became President of the United States in 1801, and by January 1803 he believed that Congress was ready to hear from him on the subject.

Congress would not be informed about the Louisiana Purchase for six months yet, so Jefferson delivered his message to the legislators in confidence. He asked that an exploring party be sent to "trace the Missouri to its source, to cross the highlands and follow the best water communication which offered itself from thence to the Pacific Ocean."

He cited as his reasons for the need of such an expedition the growth of British trade in the Northwest region, and control of the Indian tribes, whose friendship and furs were both very valuable. Congress

239

agreed; approval was given and money appropriated for the expedition. President Jefferson then acted with all possible speed.

His knowledge of the region was faulty despite the intensive and prolonged research he had made. Information he contained in the message sent Congress spoke of a mountain range 180 miles long and forty-five miles wide. This was composed of "solid rock salt without any trees or shrubs on it." While he told Congress that no reliable map of Louisiana existed, he believed that the region reached from the Mississippi to the Pacific.

The best map available to him was one produced in London in 1795 by an English cartographer, Aaron Arrowsmith. It contained several major inaccuracies having to do with latitude and longitude, the length, the courses and locations of rivers, and the non-existence of several ranges of the Rocky Mountains. There was no way for Jefferson to establish geographical fact without sending an expedition into the region. It was very easy to be mistaken; what was called Louisiana encompassed more than one million square miles.

Dr. Samuel Latham Mitchill, a member of Congress from New York, an able scientist and a strong advocate of the Louisiana Purchase, gathered an amazing array of garbled data which he presented to Jefferson. He and the President were close friends, and he was one of Jefferson's advisers. They considered together stories about a river of brine, gold mines, silver mines, a volcano on the upper Missouri, and a mountain of pure crystal. Lieutenant Zebulon Montgomery Pike of the United States Army had sent reports back from the western vastness that the mines of Santa Fe were nearly on a parallel with the mouth of the Ohio. He included the statement that he had met a man who worked in the Santa Fe mines. The miner's family lived in St. Louis, or Kaskaskia. He made a visit to his home each year. The journey only took fifteen to twenty days on foot, and ten to twelve on horseback.

President Jefferson chose Captain Meriwether Lewis of Virginia to command the expedition. The captain had served until very recently as his private secretary, lived in his home, and Jefferson had great respect for his ability. Captain Lewis chose in turn William Clark, a Kentuckian, as second-in-command. Both were veteran frontiersmen who had lived in the wilderness among Indians and were skillful boat-handlers.

Lewis took charge at once of the collection of special equipment, received thorough instruction in survey work, and organized the maps and books which had been published about the region he was to explore. Clark went into the remote parts of Kentucky, seeking the right men for members of the expedition.

President Jefferson wrote two detailed drafts of orders. He stated specifically what he wanted from the expedition. Should the party reach the Pacific, he wrote, "Inform yourself of the circumstances which may decide whether the furs of those parts may not be collected as advantageously at the head of the Missouri as at Nootka Sound, or any other point on that coast."

He was aware that the British were steadily enlarging their trade in furs on the Northwest Coast, and were being joined by the Russians. He had also been informed that the Spanish at Santa Fe were afraid of penetration of the Southwest by British traders. Parties of those men would arrive by boat, come down the Colorado River, or, in another form of invasion, make their way up the Rio Grande from the Gulf of Mexico. But Jefferson ordered the American expedition to wait for the proper time.

Lewis stowed his heavy gear aboard barges at Pittsburgh on August 30, 1803, and shoved off for Louisville. He picked up Clark and the recruits at Louisville in the middle of September. Then the combined party kept on downriver to the Mississippi. Winter camp was built on the bank of the Mississippi above St. Louis and across from the mouth of the Missouri. Discipline was carefully maintained during the inactive months. This, Captain Lewis made very clear, was a military expedition.

The formal acquisition of upper Louisiana was made at St. Louis on March 10, 1804, and with it France gave up her last territory on the continent. But Lewis and Clark were interested in history of their own making. The expedition started up the Missouri on May 14th in three heavily loaded craft.

There were forty-five men in the complement, including Lewis and Clark. Nine were young men recruited from the Kentucky backwoods. Fourteen were soldiers of the United States Army, selected from volunteers at various frontier posts. There were two veteran French Canadian *voyageurs*, Cruzatte and Labiche, and a man named Drouillard

241

who served as both hunter and interpreter. Drouillard was good-natured about the pronunciation of his name; he was soon known by his companions as Drewyer.

All of these men, with the exception of York, who was a Negro slave and owned by Captain Lewis, were enlisted as privates for the duration of the expedition. Three sergeants were drawn from among their number, Floyd, Pryor and Ordway. A detachment of seven soldiers and a corporal was also engaged by Captain Lewis, and an additional force of nine river men picked up in St. Louis.

The detachment of soldiers and the river men were needed to help in the carrying of stores, and at cordelle work, and in case of Indian attack. Lewis had been told at St. Louis that the area most to be feared was between Wood River and the Mandan villages on the upper Missouri. He proposed to send the extra force back when he reached the villages, continue with his own people.

A keelboat and a pair of pirogues formed the expedition's flotilla. Cruzatte was *patron* aboard the keelboat, and Labiche served as *bosseman* with men from the regular party at the sweeps, poles, or cordelle. The soldiers and the corporal found themselves propelling a six-oared pirogue whose hull was painted white. The other pirogue, somewhat larger, was the responsibility of the crew of river men, and was painted red. She and her sister craft were equipped with small squaresails for use when the wind was astern.

This was the first organized exploration of the upper Missouri since March 29, 1714, when a young Frenchman named Etienne Veniard de Bourgmond started his journey from St. Louis. He went back to France in 1719, and was given a royal commission as Commandant de la Rivière du Missouri. During another Missouri voyage he built a fort and made treaties with the Missouris, the Osages, the Otos and the Illinois. All of them had an implacable distrust of the Spanish and the English they had met.

De Bourgmond took advantage of the fact. He invited the chiefs of these tribes to return to France with him. They agreed, and he presented them with great success to Louis XV. The group wore tribal costume, were magnificently painted and bedizened. The Duke de Bourbon and the Duchess d'Orleans claimed them as protégées. The four erect,

gravely dignified men became familiar figures among the courtiers at Fontainebleau.

They were extremely popular. They performed their native dances at the Opéra and the Théâtre Italien in Paris. Deer were stalked by them in the Bois de Boulogne, and killed with bow and arrow. Chicagou, the Illinois chief, was the favorite among the four. He and the rest of the chiefs were induced to give up their buckskins and eagle feathers, and instead wore cocked hats and lace-trimmed velvet coats.

De Bourgmond was so pleased by the successful conduct of the chiefs that he permitted his sergeant to marry the Indian girl who had accompanied him from America. He had simply called her *La Sauvagesse*

243

when he presented her at court. But now that she was to marry the sergeant, she became *La Princesse du Missouri*. The princess was baptized at Notre-Dame Cathedral, and immediately entered into matrimony.

Chicagou told many stories about Paris when he returned to the tribe. He described wheeled vehicles, and buildings taller than trees, and rooms lit by hundreds and hundreds of candles. But he was disbelieved, and his French clothing got smoke-smirched and greasy, wore out; he told no more stories. The fort De Bourgmond had built and named for the Duke d'Orleans was abandoned in 1727, and fell into ruins. The Frenchman's presence on the river faded in tribal memory, was recalled vaguely, almost as legend.

Captain Meriwether Lewis was of a different type. He was twenty-nine years old when he started up the Missouri, and he had already made very definite decisions about the expedition and its purpose. He looked upon himself as a professional soldier under direct orders from his commander-in-chief, President Jefferson. He was, without any conscious effort, an exemplar of the Anglo-Americans who because of a great deal of courage and steadfast initiative were taking over most of the North American continent.

He accepted in totality the concept of manifest destiny. He and men like him drove back ruthlessly whenever necessary the French, the British, the Spaniards. They spent less thought about those people than they gave to the Indians. It was the tribes, after all, who still lived in the territory that held the beaver and the buffalo.

Captain Lewis was an infantry officer. He had been on active duty since the Whiskey Rebellion until he was detached to serve Jefferson as private secretary. Clark, who had been a lieutenant in the Indian campaign led by General Anthony Wayne, was under Lewis's command for some months during it. They were well known to each other, and shared the same background.

They both considered themselves wilderness monarchs. While they regarded with great respect Drouillard's ability to talk the languages of several tribes and to mingle with almost absolute freedom among the warriors, they were secretly a bit contemptuous of him. They consistently mispronounced his name. He was of French Canadian stock, and it was not important.

Lewis had not only brought along on the expedition his slave, York, but his big Newfoundland dog, Scammon. He had been certain, right from the start, of making his objective.

The lower reaches of the river were not difficult. The cordelle was seldom used aboard the keelboat, and the pirogue men bucked the current without extreme effort, were able at times to set the sails and take advantage of the wind. This month of May was the most beautiful on the Missouri. The men worked bare to the waist, swam and fished from the bank after camp was made for the night.

There was a profusion of game. The party's hunters were ashore all day long, came back with turkey, grouse, beaver, and bear and elk haunch. The broad fat tail of a beaver baked in the ashes of the campfire was a great delicacy. The men went into the wooded runs and picked wild grapes and Osage plums to eat with the meat. They raked big mussels out of the river mud, and in the river and the creeks they caught trout, bass, pike, crawfish, catfish and a fish that looked like salmon.

Then, though, it began to rain, and there were violent squalls alternated by periods of oppressive, windless heat when the flies and mosquitoes were nearly intolerable. Clark was an expert river man. He conned the boats steadily upstream with enormous assistance from Cruzatte. The French Canadian veteran had lost an eye, gouged out years ago in a fight, and could not see very well with the other. His physical power, his vast knowledge and acute river sense made up for his lack of vision, and Labiche, the *bosseman*, was always close to give a shout of warning or explanation.

The sluggish-seeming, dun river became furious under the impact of the squalls. The erratic but severe current and the wind force hurled the boats off course. They swung broadside, threatened to capsize, or crash against the snag-littered islands or the banks. Men sprang into the water and fought the craft back from what would be complete destruction. They hauled at cordelles while shoulder-deep in the river or straining from tree to tree, boulder to boulder.

The wind whipped them cruelly through the narrow gaps in the shore bluffs. Rain and spindrift struck knife-sharp against their eyes. The bank often crumbled beneath their feet as the current surged at it. There were snakes among the underbrush.

The men learned how to haul a boat through what Cruzatte called a "chute," where the current swung close past an island, and to keep course when the river suddenly formed a "boil" of air and mud beneath the surface that broke with whirlpool action. They became familiar with dangerously drifting "rafts" of flotsam large enough to sink the keelboat, sandbars that could instantly capsize the pirogues, and islands half an acre long that because of some quirk of current rapidly and totally disappeared.

But the weather cleared. The men toughened and their river skill greatly increased. Progress was steady. The flotilla reached the Grand Detour, negotiated it, and continued along the upper river. Here the party was in Indian country, with scouts out on each bank, and almost constant contact with the tribes.

Lewis and Clark made long entries in their journals. They were careful to observe and record every detail of native life. Lewis had picked up from Drouillard some of the French Canadian's diplomatic ease of manner when treating with the warriors. His behavior pattern, profoundly influenced by the circumstances of his early life in Tidewater Virginia, changed. He was red-headed, blue-eyed, and deeply tanned, dressed in worn buckskins, was an attractive figure. The chiefs were pleased to talk with him. Clark, raised in backwoods Kentucky and genial by nature, was almost as successful.

They found that practically every tribe along the Missouri had a separate, highly developed skill. The Osages were proud of a warrior group which worked as cooks. These men gave most of their time to the preparation of formal feasts, then presided over them, made sure that the rites demanded by tradition were meticulously observed. When they were free from their duties as cooks, they served as village criers, announced various events and gatherings.

The Mandans of the upper river were famous for the glass beads they produced. They manufactured, too, in the tribal kilns exquisitely thin pottery. Their artists excelled in painting battle scenes on tanned buffalo hide.

The Arikari tribe—known as Rees by the white men—had once occupied thirty-two villages along the river. Their power had declined when the Lewis and Clark expedition entered the territory that still belonged to them, but their medicine men were unsurpassed. Performances were given after gifts were offered and accepted. The members of the expedition were extremely curious; traders met in St. Louis and on the river had warned them about the medicine men's ceremonies. Those sometimes kept going for several days and nights, unbrokenly, and were so frequent the traders spoke of them as "the opera."

The ceremonies were usually performed at night, and within the huge, round-domed earthen lodges. A fire of massive logs burned in the center. Flame flung high from it, but was intermittent and flickered, subsided, was obscured by smoke. The medicine men wore buffalo-horn headdresses. Dancing gravely, very slowly, their several otter-skin bags swaying from their paint-striped shoulders, they played upon whistles fashioned from bone and small drums. The whistles and the drums were supposed to own magical powers.

The members of the expedition sat beside the chief. He wore an ermine-skin headdress. Behind him were the senior warriors, then the ranks of the tribe, silent, slightly bent forward to watch and to listen, the firelight glistening on the somber faces, the narrowed eyes.

The medicine men, when incantations had been made, took meat with their hands from a kettle that boiled upon the fire. One, wearing nothing but a breechclout, sat in the fire. Stones that had been heated beside the kettle were pulled out, and instantly a medicine man walked barefooted across them.

Lewis and Clark were wordless. It was certainly not white man's magic, and they had no answer for it. They left the lodge finally, when the chief said the medicine men wished to be alone with the spirits. But the next day, in full sunlight, they saw further evidence of what the medicine men could do to hold the confidence of the tribe.

A medicine man was bound with thongs, feet and hands tightly secured. Then he was put inside a net, the net wrapped in a buffalo robe. Robe and all, he was stuffed in a hole in the ground, and the hole covered with a large flat rock. But he managed somehow to get rid of his bonds, push aside the rock and stand free in front of the crowd.

Then medicine men danced, and restored the shards of broken gourds. Small clay dolls were induced to dance, and untouched pipes gave puffs of smoke, birds that were obviously stuffed emitted natural-sounding calls.

247

Captain Lewis shrugged and grinned. He turned to York. The tall, magnificently built Negro was a very handsome man, his skin blue-black, his hair tight upon his skull. A number of squaws had already shown their extreme willingness to get to know him on close personal terms, and warriors, with appropriate apologies, had tested his bicep muscle. York's teeth flashed gleaming when he laughed at what Lewis asked. Then he moved out from the front rank of the crowd and picked up one of the medicine men's drums.

It was a small instrument, the barrel made of cottonwood, the head loosely stretched deerskin. He smacked it with the palm of his huge hand and it resounded. He hit it again, in African rhythm, and began to dance. His feet and legs jerked with motions that were opposite to those of his arms and shoulders. His wide flat feet, pale with dust, slid back and forth with extraordinary grace. He slowed the drumming and, standing almost still, began to sing.

Captain Lewis had heard songs like this in Virginia, at night, and outside plantation slave quarters. Still, he did not understand it, had no knowledge of the meaning. York sang a chant that came from Africa. It told of the very old African gods, Damballah, who represented war, Agoué, the deity who ruled over the rivers and the sea, and Vaudoun, the creator, the greatest of all.

York stamped his feet on the bare packed earth as he sang, that sound in rhythm with the drumbeat. He stared far off, over the cottonwoods and the prairies where the river coiled. But those watching him knew that he had gone back, lived for the duration of the chant in Africa. He was alone now, kept so by his pride.

He finished and put down the drum. A young squaw made a quick but unmistakable gesture, her face and eyes shining. York followed her towards the doorway of a lodge. The deerskin over the doorway fell behind him and the squaw. No warrior moved, or spoke. It was Captain Lewis who started to talk, and then there was a lot of conversation and natural, unforced laughter.

The expedition spent the winter at the Mandan villages. Both Lewis and Clark had brought along violins, and they joined merrily in the entertainment that helped pass the monotonous months. But York remained the star of any performance, and a number of squaws maneuvered

248

for his favors. The male population accepted his popularity with complete good will; promiscuity was common in the tribe and York deserved any amorous attention given him.

The two captains—Clark shared Lewis's rank—talked at length with John Colter, one of the expedition members. Colter was an itinerant trapper and hunter with a considerable amount of experience in the Rocky Mountain region. He was able to tell his superiors in fairly accurate terms what the expedition would meet when it moved west in the spring.

Then Lewis had the great good fortune to hire as a guide, interpreter and hunter a Montreal *voyageur* named Toussaint Charbonneau. The man was spending the winter in the Mandan villages with his very attractive Indian wife, Sacagawea. She was a Shoshone, and he had bought her in 1804 from the Minnetarees, among whom he had been living on the Knife River.

Sacagawea was much more intelligent than her husband, and possessed a vast sum of geographical information about the Rocky Mountains. She knew of the Lemhi Pass that was commonly used by the tribes who made the journey between the Missouri and the Columbia. While with her clan of mountain people five years ago, during their annual buffalo hunt in the Missouri Valley, she had been captured by the Minnetarees. This was near the Three Forks of the Missouri, and she knew the country there.

Captain Lewis recognized at once her value to the expedition. He made plans for her to accompany it with her husband and her newly born son, Jean-Baptiste. The boy was born in February, and the party started west on April 9, 1805, its first objective the Great Falls of the Missouri.

The heavy-hulled keelboat was sent downriver in charge of men relieved of further duty, and carrying maps, data and voluminous reports for President Jefferson. The party used the pair of pirogues and six cottonwood dugouts built during the winter. The muster contained twenty-six soldiers and the river men, and Charbonneau, Sacagawea, and Jean-Baptiste, the baby strapped to his mother's back in regular papoose style.

The party encountered many difficulties on the upper river and was often in danger. But Lewis was a wise and courageous commander. 249 Drouillard, Charbonneau and Colter proved their ability, and were willing to take the advice offered by Sacagawea. The Lemhi Pass was reached, and the expedition went down the western slope of the Rockies towards the Columbia. They came to the Columbia where it joined the Snake, and found it filled with thrashing masses of silver-bodied salmon.

Portages were used around some of the rapids met on the way to the coast, and at others the entire party rode the white water in the canoes. There was one set of rapids in the Cascade Mountains where the river flung through a channel only forty-five yards wide. The *voyageurs* whooped when they entered it and took the canoes out of it intact in single file while from a pinnacle of rock, where they had gathered for the salmon catch, the local Indians stared unbelieving.

The final stretch of the rapids was reached on October 30th, and could not be navigated. It was three miles long, and they were forced to portage their gear, ease the canoes downstream checked by elkhide ropes made for the purpose. Then, though, below the rapids, they saw sea otter. This was tidewater. The party was exultant. The journey was almost finished.

Fog blocked their passage on the lower river. They slept wet, cold, wracked by dysentery. Their rations were reduced to smoked salmon, and the best firewood available was soggy willow twigs. The Indians encountered were not outrightly hostile, although they systematically and stubbornly stole.

A strict guard was kept over the gear when a village was visited. Each village and even the fish-racks were infested with fleas. The men scratched and cursed while they lay shivering at night. Sacagawea was kept busy cleaning Jean-Baptiste's poll, and heavy-coated Scammon was repeatedly attacked.

The fog lifted November 7th and men with exceptionally keen vision said they saw the sea. Lewis and Clark were not certain, though. The river estuary had become so wide that the canoes were pitched by heavy rollers; it was raining, and the entire party was seasick, thirsty, hungry, and tempted to express wish-fulfillment.

It was from a sheltered camp on the north shore that the sea was observed across the rush of breakers at the river bar. This was November 15th, and Lewis made a notation in his journal that the camp was in "full view of the ocean."

The men felt abruptly the full weight of their exhaustion. They were almost speechless. Here was their objective, and now that they had achieved it they lacked the energy to shout, cavort, fire off their muskets. They sat instead by the small fire, dull-eyed, gaunt with dysentery, and appalled by the distance they had come.

Lewis and Clark understood the magnitude of the achievement, though. They had accomplished much more than Mackenzie or any other men who had made the transcontinental traverse. Mackenzie's route was almost impassable, could not be used for trade purposes. This which they had opened gave direct connection with the Missouri basin and the tremendous wealth in furs, fish and timber along the Pacific Coast.

The achievement was too great to be blemished by sickness or disease among the people of the party. Lewis took them back from the sea and a short distance into the forest, prepared for winter. Large timber was needed for the fort he wanted to build, and inland the hunters could find elk to vary the diet.

The fort was built in the unremitting rain, and named Clatsop for the local tribe. A number of the Clatsop and the nearby Chinook people visited at the installation during the winter. Cruzatte and Labiche openly admired the superb dugouts the Indians used.

These bore carved figureheads of weird birds and animals, were generally made from a single log of white cedar or fir, and fifty feet long. They held as many as thirty passengers, and would take four tons of cargo. Squaws were just as expert canoe-handlers as the warriors, and often a big dugout arrived at the fort landing with a squaw in the steering position.

A canoe was very highly valued among the Indians on the coast. When a young warrior sought a wife, he offered her father a canoe in exchange. There was nothing else that had the same worth. The Clatsops, the Chinooks and the other coastal tribes buried their dead in canoes. The corpse was laid out on mats in the craft, alongside it all personal gear. Then another smaller canoe was placed on top and used as the cover for the coffin. The coffin was raised from the ground on stakes, and the following year the bones were buried at the same site. 251

But even the river men became bored with Indian canoe-making and burial rites. Lewis knew that with fair weather the party must start the return journey. There was plenty of evidence, pieces of red cloth, empty rum kegs kept hopefully by the warriors, and hatchets, knives, awls and files, that showed British traders were busy on the coast. A full report should be given to President Jefferson. The right to possession of this immense and fabulously rich territory was still in doubt.

Lewis and Clark took the party back over the Great Divide, and at the mouth of the Yellowstone River met a pair of American trappers. These were the first men to follow the expedition's trail, and they asked for a guide to go with them into the maze of the far ranges. John Colter was given his discharge. He was an ideal man for the job, and the other members of the expedition were happy to have him get it. He was outfitted with what the expedition could spare, and led his new companions, Dixon and Handcock, westward.

The expedition kept on, reached the Mandan villages, rested briefly, then rode the Missouri towards still distant St. Louis. But Lewis and Clark were already compiling their final reports. The venture was a great success, and there were no incidents of any consequence along the river.

The party returned to St. Louis after an absence of three years. It had lost only one man, Sergeant Charles Floyd, who had died early of a ruptured appendix. Lewis and Clark and the rest of the party were greeted as heroes. They had done more than secure the Louisiana Territory for the United States. They had opened up the natural land route to the Pacific. It would be used by thousands of pioneers.

## 15

SHE WAS STILL KNOWN ONLY AS "THE STEAM-boat," and she was an awkward craft. John Astor stood on the Battery promenade and watched with interest as she came in through the New York harbor traffic to make her landing. She was the first vessel of her kind to be put in operation here, and she had wealthy influential men as her owners. This was August, 1807, and Astor, whose fur business depended almost entirely on water transportation, was very curious about her performance.

Her tall and thin iron-plate stack was scarlet with heat. Smoke gusts flung from it, and sparks. There were already spark burns on the furled foresail and mainsail and on the glossy paintwork. Steam escaped rumbling from the boiler that was covered with blankets and carpets as a protective measure.

Robert Fulton, the man in command of the steamboat, stood tensely braced on the upper deck. When he wanted the paddle-wheels

Wash drawing of Robert Fulton's *Clermont*.

reversed, he stamped on the deck planking right over the engineer's head. The visored cap that Fulton wore and the shoulders of his long velvet-collared coat were scarred by sparks. He was a very anxious man. The landing was made successfully, but after Fulton had backed off from the wharf to save his inboard paddle-wheel.

Gashes were in her paddle-wheel guards and side rails from collisions with various craft met out in the bay. Astor suspected that most of these were deliberate. Sailing-craft operators were not too happy about the arrival of a steamboat as a competitor. Astor turned away; it would be some time yet before vessels like this replaced keelboats and hauled the fur cargoes on the Missouri and the other western rivers.

Fulton's steamboat made her first official voyage on August 17, 1807, started up the Hudson from New York bound for Albany. There was a large group of guests aboard, and Fulton, handsome and gracious, proved himself a fine host. A great deal of his time, though, was given to the handling of the vessel.

She was of wood construction throughout, with 136-foot length, 16.5-foot beam and a seven-foot draft. Her engine, made by Watts in England, had a cylinder two feet in diameter with a four-foot piston stroke. The boiler was twenty feet long and built of wood bound with heavy iron bands. Her paddle-wheels were fifteen feet in diameter, and the floats four feet long, with a depth of two feet.

The major problem for Fulton was the boiler. It had a seven-foot depth and was eight feet wide. But when the furnace had been well stoked with pine cordwood and a head of steam raised, the boiler changed dimensions. The lozenge-shaped contraption shrank beneath the constricting iron bands and swelled elsewhere, and leaked, and threatened to explode. Fulton could only hope that the workmen at Charles Brown's shipyard on the East River had used really sturdy material.

The boiler held. Smoke and sparks swept astern free from the vessel as she gathered way and proceeded north of Manhattan Island. There were eight girls aboard, all of them from the Livingston family. They sang, laughed, gave admiring glances to curly-headed, brown-eyed Fulton. He kept his smile for Harriet Livingston. Their engagement, still a secret, was to be announced when the party reached Clermont, the Livingston manor.

255

Chancellor Robert R. Livingston rested a bit aside from the other passengers and regarded with satisfaction the way Fulton navigated the vessel. He and Fulton were partners in this venture. He knew of the love affair between Harriet and Fulton, would announce the engagement at Clermont.

The Chancellor was red-headed in the family tradition, and just as predatory in his business dealings as any of his ancestors. He maintained at considerable expense, in the form of bribes to the State legislature, the steamboat monopoly on the Hudson. He and Fulton shared in the patent rights for the vessel and had as a partner in those Nicholas J. Roosevelt. But Roosevelt had relinquished all but a negligible interest. The Chancellor envisioned a considerable amount of wealth coming soon to himself and Fulton.

There was no opposition. John Fitch, who before the Revolution had built a steamboat, was dead, a suicide. Fitch had run a regular but profitless service on the Delaware River, with stops at Trenton, Bordentown, Bristol, Burlington and Philadelphia. Hoping to raise funds for his failing business, Fitch brought the steamboat to New York. The Chancellor distinctly recalled a ride aboard the vessel around Collect Pond.

Then, in 1796, another steamboat inventor, Captain Morey, from New England, took the Chancellor for a ride. It was upstream along the Hudson, from the Battery to Greenwich Village. Morey's venture failed for lack of backers and popular interest. Wealth was needed to build successful steamboats, the Chancellor realized.

This was true in the instance of his brother-in-law, John Stevens, who built a number at Castle Point, Hoboken. The two Stevens boys, Robert and John, helped their father with the construction. They took the twin-propeller craft *Little Juliana* across the Hudson from Hoboken in May, 1804, and safely back from Manhattan.

All of the knowledge gained from Fitch, Morey and Stevens was passed along to Fulton. There was no legal restraint, the Chancellor understood, upon such ideas. It was Fulton who had drawn them together, selected the best, and built a boat that could be successfully operated. Fulton was a smart fellow, and smart enough to marry Harriet.

256

The boat rounded Kidd's Point. Wind from off the Highlands sent a flick of white caps across the sapphire water. Fulton checked his bearings. The boat was making an average speed of almost five miles an

Robert Fulton

hour. He gave her helm against the wind pressure. Then he raised his pleasant tenor in a song he cherished:

> *Ye banks and braes o' bonny Doon,*
> *How can ye bloom sae fresh and fair?*
> *How can ye chant, ye little birds?*
> *And I sae fu' of care!*

The passengers sang with him, the Chancellor's staid men guests caught by the grace of the Livingston girls as they joined in, sweet and true. Harriet gazed bright-eyed upward at Fulton. She smiled to dispel the sadness of the line:

> *Ye break my heart, ye little birds.*

Fulton was jubilant. He had given more than twenty years of his life for this moment. Now he would not die like the other steamboat men, broken, miserable and alone.

There was a prolonged business conference at Clermont after the engagement toasts were drunk and Fulton could get away from Harriet. It was the Chancellor's opinion that an immediate investigation should be made of western river conditions. Much more money could be realized from steamboat traffic in the west than on the Hudson. An experienced man was needed to conduct the survey, and Nicholas J. Roosevelt was preeminent. He was already a partner, and a born river man, belonged to the Roosevelt family that had been on the Hudson since Dutch colonial days.

Roosevelt was engaged in other activity, and drove a shrewd bargain with Livingston and Fulton. He wanted, he said, a full third share in the partnership if he discovered that the western rivers were suitable for steam navigation. The Chancellor and Fulton were to supply the capital, and Roosevelt was to superintend the building of the boat and her engine. An agreement was reached on Roosevelt's terms, and partnership papers signed.

258 Then Roosevelt and his wife left in May 1809 for Pittsburgh. They were newly married, and Mrs. Roosevelt insisted upon accompanying her husband. He planned to go by flatboat from Pittsburgh to New

Orleans. The voyage would take months while he tested the Ohio and Mississippi currents, checked soundings, bearings and charts.

Roosevelt ordered built in Pittsburgh a flatboat to his own specifications. The forward cabin served as the Roosevelts' private quarters, contained a fireplace and furniture bought by them. The crew were carefully chosen veterans, and the voyage was uneventful.

The Roosevelts spent six months aboard, and the craft became their home. They were ashore for three weeks at Louisville. Then, on the lower river, between Natchez and New Orleans, they passed ten days in a rowboat so that Roosevelt could make extensive calculations of river velocities. It was the current that would defeat any steamboat venture, he was told. The report was always the same—this river was too big, too tough. The warnings were from merchants, and planters, and pilots and keelboatmen and flatboatmen. But Roosevelt remained unconvinced.

He and his wife passed a few days of relaxation in New Orleans at the end of the voyage. Then they took a full-rigged packet ship for New York and arrived there in January 1810. The partners immediately met in conference. The data Roosevelt presented to Livingston and Fulton greatly impressed them. They decided to build a steamboat to be used in western river navigation.

The Roosevelts went to Pittsburgh in the spring of 1811 and he began the construction of the vessel in a local yard. The hull plan and all of the dimensions had been determined by Fulton in New York. The steamer was 116 feet overall, with a twenty-foot beam and a very shallow draft. Her engine had a thirty-four-inch cylinder, and her entire construction was white pine.

She cost more than $38,000 before the shipyard was finished. The vessel's name when launched was *New Orleans*, in honor of the ultimate port of call. Mrs. Roosevelt insisted on making the initial voyage. She said it was her habit to accompany Mr. Roosevelt, and the idea appealed to her very much.

Family friends pleaded with Mrs. Roosevelt. When she failed to be dissuaded, she was told that she was out of her mind. The fact of her pregnancy was mentioned; she was soon to become a mother.

Mrs. Roosevelt sailed with her husband aboard *New Orleans*. The

259

vessel took a short experimental run up the Monongahela in late September 1811, turned around with the current and headed for the Ohio and the Mississippi. The Roosevelts were the only passengers, occupied the after cabin. The pilot was Andrew Jack, the captain Henry Shreve, and the engineer a man named Baker. Six deckhands were in the crew, two women servants, and a male waiter. A very large and very friendly Newfoundland dog called Tiger was also aboard, as a guest.

The pilot, Captain Jack, had been worried about the vessel's performance. But she responded easily to her helm, and maintained a regular speed of between eight and ten miles an hour. When the people in a small village turned out along the bank and cheered the steamer, Captain Jack led the cheers of the crew, gave long blasts on the whistle.

Cincinnati was reached two days after leaving Pittsburgh. The steamer rounded up against the current and anchored offshore. It seemed to Mrs. Roosevelt that the whole town was either on the levee or coming off in small craft. The vessel was surrounded. Men from keelboat crews shouted that *New Orleans* might go downriver fine, but to get back up, that was a joke.

Roosevelt stayed at Cincinnati only long enough to take cordwood aboard. Then the steamer hauled anchor, maneuvered away from her admirers and detractors and started for Louisville. She was abreast of Louisville on the splendid moonlight night of October 1, 1811, and again Roosevelt kept her out in the stream. He had explained to the master, Captain Shreve, and to Captain Jack, that he did not want unwieldy crowds tramping all over the vessel.

A very warm welcome was given the Roosevelts ashore. They returned the courtesy with a banquet served aboard, and regret was expressed that *New Orleans* would not make another call at Louisville. It was Roosevelt's intention to take her to New Orleans as fast as possible. Then she was to enter into service on the lower river between New Orleans and Natchez.

But Roosevelt found that he could not move the vessel below Louisville. There was not sufficient depth of water to give her clearance in safety on the falls of the Ohio. There must first be a rise in the river. *New Orleans* waited at her anchorage off the town for weeks. No rain fell, although the weather was heavy and overcast. Roosevelt went every day in a skiff to sound the water at the falls.

He decided to make the run when there was only a five-inch clearance at the shallowest part. He had hired the best available local pilot to work with Captain Jack, and the man had advised him that the water would not rise any further. This was also the last week of November, and the river was soon going to be filled with ice.

*New Orleans* took in her anchor. Captain Jack and the local pilot stood in the bow of the vessel and gave helm direction to Henry Shreve. He stood above them in the pilot-house, hands firmly on the spokes of the head-high steering wheel. It had been suggested by people ashore that, because of the risks involved, Mrs. Roosevelt should leave the vessel for the run through the falls. But, she said, she belonged aboard, and during the run she stood on the after deck. Tiger crouched at her feet. The big Newfoundland dog seemed to sense fully the degree of danger.

The Indiana channel had been chosen by the pilots. It was the most navigable, but to enter it *New Orleans* was forced to make a wide sweep across the current before she could gather her maximum steerage way. She needed all of her speed to exceed that of the current; if she did not have it, she would not respond to her helm, and would pile up, a total loss.

*New Orleans* vibrated in her length, and excess steam shrieked through the safety-valve vent. Baker, the engineer, heaved cordwood into the furnace and kept the door wide open. The paddle-wheels slapped the shallow water with a blur of sound and movement, a fine spray whipping upward and aboard from the floats. It was impossible for Shreve to hear the pilots; he followed their hand signals.

Roosevelt stood near his wife. He watched the black rocks alongside, and the frothy eddies that might deflect the vessel from her course and smash her bottom planks in a single blow. He gripped the rail, and indicated that his wife should brace herself. This was the worst, the narrowest stretch. *New Orleans* came through it, and out into calm water below the falls.

Baker reduced the steam pressure. The vessel drifted in the quiet-

261

ness of the broad pool. Then the crew began to shout, and the waiter banged on a dishpan. This was a great triumph. But Captain Shreve stood solemn in the pilot-house. He called down to the fore deck and ordered an anchor let go. The day was so overcast that it was difficult to see the forested bank, but the trees there were shaking, bending, and an enormous tremor passed through the ground that reached out into the river.

It was the first shock of the 1811 earthquake, the worst in the history of the country. The *New Orleans* crew found many signs of it as the vessel proceeded downstream. Both Shreve and Jack observed some miles above the mouth of the Ohio that the river's speed was considerably less than normal. That could only have been caused by unusual flood conditions in the Mississippi.

The earthquake whose tremors continued day after day caused inestimable damage in the Mississippi Valley. Bottom lands were under water for hundreds of miles. Chickasaw Indians in pirogues paddled forth from between the boles of trees and hailed *New Orleans*, invited themselves aboard. Carrion crows rode the carcasses of drowned animals; wreckage from houses, barns, boats cluttered the banks, and bodies floated swollen and hideous.

New Madrid was a mud-slimed shambles. The spacious, lovely Missouri town had been almost completely inundated. Here the shocks had been so great that the river reversed itself in its course, and millions of tons of water that poured south roiled, convulsed, and rushed north. Fissures in the earth had taken homes and inhabitants; no trace was left. People wept when they tried to tell of their losses. The crew of *New Orleans* went ashore and helped. But there was not very much they could do. They lacked supplies and medicines.

*New Orleans* got under way again in the weirdly disturbed and treacherous river. Pilotage was guesswork. The channel had disappeared. All landmarks were destroyed, and navigation was among semi-submerged trees, stumps and drifting islands of tangled flotsam.

The town of Henderson was reached in safety, though. It was downstream from New Madrid, and the people were at first incredulous. They could not quite accept the fact that the steamer had survived the hazards of the upper river. Then a tall and sun-brown man with shoulder-

262

The great earthquake at
New Madrid.

long hair dived from the town wharf. He swam with great ease beneath
*New Orleans*, came up splashing and laughing on her outboard side.

The people on the wharf began to laugh. The Roosevelts were
invited ashore. They were told that the swimmer was a local storekeeper
named Audubon. He was supposed to be a little cracked. Most of his
time was spent out in the woods chasing birds.

*New Orleans* left the earthquake disaster region beyond Henderson. The next port was Natchez, where people lined the bluff and
hoarsely shouted. Then, for the Roosevelts, the rest of the voyage was
familiar. They had gone by skiff from Natchez to New Orleans during
the last voyage, spent days on this stretch of the river.

The city was very welcome to them now, and they finally recognized how intense their nerve strain had been. The steamer had succeeded in her purpose, though, and that was what counted. The keelboats, the flatboats, the barges and pirogues might serve on the river for years yet, and make money for their owners. Then they would give way to steamers like *New Orleans*. Steam power was cheaper than man power, and more effective.

The Roosevelts took passage for New York, carrying the news for the partners.

Astor heard about the steamer's successful performance right after the couple arrived. He correlated it with the immense mass of information that was brought daily to his Pine Street office. His own vessel, the 280-ton brig *Tonquin*, had reached the Pacific Coast on March 22, 1811, at the entrance of the Columbia River. He could still see no need for steam navigation to forward the interests of the American Fur Company, of which he was the principal stockholder. Any steamer that resembled *New Orleans* could not withstand the weather around Cape Horn, and inland the wages paid river men to haul and heave were not yet too high.

Astor was rapidly expanding his fur empire. He was about to become the wealthiest man in North America. The fur trade, in his manipulation of it, returned 1,000 per cent profit to the investor. It was so great that national policies were involved, and acute antagonism between firms, tribes and individuals created. Trappers or traders that invaded fur-bearing territory claimed by other men were summarily shot, killed from ambush without warning.

During the early years of the nineteenth century, six million pelts were sold annually at prices that ranged from fifteen cents to $500 apiece. International style insisted that every "gentleman" in Europe, Great Britain and North America must wear a beaver hat, and many other men below that arbitrary rank believed that they were forced to invest in the same headgear.

Astor did not participate in open warfare to take over the fur-bearing territories. He weakened opposition companies through competitive bidding, then hired their best operatives, factors, trappers and *voyageurs*. Most of his depredations were in Canada, where he had many connections. He had waited impatiently for the Lewis and Clark reports, soon afterwards began his bold design of western expansion from Michilimackinac to Grand Portage, and on down the Mississippi to St. Louis, from there up the Missouri to the furthest reaches of the tributary rivers, and then across the Rockies to the Columbia and his post at the mouth of that river.

Advertisement in the U.S. Directory.

Astor used bribes with shrewd effect. Among his close collaborators was Governor De Witt Clinton, a Hudson River man who understood the basic requirements of the fur trade. Governor Clinton made representations in Astor's favor in Washington, where his uncle, George Clinton, served as Vice President. It was Astor's idea to take over from the government all of the trading posts that had been established to strengthen the bonds of friendship with the frontier tribes. The government would thus be saved the maintenance cost of the posts, and widening of trade with the Indians would soon make many friends. The warriors were tempted at present, Astor pointed out, to take their pelts to British-owned posts.

President Jefferson, after due investigation, gave his approval on April 13, 1808, and a charter was issued to Astor. It allowed him to establish a virtual monopoly of all of the western fur trade. Astor was intensely pleased. President Jefferson had not only put the trade in the hands of an American citizen, but of an American citizen born in Waldorf, Germany, in 1763 and who in the spring of 1784 came to the United States from London. Astor was quite sure there could be no doubt about who that man was.

Armed with the monopoly, he finished his recruiting of Canadian fur-company personnel. He hired away from the Northwest Fur Company five of its best factors. These were all Scotsmen—Donald McKenzie, Alexander McKay, Duncan McDougal, David Stuart, and Stuart's nephew, Robert. He brought them to New York and made them partners

265

in his newly formed Pacific Fur Company, formed in July 1810 as a subsidiary of the parent company, the American.

He hired also a number of sturdy young Scots clerks, took them from behind the counters of the Northwest Fur Company. They would serve very well on the Pacific Coast, he believed. His early experience as a trader at Grand Portage had impressed him with the special qualities developed in the High Country. He added a force of fifteen *voyageurs,* and these men left Montreal by canoe, paddled to New York.

Astor was already embarrassed by his Scottish partners. Donald McKenzie, who was a veteran High Country trader and a famous rifle shot, was busy preparing for the journey to be made from St. Louis up the Missouri and across the Divide to the Columbia. A citizen of New Jersey, Wilson Price Hunt, who was Astor's major partner in the enterprise, would serve as co-leader of the inland expedition. He kept McKenzie occupied.

The other four, assigned to sail aboard *Tonquin,* made a very thorough tour of New York's taverns and public gathering places. There was trouble with the police, which Astor settled, but only after considerable expense. He induced the quartette to board the brig and conduct their drinking in private. They came over the gangway bearing pistols, daggers, large whiskey flasks and enormous conceptions of their own importance. The master of the vessel was Lieutenant Jonathan Thorn, who was on leave from the United States Navy. He complained to Astor that the Scots were insisting upon their occupation of nearly the entire quarter deck and the passenger accommodations.

Astor had little time to answer Thorn. The fifteen *voyageurs* had just arrived from Canada. Their voyage along the Hudson had been interrupted by quite a few shore visits. They had fired off their muskets, shouted Indian scalping cries, acted drunkenly, and made lewd proposals to farmers' wives.

Their approach to Manhattan had begun in triumphal style. They paddled around the Battery to the punctuation of musket volleys answered by the shouts of the pleased crowd on the promenade. The *voyageurs* wore buckskins and red eagle feathers, the feathers supplied by Astor as a sign that these were top men.

The people they met in the streets were at first friendly. The Canadians sang *chansons*, and were gay and funny. But they stayed too long in the taverns. Fights started, and the watch was called. The *voyageurs* fought the members of the watch and were subdued and roughly taken to jail. Astor settled the damage claims, paid the fines. It was time, he told Thorn, that *Tonquin* sailed.

She cleared the port September 8, 1810, bound around Cape Horn. The Scots partners, the clerks and the *voyageurs* stood on deck and vigorously waved. But only a few people along the Battery waved back. The ship had left bad memories.

The voyage, for Captain Thorn,* held more danger from the partners than from the sea. His life was threatened a number of times when he was reluctant to obey orders issued by the quartette, and he was rudely instructed in a Highlands version of ship handling. But *Tonquin* reached Oahu in the Hawaiian Islands on February 11, 1811, and anchored offshore. Astor had designated it as a port of call because of his expanding trade between China and the Pacific Coast. The island served as an excellent transshipment point for his cargoes.

The partners demanded a boat from Thorn and went ashore in a separate group. They wore their kilts in the dress tartans of their clans, and plaids carefully draped across their shoulders and secured with cairngorm brooches. Pistols were left aboard, although they carried their long, basket-hilted Claymore swords, and wore daggers in their stocking tops. They informed Thorn that they, all four of them, were *eris*, chieftains of noble blood, and on their way to make a ceremonial call upon King Kamehameha.

The king was so impressed by the call that he considerably increased the price of the fresh provisions Thorn had requested. The famous island hospitality was unstinted, though. Kilts swung in time with grass skirts in the white moonlight on the beach. While the drums thudded, *voyageurs* gave up dancing and love-making momentarily for further investigation of the effects of palm wine.

*Tonquin* sailed from Oahu with twenty-four island men aboard,

267

* The term of captain is used here in the full maritime sense. Any man who commands a vessel, no matter his naval rank, is her captain.

recruited by the partners. The Polynesians were powerful, massive-shouldered, and had displayed their canoe skill in the maelstrom surf along the
island beaches. They would be of great assistance to the *voyageurs* in
the complicated small-craft operations at the mouth of the Columbia
where the tide rip was known as extremely treacherous.

Thorn proved himself incompetent when on March 22nd he made
his Pacific Coast landfall and tried to enter the Columbia River. He lost
seven men from two boat crews at the river bar, among them the chief
mate. It was Duncan McDougal who took charge of the landing parties
and put boats ashore. They navigated the channel under his command
and he chose Point George on the south side of the stream as the site for
the post.

Cargo was landed by the combined boat crews, *voyageurs* and
Polynesians working easily together. They brought ashore stores, and a
large amount of equipment, and tools and materials for the construction
of a small schooner. The post was finished, and the region now belonged

Astoria as it was in 1813.

without question to the United States. But the quarters were occupied by a polyglot assembly—Americans, Scots, *voyageurs* who still preferred to speak French, Polynesians who disliked trousers and talked very poor pidgin English, and squat, bow-legged Clatsops and Chinooks who did not talk much at all, but stole anything they could lift, hide or swallow.

Members of the overland expedition that Astor had sent out from St. Louis arrived February 15, 1812, at the post. The men, led by Astor's principal partner, Hunt, were in poor shape, and gave accounts of repeated disaster. It had taken 340 days from St. Louis, and 140 of those were spent in camp. Fugitive groups, sick, lame, dispirited, were scattered anywhere from the Missouri to the headwaters of the Columbia. The trail was marked with a litter of wantonly discarded provisions, stores, arms and ammunition.

Audubon, when he came years later to the Missouri, heard of that sorry journey. It was Astor's greatest single defeat. He had failed absolutely in his objective to build a chain of posts linking St. Louis with the Pacific Coast.

Audubon was on the Missouri in March 1843 as a guest of the American Fur Company. He spent six months along the river and its tributaries while he made sketches for his *Birds of America* series. His life was assured now; he was at last completing the work he had begun as a teenage boy at Mill Grove Farm on the Perkiomen.

The scenes here on this great river both delighted and saddened him. He was still enough of a frontiersman to be enormously interested in the people he met. He wrote in his journal about his fellow passengers, bound upriver aboard the rattle-trap steamer *Gallant*:

> Our *compagnons de voyage*, about 150, were composed of Buckeyes, Wolverines, Suckers, Hoosiers, and gamblers, with drunkards of each and every denomination, their ladies and babies of the same nature, and specifically the dirtiest of the dirty. We had to dip the water for washing from the river in tin basins, soap ourselves all from the same cake, and wipe 150 with the same, solitary towel rolling over a pin, until it would have been difficult to say whether it was manufactured of hemp, tow, flax, or cotton.

269

When he was a passenger aboard the steamer *Omega* he wrote:

We had a night of rain, thunder and heavy wind from the Northeast. The country was water-logged, wolves eating carrion on the sandbars.

*Omega* passed the mouth of the Little Sioux River, "a stream formerly abounding with Beavers, Otters, Muskrats, etc., but now quite destitute of any of these creatures."

He noticed how the turkey buzzards tore at the river carrion, and black-tailed deer fought on the bank. The two largest deer, he wrote, were probably males, and "raised themselves on their hind feet and pawed at each other after the manner of stallions."

Heron eggs, he remarked, were often eaten by ravens. Then his years of service as a river man pushed aside his ornithological interest. He reported in the journal:

> We saw this morning eleven Indians of the Omaha tribe. They made signs for us to land, but our captain never heeded them; for he hates red-skins as most men hate the devil. In another place saw one seated on a log, close by the frame of a canoe; but he looked surly, and never altered his position as we passed.
>
> The frame of this boat resembled an ordinary canoe. It is formed by both sticks giving a half circle; the upper edges are fastened together by a long stick, as well as the center of the bottom. Outside of this stretches a Buffalo skin without the hair on; it is said to make a light and safe craft to cross even the rapid, turbid stream—the Missouri. By simply looking at them, one may suppose that they are sufficiently large to carry 2 or 3 persons.

Audubon's description of the famous bull boat used by all of the tribes west of the Mississippi was very accurate. So was his account of the flotilla of four bateaux that passed the steamer, headed downriver from Fort Pierre for St. Louis. The crews, he wrote, lived entirely during the voyage on buffalo meat and pemmican. The men were the last of the *voyageur* breed and handled the craft with easy confidence:

> These boats are strong and broad; the tops, or roofs, are supported by bent branches of trees, and these are covered by water-proof Buffalo hides; each has 4 oarsmen and a steersman, who manages the boat standing on a broad board; the helm is about ten feet long, and the rudder

The elongated bull boat was an adaptation of the circular ones used by the Mandan Indians when the first fur traders of the Hudson Bay Co. visited them in 1790.

itself is five or six feet long. They row constantly for sixteen hours, and stop regularly at sundown.

The flotilla that Audubon saw carried an aggregate cargo of 10,000 buffalo hides. Astor's estimate of the cheapness of labor on the interior rivers had been correct. Even in 1843, men could be found to pull on sixteen-foot sweeps for sixteen unbroken hours a day, and subsist on slabs of buffalo meat and pemmican. But the *voyageurs* were rapidly being absorbed, and losing their identity as they became steamboat deckhands.

Audubon was proud to record the fact that during his Missouri River voyage the senior pilot was Captain Joseph La Barge. The pilot was of French parentage, his father having come to St. Louis from Canada, and his mother from the Acadian region of lower Louisiana. The family

271

had been connected with western river navigation for fifty years. There were in St. Louis seven licensed river pilots who bore the La Barge name.

Audubon when he finished his Missouri River tour had been upon almost every stream of consequence on the continent. Back several years ago, when success first came to him, he was assisted by the United States government and made a voyage along the St. Johns River in Florida. He was a guest aboard the government schooner *Spark*.

Sunlight seldom reached the surface of the Florida river. The tall live-oaks were hung with matted, flower-bedecked tangles of moss, and lianas and creepers trailed in a thick confusion among the mangroves and cypresses. He made sketches in the strange, crepuscular light. Heron perched on the grass hummocks at the center of the current, and water turkeys dived industriously for fish, whooping cranes gave their harsh cry, and alligators barked.

It seemed to Audubon that all of the wild life of this region was noisy, and only the Seminoles were quiet. The proud and handsome Indians emerged silently from the tunnel-like shadows of the side creeks, the warriors standing erect in the narrow, extremely cranky dugout canoes. Squaws and the children sat motionless in the bow and balanced the craft, and stared up at the white men aboard the schooner with no indication of interest. This was not their world; they existed aloof, apart, deep in the Everglades.

Then, singing, the timbermen came down the river. They were the "live-oakers," the crews that had worked for months in the pine barrens upstream. The timber-cutting was finished, and the crews were rafting out the chained logs to the coast. They were Negroes, and their favorite song was:

> I pole dis raft way down de ribber
>   Oh-o! Oh-oh-oh! A-haa!
> De sharks and de sawfish make me shibber
>   Oh-o! Oh-oh-oh! A-haa!
> De fish hawk kotched a big fat mullet
>   Oh-o! Oh-oh-oh! A-haa!
> But it found its way down de eagle's gullet
>   Oh-o! Oh-oh-oh! A-haa!

Audubon rejoined Lucy when the St. Johns' voyage was finished and he had filled several sketchbooks. He took Lucy, his son John and John's wife to Scotland. He could afford such travel these days; the sale of his *Birds of America* book made it possible. Scotland was where success had first come to him and where on his previous visit he had found the original subscribers for the series. He had met Sir Walter Scott and all of the other leading Scottish figures; he was a celebrity in Edinburgh.

Lucy was both greatly impressed and joyously happy. Audubon was able on their return from Scotland to buy property and build a home

American Snipe, near a South Carolina Plantation—from Audubon's *Birds of America* series.

for her. It was on the Hudson, near Harlem village and just beyond the northern limits of New York City. They called the place Minnie's Land, using the Scots term of endearment.

There was a view of the river and the vast buttresses of the Palisades. Elms and beeches stood tall around the house. A stream ran through the property, and Audubon put up a dam and made a pond and a waterfall. The lawn sloped gradually towards the river, and deer and elk he had captured as fawns grazed untethered. Foxes, wolves and badgers were kept in a large enclosure, but taken out often and treated as pets.

The house was square, simply designed. High piazzas were designed for the river view. Lucy loved the place. When Audubon came home from the Missouri in 1843, Captain Cumings was waiting for him. The old Mississippi River pilot and cartographer had brought a large amount of very valuable data that Audubon might use. The captain, in most natural fashion, wore a suit of fringed buckskin.

Audubon spent the rest of his life at Minnie's Land. There were four or five years of contentment, further work and substantial rewards until in 1851 he died. He was internationally famous. But he represented much more than his achievements as an artist and an ornithologist. Within the span of his life, the forces of several societies had clashed, and finally been merged and given superb, lasting expression.

The same hands that had thickened while straining on a keelboat pole could also perform with exquisite delicacy the detail of the paintings in *Birds of America*. The man who had made Daniel Boone's portrait at Femme Osage when the doughty old-timer was eighty, and had talked with him as a close friend and fellow wilderness hunter, had been adroit, correct, even suave in the homes of the wealthy in Edinburgh and London and Paris.

Audubon, at the end of his life, though, felt a greater affinity for the frontier. He was in his essences a wilderness man.

He ranged back in his mind, gently, sometimes randomly touching the multiple textures of the fabric of memory. Fiddles played jigs and reels. He heard the notes of his own flute. There was the smell of frying catfish, and of Osage squaws who had not washed during a long winter. A Yankee in a wide-flopping hat walked the New Orleans levee; the coat he wore was light green, and he had nankeen trousers, a pink waistcoat.

274

Audubon remembered turning to watch the Yankee. A number of people on the levee stared at the man. The Yankee's frilled shirtfront was decorated with a bunch of magnolias, and among the flowers, swaying right, then left, appeared the head of a young alligator. The Yankee carried a bright silk umbrella in one hand, and in the other a cage of vivid-colored birds. He sang in broad Scots accent the song which began, "My love is but a lassie yet."

There were memories, too, of flatboats that were loaded entirely with turkeys held in crates. The gobbling croak of the fowls was taken for miles along the wind. Then there were the blacksmith boats where the horses were shod, and whinnied and resoundingly stamped. Six or eight boats were sometimes lashed together, hull to hull, and floated downstream to New Orleans. A boat that served as a tavern was usually near the middle, and close alongside a whoreboat. The fighting and the singing and the yelling went on all night long.

But those were vibrant memories. The one that remained clearest in his mind emerged from quietness. It had been formed in almost total dark.

A showboat had been poled up a small Kentucky river. Quite a few of the kind worked their way from the Ohio in summer. This might have belonged to the Chapmans, the family which started the showboat trade. Audubon was not sure. He recalled fully, though, the Kentucky night, and the boat tied to the bank, and deserted.

The performance was up-slope from the river. It was given in a clearing around some cabins. Moonlight illuminated the space the company had chosen for a stage. The acting was done in a low-roofed passageway between two cabins. The audience sat on both sides on the ground.

The play was a melodrama, perhaps *The Iron Chest*, or *Pizarro*, or *The Spectre Bridegroom*. It was long, with several acts. The moonlight faded. The audience could not see the actors. But the performance continued. People in the audience talked in low voices about the characters of the play, and the actors answered them, and it was finished like that. The spoken lines came stilted and deliberate, and the murmurous slow talk of the mountain folk, and the actors again, either answering or going on with the next lines.

275

Early types of river craft near Caldwell's Landing on the Hudson.

Audubon liked to recall the memory. It held a simplicity and an understanding that seemed afterward to have vanished. He could not, he realized, ever go back to that Kentucky world. Somehow, the people would not welcome him.

When in his uneasy sleep, late at night, he awoke, he listened to the river sounds. They gave him the same sense of calmness that Champlain had found.

# ILLUSTRATION CREDITS

The New York Public Library, pp. 12, 76, *The First Edition of the Voyages of 1619*; 23, 165, Campbell, P., *Travels in the Interior*, Edinburgh, 1793; 38, Willis, N. P., *American Scenery*, 1840; 49, Shortt, A. and Doughty, A. G., *Canada and Its Provinces*, Toronto, 1917; 98, Smith, John, *Generall Historie*, 1624; 115, Bryant, William, *Picturesque America*, 1872–74; 127, 173, Collot, *Voyage dans l'Amerique*, Paris, 1826; 139, Lossing, B. J., *Pictorial Field-Book of the Revolution*, 1851; 141, McKenney, Thomas L., *Sketches of a Tour to the Lakes*, 1827; 162, *The Papers of Sir William Johnson*, Albany, 1928; 175, Croft, William A., *Pioneers in the Settlement of America*, 1876; 185, *The Portfolio*, 1810; 233, Hall, Basil, *Forty Etchings from Sketches Made with the Camera Lucida in North America*, 1829; 263, Howe, Henry, *Historical Collections of the Great West*, 1854; 79, 89, 273, Picture Collection; 71, 122, Prints Division; 37, Prints Division, The Phelps Stokes Collection; 7, Champlain, S., *Les Voyages*, Paris, 1613, Rare Books Division

The Public Archives of Canada, pp. 5, 182-183, Bouchette, Joseph, Map of the Provinces of Upper and Lower Canada, 1815; 188, from a water color by Mrs. M. M. Chaplin

Scribner Art Files, pp. 75, 149, 268, 276

Toronto Public Library, John Ross Robertson Collection, p. 70

MAP BY LE ROY H. APPLETON

Mask of braided corn husks;
of the Cayuga *Husk Face Society*—
Iroquois Indians

# INDEX

279

283

284